D1569386

NUCKY

THE REAL STORY OF THE ATLANTIC CITY BOARDWALK BOSS

By Frank J. Ferry, Esquire

COMTEQ PUBLISHING

MARGATE, NEW JERSEY

Margate, New Jersey

A division of ComteQ Communications, LLC

www.ComteQpublishing.com

Printed in Canada
10 9 8 7 6 5 4 3 2 1

ISBN 978-1-935232-62-9

ComteQ Publishing
101 N. Washington Ave. • Suite 1B
Margate, New Jersey 08402
609-487-9000 • Fax 609-487-9099
Email: publisher@ComteQpublishing.com

Book & cover design by Rob Huberman

This book is dedicated to my mother,
Louise Antoinette (Kirby) Ferry,
who was raised in Atlantic City,
knew Nucky Johnson,
and shared her stories of Nucky's past.

I'm so glad I listened.

TABLE OF CONTENTS

LIFE BEHIND BARS

THE FINAL DAYS

ACKNOWLEDGMENTS

It has been an enriching experience to explore the past and to resurrect the interesting characters who shaped Nucky Johnson's life. As the Roaring 20s arrived with gusto in our country, Nucky symbolized the excitement of the times and will long be remembered as one of the great political bosses of this era.

I am grateful to the many people who supported my research and writing effort wholeheartedly for the past 12 years. Some contributors had never heard of Nucky, some indeed had, and some were his personal acquaintances. But all of them gladly contributed to his life story in some way.

I would like to extend my special thanks to the Staff of the Atlantic City Free Public Library, particularly Heather Halpin-Perez and Pat Rothenberg, for their efforts in consistently going above and beyond the call of duty in helping with our research and sharing their expertise with us.

Thanks, too, to my daughters, Mary Lou Ferry and Anne Marie McGinty, who encouraged my efforts enthusiastically, which added to my satisfaction in undertaking this effort.

I also extend my gratitude to my special friend, Audrey L. Foster, for her companionship and helpful suggestions from the inception of my project.

It was my good fortune or perhaps just Irish Luck to have found Rob Huberman at ComteQ Publishing in Margate, NJ, who showed a special interest in preserving Atlantic City's colorful political history. With Rob's encouragement, this became the first book ever written that is devoted entirely to Nucky Johnson and his life and times.

Most contributors are mentioned in the bibliography, but the in-depth research was done by Carol (Boyce) Heinisch, my longtime legal assistant, with enthusiasm and dedication, which made the thoroughness of this work possible and enjoyable to read.

PREFACE

Enoch L. "Nucky" Johnson, the Republican powerhouse from Atlantic City, dominated New Jersey's political landscape in the early part of the 20th century. This book is dedicated to preserving and celebrating his real life story and legacy before these recollections are washed out to sea with the sands of time.

In the early part of the 20th century, America was bursting with raw energy, especially in politics and crime that were often intertwined for their mutual benefit. It was the time of the horseless carriage, the airplane, victory in the Spanish-American War and World War I, the "talking" moving pictures, and the excitement of Broadway Shows. Elegant hotels sprang up in New York and propelled the country into cultivating a taste of excitement and a desire for the good life. The days of high society and the Gilded Age had arrived with gusto. Politicians and criminals were eager to give the people what they wanted, legal or not.

From coast to coast, the U.S. was a hotbed of political intrigue and criminal turf wars. By the 1920s, the U.S. government was spurred into action. The federal agencies were intent on tracking the most notorious lawbreakers, bringing them to justice, and restoring some semblance of peace in city neighborhoods. It was a time when city governments were synonymous with corruption, and thugs were calling the shots in and out of office.

In 1921, William J. Burns became head of the Federal Bureau of Investigation, shortly before J. Edgar Hoover took over. The FBI became the top investigation agency in the world. Burns gained notoriety for investigating corrupt public officials, and every part of the country was clamoring for his services. He teamed up with Francis J. Heney, the nationally known prosecutor of graft and corruption, to investigate and prosecute California's Abe "The Boss" Ruef's San Francisco Union Labor Party. Every branch of the California government at the time was honeycombed with graft. The Labor Party's creed was "Let no dishonest dollar escape." More than 300 indictments were returned, and at the end of a sensational trial in 1908, Ruef was sent to the penitentiary for 14 years. A

Ruef supporter shot and wounded Heney during the trial, but Hiram Johnson, his co-counsel, took over and successfully completed the case.

In the Midwest, Tom Prendergast's Democratic machine controlled Kansas City; alcohol flowed during Prohibition, gambling flourished, and elections were rigged. Boss Prendergast could always count on his "graveyard" precinct to vote the straight Democratic Party ticket. He also spearheaded contracts for numerous public buildings to provide much-needed jobs during the Great Depression. Although he was eventually sentenced to federal prison for failing to pay income taxes, he was powerful enough to handpick Harry S. Truman for U.S. Senate in 1934, the senator who later became the 33rd U.S. President in 1945.

In 1949, Governor Adlai E. Stevenson appointed a young aspiring Democrat by the name of Richard J. Daley as state revenue director for the state of Illinois where he gained a keen insight of government, budgets, and revenue sources. In 1955, he was well-qualified to become mayor of Chicago, the nation's second-largest city, and he wielded the power of that office and as Cook County Democratic chairman.

He won re-election easily from 1959 to 1975 and pursued the dual role as mayor and party chairman for 21 years, ruling his domain with an iron fist. Party workers who delivered the vote were generously rewarded, and those who did not, lost their jobs and were told to "tell your story walking and hit the bricks of the Windy City."

His organization, which delivered large blocks of votes for state and presidential candidates, made it possible for him to seek and receive billions in federal dollars for highways, public transit, and housing for the poor in Chicago. This funding contributed to the renaissance of Daley's city when other northern cities were experiencing declines. It was the time O'Hare Airport and McCormick Place were built. Daley will be remembered as the last of the great city bosses who provided John F. Kennedy with a substantial vote, most of it legal too, in a narrow victory over Richard M. Nixon in November 1960.

In New England, the power base of James Michael Curly had controlled Boston's Democratic politics for almost 40 years. He held public offices in the state house of representatives and as governor, as a member of Congress, and as mayor of Boston at the end of his political career in 1950.

A new leader was emerging in the Boston area, a man who controlled the Democratic Party as president of the Massachusetts Senate from 1961 to 1970: William M. Bulger, aka the Good Bulger. His older brother, James I. "Whitey" Bulger, chose a different path to notoriety, leading to murder and drugs as the head of the Winter Hill Gang. He received his recognition as a name on the FBI's Most Wanted List and was eventually captured in 2011.

In New York, the Society of St. Tammany, founded in 1789 for patriotic and fraternal purposes, turned into a Democratic political machine, thanks to William March Tweed, who controlled New York City government for 70 years. Boss Tweed, a title he never resented, converted the early saints of the society into full-time sinners who preyed upon the gullible new arrivals passing through Ellis Island to Manhattan. As president of the board of supervisors, he controlled the financial purse strings, and as New York state senator, he dispensed state patronage to the faithful.

More than half of the residents in the Big Apple were foreigners who readily followed the solicitous Democratic election district committeeman's political choices. Tweed's name became synonymous with "bossism" in American politics.

On the other side of the Hudson River in New Jersey, the dapper Irish teetotaler Frank Hague kept unchallenged control of the Democratic Party for more than 30 years. From his powerbase as mayor of Jersey City in Hudson County and as vice chairman of the Democratic National Committee, he will long be remembered when he declared, "I am the law in Jersey City!" in a speech on November 10, 1937. His comment drew criticism from the press, but in reality, he was speaking the truth. John V. Kenny, his Democratic successor, inherited a system that seemed to work, and he saw no reason to change it.

In the Deep South, the Kingfish (Democratic Governor) Huey P. Long who later became the U.S. Senator for the state, controlled Louisiana. He fought to protect the rural poor and fought off attempts to impeach him during his term as state senator, and his success in doing so made him more powerful than ever. He was colorful and charismatic, but his tumultuous career was cut short by an assassin's bullet during a legislature session in Baton Rouge on September 8, 1935.

At the turn of the 19th century, the Gas Gang controlled the political process in the Philadelphia, later known as the City of Brotherly Love. Fraudulent voting on a scale that America had never seen before assured victory over any opponent. Even dogs, cats, horses, and tombstones were on the list of registered voters. One home was actually credited with having 62 registered voters. In 1903, Mayor Samuel Howell Ashbridge (aka "Stars and Stripes Sam") left office after four years of total political control he garnered through election fraud that eventually spread across the Delaware River to the Jersey shore.

As the great failed experiment of 1920, the Volstead Act (better known as Prohibition) launched the careers of notorious criminals from coast to coast. Johnny Torrio took over Chicago and then brought Brooklyn's Al Capone on board before rising to new heights in national infamy. New York had Frank Costello, Lucky Luciano, and Albert Anastasia; Cleveland had Dutch Schultz; North Jersey had Abe Zwillman; and their brain trust was none other than Meyer Lansky. These men eventually formed the crime families known as the Mafia. Law enforcement officials patiently watched the action from the sidelines, only getting involved when absolutely necessary. Why should they? Everyone was having a good time. This panoramic view of crime and politics across the U.S. was personified in the life and times of Enoch "Nucky" Johnson.

Nucky controlled his own world from his political base in Atlantic City, known as the World's Famous Playground. He proudly carried the Republican banner into the political battles that he usually won. He entertained lavishly and supported anyone who enhanced his power, from U.S. senators, congressmen, governors, mayors, and attorney generals to sports figures and Broadway celebrities. When he hosted the first national crime convention, Nucky's picture was plastered alongside that of Capone on the front pages of most national newspapers in May 1929.

But Nucky was much more than a political leader. He gave Atlantic City style, excitement, and pizzazz, turning it into the place to be and the place to be seen, where the good times rolled, where real estate speculation was booming, and where everyone in town had a piece of the action. He made Atlantic City the playground of the world. In fact, Monopoly, the world's biggest selling board game, is an enduring tribute to his leadership in building the Boardwalk Empire.

The neighborhood candy store, grocery market, and barbershop offered gambling on "punchboards," and store operators wrote numbers, the precursor of the state lotteries, to anyone who walked in the door with pocket change. It was common for a uniformed police officer to stroll into a numbers parlor without arresting anyone and get in line to buy his own daily number. The numerous and wide-open "horse rooms" offered comfortable seats, free drinks, and tasty snacks to the high rollers who spent the entire day enjoying the Sport of Kings.

Atlantic City became a hub for illegal activity. Moses L. Annenberg, from his base in Chicago, extended his financial tentacles into every horse room in Atlantic City and across the country. He supplied horse-racing results by wire after winning the needed mob approval at the first convention of organized crime figures in Atlantic City in 1929.

Getting a drink on Sundays or during Prohibition was never a problem in Atlantic City. Nucky was a member of The Big Seven, a cartel that controlled the flow of untaxed liquor into the country. Atlantic City was one of the leading ports of entry for illegal liquor on the East Coast, and laws were totally ignored. Many of those who crossed the Delaware River and the salt marshes to the shore were determined to get some Jersey lightning.

In order to make Atlantic City grow, Nucky needed cash. And the appreciative gambling fraternity was only too eager to support and to contribute to such a worthy cause in hopes of keeping the tourists coming to the Jersey shore and keeping their hot dice rolling. After all, this is the way it always was. Gambling brought prosperity to the city; the results were obvious from the smiling merchants with their cash registers brimming to the happy residents who saw no need to change.

When his friends asked Nucky what he did with all his money, he proudly said, "I spent it on booze and broads—the rest of it I wasted."

Nucky's cash disappeared as quickly as he made it; he spent some money on himself, some on elections, but most of it went to the locals who fell on hard times. Welfare and Social Security laws didn't exist until the late 1930s, and Nucky's boundless generosity made him a local hero. His gala parties were legendary, along with his winning local and statewide campaigns where he always spent more than his opposition to elect U.S. senators, congressmen, and governors. The residents of

Atlantic City fondly remember Nucky's lifetime as "the good old days."

The Atlantic City Boardwalk Auditorium, the largest in the world at that time, became a reality through Nucky's political muscle. He countered intense opposition in the process until the building was dedicated in grand style in 1929. The Oceanside auditorium, the original home of the Miss America pageant, is still a testimony to Nucky's power politics and dynamic leadership for 30 colorful years.

The spirit of the era was best expressed by the words, "Laissez les bons temps rouler!" ("Let the good times roll!"). That's when Nucky took center stage and gave Atlantic City its place in the sun and its colorful chapter in history.

In full disclosure, I have taken the liberty of recreating some of the dialogue between Nucky Johnson and others. I based these conversations on details I discussed with Nucky during the two-year period I represented him during his criminal fine case. I also used excerpts from Nucky's testimony in his 1941 criminal trial, along with his depositions in his claim against *The Saturday Evening Post* and David Niven, and his interviews with the FBI in his application for pardon. These testimonies give us insights into Nucky's true character through his own words.

Many people also told me about the specific personal incidents they shared with Nucky that are also contained in this book. For instance, Marie Boyd, who worked in the Atlantic City Treasurer's Office, was very close to Nucky and his wife Floss for many years. Boyd attended Nucky's criminal trial, and she and her husband, Jimmy, who was Nucky's right-hand man, were my longtime clients. And Senator Frank S. "Hap" Farley, Nucky's successor and my law partner for 15 years, also shared a great deal of what he knew and remembered about Nucky. Even John Mooney, who was the head of the vice squad in Atlantic City, was my client and friend for most of his life; he often spoke of Nucky in glowing terms.

I also used the basics of the actual events in Nucky's life from FBI reports, IRS records, trial transcripts, as well as those listed in the bibliography at the end of this book. All of these sources served to re-create the life and times of Nucky Johnson.

—*Frank J. Ferry*

THE EARLY YEARS

CHAPTER 1

THE MAN IN ALL HIS PLUMAGE

Long before Atlantic City became synonymous with casinos, high rollers, shopping outlets, and saltwater taffy, this stretch of prime beachfront along New Jersey's Absecon Island long remained a hidden treasure. It stayed a secret to all but the locals until the early 1900s, when Philadelphians who began making the long journey eastward by stagecoach, train, or automobile discovered the comforts of this "Atlantic playground." Miles of sand and surf kept visitors coming back for summer fun year after year, and local entrepreneurs sweetened the deal by extolling the benefits of the resort's restorative powers for mind, body, and spirit.

One local man saw this diamond-in-the-rough for exactly the natural treasure it was. As the resort grew, so did his vision for the untapped potential of this seaside resort. By the Roaring Twenties, this man earned his day in the sun as the true boss of Atlantic City, and all the locals knew him well. The Boardwalk was his home turf, a place where his shrewd business know-how and political prowess grew to legendary heights. During the heyday of the Prohibition, the decisions he made and the deals he wrangled kept Atlantic City riding high on a seemingly endless wave of prosperity from legal and not-so-legal pursuits.

The man was Enoch Lewis Johnson, better known as "Nucky" to friend and foe, and he was a man who had many of both. His charm attracted people to him like moths to a flame. He staked his claim in this burgeoning resort by backing key political bigwigs and investing in enterprising ventures of every dearth, from bootlegging to gambling to prostitution. Part mobster, part philanthropist, Nucky rejoiced in politics and big business, was quick to lend a hand to those in need, and counted the nation's notorious partners in crime among his many friends, including Al Capone. Whenever Nucky strolled along the Boardwalk, people whispered in awe, "Here comes the man! Here comes the man!"

But it wasn't only his reputation that turned heads along the Boardwalk. Tall and stately at 6'2", Nucky stood out in a crowd in physical appearance, too. Like the old adage that says, "By the plumage, you can tell the bird," Nucky was a rare and endangered species, truly one of a kind. Using his commanding physique and powerful reputation to full advantage, he always made sure he was dapper and dressed for the part of the "boss."

His attire consisted of a full-length black coat with a velvet collar, kid gloves, and pearl-gray spats. He topped it off with a cravat and diamond stickpin, along with his trademark boutonniere: a single red carnation. For the finishing touch, he tucked a white, four-point hankie neatly into his lapel pocket and set a wide-brimmed Borsalino hat on his head, tilted at just the right angle for an air of sophistication and hauteur.

When he wasn't twirling his signature Irish Blackthorn walking stick during his strolls along the Boardwalk, he loved to don his full-length raccoon coat and ride around Atlantic City in his powder-blue limousine. His chauffeur and bodyguard, Louis "The Russian Bear" Kessel, was Nucky's constant companion and confidant. Dressed in a chauffeur's gray flat cap with a shiny black-leather visor, Kessel kept Nucky's cache of vehicles road-ready, and there were plenty of options to ferry him to his next appointment. Nucky often chose his vehicle depending on his mood and the day's agenda. His collection included two 16-cylinder Cadillacs, a black Chrysler convertible coupe (complete with rumble seat and red leather upholstery), a Lincoln, a Rolls Royce, a Hudson Super-Six, as well as a large Pierce Arrow, and a small Ford.

Yep, Nucky liked the good things in life, and friends and acquaintances spoiled him with material comforts every chance they had. In 1929, as Wall Street crashed, Nucky was raking in big bucks through his assortment of enterprises, some legal, some not. Over the years, he earned the respect of the Atlantic City locals, many of whom he personally helped through rough times during the Depression.

In return, his assembly of well-wishers showered him with hundreds of gifts and thousands of Christmas cards and telegrams during the holidays and plenty of tokens of appreciation in-between. His squad of

Western Union messengers routinely sprinted through the Ritz-Carlton Hotel, whisking news to Nucky's ninth floor headquarters overlooking his Boardwalk empire and the Atlantic Ocean. This is where Nucky sat with his entourage, skillfully negotiating with players and pawns to expand his political empire in Atlantic City.

Nucky's political reach extended far and wide. As the recognized Republican political kingpin of New Jersey for more than 30 years, Nucky helped orchestrate the elections of governors and U.S. senators during their rise to public office. During Prohibition, Nucky controlled the reins of big business in town, which translated to all of the gambling clubs and liquor trafficking operations in Atlantic City.

Nucky's foothold in politics and big business in South Jersey carried a hefty price. While he was busy watching over his enterprises, U.S. government agencies were watching him. But his business savvy kept his dealings operating well under the federal radar. It took years of tracking and surveillance for the Internal Revenue Service to seal the government's case against Nucky, which happened at the pinnacle of his political power: Nucky was convicted of income tax evasion and was sentenced to a term of four years in Lewisburg Federal Penitentiary starting in 1941.

Looking back, however, it was Nucky who actually laid the groundwork for legalized gambling in Atlantic City. The state of New Jersey tried to block gambling in all forms for many years. After all, the government billed gambling as destructive to family life and opened the seaside resort to criminal activity.

But it took years before New Jersey realized that gambling could actually infuse money into the state's troubled economy and breathe life into this fading shore community. Suddenly, gambling wasn't so bad after all. By 1976, the New Jersey State Constitution was amended, and neon-laden casinos began to pop up along the Atlantic City Boardwalk and beyond.

Today, there are 13 casinos pumping millions of dollars into the state treasury, and gambling has diversified its activities on all fronts: New Jersey television stations simulcast horse-racing results from all over the country, lottery machines are fixtures in just about every store, and New Jersey has joined 12 other states in offering Mega Millions with colossal jackpots. Churches even sponsor charter buses to casinos and give parishioners a complimentary roll of quarters and a meal coupon to spend the day with one-armed bandits or at the roulette tables—even on Sunday.

The Atlantic City that Nucky once knew has changed dramatically in form and function from its halcyon days before the turn of the century. The famous Boardwalk, originally built in 1870 to keep railcars and hotels sand-free, once stretched for seven miles from Atlantic City to Longport in its heyday. After the hurricane of 1944 stormed into town and devoured a chunk of the Boardwalk on its way out, the walkway was fortified with reinforced steel and concrete for added stability. Today, the herringbone-pattern wooden pathway measures 60' wide and more than 6 miles long, affording plenty of room for strolling tourists both in and off season. The landmark oceanfront amusement sites on the piers that jutted out into the ocean like fingers on a hand are long gone. These havens of fun and festivities once dazzled working families for almost 100 years: the Steel Pier, Young's Million Dollar Pier, Heinz Pier, Steeplechase Pier, Garden Pier, and Central Pier. Casinos with their bright neon lights have sprouted up along the Boardwalk as the modern-day playground for adults who dare to match skills with one-armed bandits, blackjack, craps, and roulette.

Nucky dreamed that Atlantic City would someday grow into a world-renowned metropolis, a haven for the rich and the famous where fortunes could be made. And his mission was to make this dream come true. His vision was limitless, and he refused to let obstacles block his path to success. He knew how to pull the right political strings to make the Atlantic City Convention Hall a reality in 1929, even in an era when the nation was entering the Great Depression.

Building Convention Hall was a monumental feat that changed the skyline and pulse of Atlantic City and it became the longtime home to the Miss America Pageant. The parade of beauties originally started in 1921 as a way of keeping summer tourists in town until after Labor Day. The pageant not only succeeded in keeping tourists around longer, it managed to turn the eyes of the world to Atlantic City each September. When Nucky was interviewed on his 84th birthday on January 20, 1967, *Atlantic City Press* columnist Sonny Schwartz reported that Nucky's eyes sparkled when he talked about the convention hall. Nucky called it the lifeblood of Atlantic City's winter economy. "That Convention Hall," he said, "that was my pride and joy, ya know...my baby."

Despite Nucky's passion and pride, nowhere is the name of Enoch L. Johnson ever mentioned in brochures or in the pronouncements from public officials about the convention hall contributing to Atlantic City's prosperity for the past 80 years. His name was never inscribed on a plaque in a place of honor in the hall; in fact, the city fathers didn't even formally recognize Nucky as ever existing and never quite gave the Boardwalk Boss credit for all he had done to put Atlantic City on the map and to keep it there. But those who Nucky helped and those he made rich and powerful remember the moxie of the real Boardwalk Boss and how he accomplished whatever he set out to do at whatever the cost.

After all, Nucky had a hometown advantage and a deep-seated love of the land. His roots were entrenched in the Pinelands, an area he worked to preserve and protect. He was a local boy, a South Jersey native born in the heart of the Pinelands on January 20, 1883. His father, Smith E. Johnson, and his mother, Virginia (nee Higbee), welcomed Enoch Lewis, the Johnson's third child who joined his older brother Alfred; Nucky's firstborn brother had died of hepatitis at age 3, and a little more than a year after Nucky was born, his mother gave birth to a daughter who was stillborn. The family was living at Leeds Point in Jersey's rural Galloway Township when Nucky arrived, but within three years, the Johnsons relocated to Mays Landing near Atlantic City when Nucky's father was first elected sheriff of Atlantic County in 1887.

Nucky's father tried a few different careers before discovering his true calling in life as a law enforcement officer. The elder Johnson was raised in Johnsontown, near the historic Smithville stage stop, about 15 miles from Atlantic City. While it would have been natural for Johnson to become a career seaman amid this region's maritime heritage, he didn't. He tried a stint at sea in his youth but quickly decided that it wasn't for him. He set his sights on looking for work ashore.

Johnson tried working as a salt hay farmer for a while, but that didn't work out either. Living off the land as a local woodsman, or "stump jumper," a trapper, or a salt hay farmer was a constant struggle for survival. Like most families in the Pinelands, the Johnsons lived off the land and bartered with neighbors to make ends meet. The meadowlands flanking the Mullica and Egg Harbor rivers produced plenty of salt hay, a versatile grass used for everything from bedding livestock in commercial livery stables to insulation to protect freshly poured concrete from frost to packing material for glassware shipments from the South Jersey glass factories. Though Jersey earned the nicknamed "The Garden State," the Pinelands were anything but Eden-like. This area was called the "barrens" for good reason: Vegetation struggled to sprout in the dry, sandy soil. Back in the late 1800s, laborers earned $.22 per hour. And Johnson soon grew tired of salt hay farming and scratching the land for a meager seasonal living.

But when Johnson delivered salt hay to Atlantic City, he was captivated with its sights and sounds. It didn't take him long before he struck up a friendship with Louis Kuehnle, better known as "the Commodore." The local Republican political leader who operated Kuehnle's Hotel and The Corner, a favorite local watering hole at the corner of North Carolina and Atlantic Avenues, was a good person to know. Through Kuehnle, Johnson expanded his circle of friends quickly, from farm workers and baymen to merchants and local politicians. The Commodore also ushered in a new level of sophistication and modernization around town. He started the first electric company in Atlantic City and made sure his hotel had the first gaslights decorating the ceilings in 1882. Kuehnle and Johnson became close friends and even closer political leaders.

Though Johnson wanted more than the struggling life of a farmer or bayman could offer, his family roots still ran deep in Atlantic County. He didn't want to stray too far from where his father, Enoch J., had settled after serving two years in the Civil War with the Union Army, according to his obituary. The elder Enoch was Nucky's namesake, and the Johnson's good name and personal integrity was a given for local folks. Johnson decided to take a gamble and run for public office in hopes of building a better life for his family in the big city. His goal was to run for sheriff, and the first step was moving his family, with the help of friends and relatives, to a cottage at 9 South New Hampshire Avenue in Atlantic City. He wanted to be near the hub of activity and devote his full attention to the election campaign.

Johnson's longtime neighbors in the South Jersey Pinelands and the new contacts he met via the Commodore helped him bridge the gap between country and big city communities. This proved to be just what he needed to win a landslide election in 1887, which launched his first three-year term as sheriff. Little did he know that this would be the start of a longtime family tradition: Johnson and his two sons eventually took turns serving as sheriff and undersheriff for the next forty years.

Johnson found his true calling in law enforcement. He liked the respect and prestige that came with being sheriff and decided he wanted to stay in the post forever, or at least as long as he legally could. But he also knew that the N.J. Constitution of 1844 only allowed a sheriff to a serve a three-year term, so he could not reapply for his post until he was out of office for three years. With a little ingenuity, Johnson found a way around the problem. After three years as sheriff, he decided to work as undersheriff for another three-year term. Then, he would campaign for his successor under one condition: After those three years, Johnson would return to his post as sheriff for another three-year term. The rotating terms in office served to be a way to buck the system, and the election cycle continued year after year and term after term. When Nucky and Alfred were of age, they joined in the rotation, alternating the roles of sheriff and undersheriff with their father and adding a few outsiders as needed to keep the key position of power all in the family.

After winning the first election, Johnson moved his family into the sheriff's official residence in Mays Landing, which was attached to the Mays Landing county jail. Though Nucky and Alfred were smart enough never to question their father's authority, they still knew the fine points of the law and learned plenty of ways around it. Nucky was fond of telling his mother that there wasn't much his father could do to him, "After all, we already live in a jail."

Since Nucky grew up on a daily diet of politics with his father as sheriff, he also was baptized into the local political process at an early age. Nucky saw the prestige that came with the job firsthand. As sheriff, Johnson commanded an all-powerful position in the county; he was the law. With Nucky growing up in such an environment in the 1880s, it wasn't hard for him to pick up the political intrigue around him through his father, his connections, and the locals he had come to know.

Nucky often said that he learned as much talking to his father and their neighbors in the community as he did in school, especially the sea captains and messmates who sailed the seven seas before they settled down in Mays Landing.

Mays Landing was steeped in rich maritime traditions in a region where seaman and shipbuilders arrived as early as 1695 and built log cabins in clusters that eventually grew into villages and cities along the waterfront. The Pinelands of South Jersey provided plenty of raw materials for shipbuilding. The tall straight oak and cedar forests held treasures for boatbuilders. Stands of hard solid oak were used for ship ribs, frameworks, and keels because the wood's strength, density, and resistance to decay could weather the constant pounding at sea. Woodjins, or the local woodcutters, felled the prime pillars with broad axes and hauled the logs via horses and oxen to the shipyard where the boatbuilding began.

The Johnsons were friends with many of the seamen and boatbuilders and their families who settled in the area. But by the close of the 19th century, that was all changing. The steam engine provided a faster and more economical means of transporting people and products by rail. The Atlantic City Railroad, operated by the Reading Company, chugged along from the station at Chestnut Street in Philadelphia to Egg Harbor City in the Pinelands of New Jersey, a route that included a spur to Mays Landing and then to Atlantic City. With the focus on shipping by sea coming to an end for the region, many seafarers were eager to find other work in their homeport of Mays Landing.

Though the Johnsons moved to Mays Landing in 1887, the elder Johnson taught the boys firsthand how most people in the Pinelands survived off the land. Nucky and Alfred learned to fish, hunt, and shoot guns. The boys became excellent marksmen and even more proficient at handling their father's Kentucky long-barrel single-shot rifle. Nucky took his father's prized long rifle to every local shooting competition. The hand-rubbed oil finish on the curly dark maple rifle stock was a sight to behold and the envy of every young local marksman. Some said that the Kentucky rifle was called a hog rifle because it could hit a wild hog more than 100 yards away. At least that's what Nucky often said. He reveled in sharing the bragging rights that came along with the rifle: "That's why buckskin-wearing Daniel Boone carried one of these babies in the frontiers of Kentucky."

Young Nucky became a legend around the Pinelands not only for the Kentucky long rifle but for his expert aim as well, especially at the local turkey shoots. He credited his success with a trick his father once taught him. Nucky had learned how to imitate the high-pitched call of a turkey, so when he was ready to fire, he wet his middle finger, touched the front sight to deaden the sun's glare, and then he cajoled loudly. His call was as dead-on as his shot; the curious turkey didn't have a hope of running into the woods after it raised its head from behind the stump to see what the commotion was. With sure-shot Nucky at a shooting event, the Johnson family always had a fresh turkey for Thanksgiving dinner.

As for formal education, the local schools were simple but structured. Nucky attended a four-room schoolhouse, where students often sat at a two-seater desk to save space. Every room had at least one sailor's son or daughter who Nucky befriended while he learned more about seafaring customs and routines. Every student from a seafarer's house usually arrived a half-hour before the school doors officially opened, following a time-honored maritime tradition of arriving early to be ready to relieve a sailor at the end of a shift. When Nucky visited his school friends at their homes, he discovered just how different life was from his own at the Mays Landing jail. In a sailor's family, life was very organized and strictly regimental: Chores were assigned, and work was completed on time. The children answered with "Aye-aye, Sir!" and no one questioned the captain's orders. In comparison, Nucky and Alfred knew they had it easy.

When the school day ended, Nucky often perched himself on the wrap-around porch of a Victorian home, waiting with his schoolmates for the captain/father to come home. When a captain strolled in the door, Nucky asked about him about his world travels, the people he met, and the countries he explored. The captain enjoyed recounting his glory days at sea, and Nucky proved to be the perfect audience.

While every captain shared his experiences sailing the seven seas, Nucky had a tough time figuring out whose stories he liked the best. One of his favorites was Captain Shepherd Hudson who commanded a Union ship during the Civil War that carried troops and ordinances. Nucky felt a special kinship with Hudson since Nucky's grandfather also served in the Civil War. Before he entered the captain's house, Nucky routinely stood at the front door at attention and said, "Permission to come aboard, Sir."

Though Hudson's first love was the sea, his second was politics. As a member of the Whig or Republican Party in his younger years, he was elected to the N.J. Assembly in 1889 and served for two years before he built a new ship and set sail again. Nucky's father eventually took Hudson's post on the N.J. Assembly for one term before resuming as sheriff.

In those early years, Nucky often daydreamed of becoming part of Hudson's crew and sailing around the world. One afternoon when he was sitting on his friend's porch, Nucky saw Hudson walking toward the house from the water's edge carrying a handmade wire clam basket filled with bricks caked with Great Egg Harbor riverbed mud. When the captain reached the steps, Nucky asked him jokingly, "How long do you have to cook those bricks before you can eat them, Captain?"

The captain stopped and countered Nucky's joke with a tale that Nucky would hold dear for the rest of his life. These were "Irish bricks" for good luck, according to the captain. He explained that as ships left Ireland without a full cargo to keep the ship stable, some of them needed ballast in the hull to keep the ship steady while the vessel crossed the rough Atlantic. So the industrious Irish merchants in the foundries sold their defective bricks to the ship owners. The defective bricks had split when they were baked in high heat because they contained too much clay, but they were put to good use.

When ships from the Olde Sod arrived in America and sailed up the Great Egg Harbor River to pick up cargo in Mays Landing, they didn't need the Irish bricks as ballast anymore, so they dumped them along the river's edge into the salt marshes. Legend has it that every Irish brick that is recovered brings seven years of good luck. With six bricks weighing down his wire clam basket, the captain said he was now carrying 42 years of good luck, which was more than he needed at his age. He reached into the basket and gave Nucky one of the Irish bricks and a blessing: "May you have all the luck you need and not need all the luck this Irish brick will bring you."

Nucky cherished that brick for the rest of his days. In fact, he once told his bodyguard Kessel that when life was rough, he would pull out that treasured brick, put it on the nightstand next to his bed, and then take a nap. When he awoke, he usually discovered that he had found a solution to his problem and the energy to tackle it. Since he didn't want to use up all his good luck at one time, he put his treasured brick away for safekeeping so he would always have some good luck in reserve, much like a savings account in a bank.

Later in life when Nucky would reminisce about Hudson's stories, he came to realize that their meaning ran far deeper than as the simple tales about life in faraway lands. Hudson's adventures were parables about human nature and molding character. For the next 70 years, Nucky loved to drop anchor when making decisions and muse, "What would the captain do? How would he solve a problem or avoid creating an enemy?"

Nucky naturally credited part of his wisdom and understanding of human character to these former sea captains who had seen the world, worked their way up the ranks, and survived not only rough seas and plenty of treachery along the way. Nucky considered all men to be captains in command of their own ships in life, and "each charting his own course only to counter the unexpected storm that suddenly changes his direction and life." The tales he heard early in life served as Nucky's compass, which he believed served to mold his success in leadership and public life. These stories were also the ballasts that kept him on course during the difficult times he endured, and there were plenty of rough seas.

Nucky decided to pursue higher education after graduating from high school in Atlantic City. He enrolled in State Normal School College in Trenton with his childhood schoolmate and sweetheart, Mabel Jeffries. Born in Steelmanville near Mays Landing, Mabel came from a long line of sea captains; her father, Lewis E. Jeffries, was the son of sea Captain James Jeffries, another captain who made Mays Landing his home.

But college didn't hold Nucky's attention for long, even with Mabel attending with him. After a year, Nucky left college to begin a law clerkship in Atlantic City with George A. Bourgeois. As a graduate of University of Pennsylvania with a thriving trial practice, Bourgeois welcomed Nucky to his office and urged his new protégé to be patient as he learned the legal ropes. Bourgeois thought Nucky's natural gift of public speaking would make him an excellent trial attorney.

In those days, law clerks were required to "sit for the bar," which meant spending every day in the preceptor's law office without compensation. The day-to-day experience and work was a good proving ground for clerks to learn the ins and outs of the law before taking the bar examination. But feeling trapped and penniless, Nucky's restlessness won out again, and he left to work in the sheriff's office with his father as a paid clerk. By the time he was 21, Nucky had settled in as undersheriff and took his part in the family tradition.

Nucky patiently waited for Mabel to graduate from college and start her teaching career at a grammar school in Mays Landing. Their long-term courtship won the blessing of both families, and on September 12, 1906, 23-year-old Nucky married Mabel, who was just 21. By that time, Nucky had been promoted from undersheriff to deputy sheriff and was earning a good living. The newlyweds even bought a house with a veranda in Mays Landing. Mabel's stepmother, who had raised her from age 7, gave the couple a "bridal elm" as a wedding gift, which the couple planted in their front yard. The small tree served two purposes: First, it was designed to protect the home, and second, it was a living sign to the neighborhood that they were newlyweds. According to legend, as the elm grew, so would their love. In fact, this elm was reported to have "sprouted vigorously and sped to maturity faster than a busy farmer could swing an ax in protest," according to Nucky. He considered the tree to be a good omen. It was a living testament to the long life he expected to share with Mabel in the years to come.

CHAPTER 2

HANGING A MURDERER

During his terms as sheriff, Nucky's father dealt with the usual petty crimes and misdemeanors, but he also had to hang three prisoners who were condemned to death by juries in Mays Landing. For each hanging, Johnson received a $500 bonus from the Atlantic County Board of Freeholders, money that he said never fairly compensated him for the mental anguish he experienced before, during, and after the hangings. Johnson had only been at his post for a year when Robert Elder was accused of patricide (killing one's father) on August 4, 1888, in Hammonton.

Traditionally, the bell in the belfry rang at the Mays Landing Court House when the jury reached its verdict. On October 23, 1888, the jury foreman announced that the jury found Elder guilty as charged. Although Elder appealed his conviction, the death sentence was carried out on January 3, 1889, a total of 72 days from conviction to execution. Justice was swift. The rapid appeals process gave birth to the phrase "Jersey Justice."

The responsibility for making the arrangements for the hanging fell on the sheriff. The only other executions that took place in the history of the county were 13 years before on October 7, 1876. That was when Sheriff Samuel Adams hanged John Fullen and John Hill on the same day; both men were convicted of murdering an elderly farmer for his money. A third man, Isaac Dayton, was implicated in the crime, but he turned state's evidence and was given 20 years in prison instead. The victim's small change purse, which was introduced into evidence, contained one penny for a senseless crime.

Johnson rounded up his deputies for Elder's execution; he wanted the ordeal to be quick and orderly. And it was. At 12:05 PM on January 3, 1889, Elder was dead. The local *The South Jersey Republican* newspaper described the hanging as "a very quiet affair, no fuss, no excitement. If capital punishment is justifiable (which we cannot believe) may the work always be done as neatly as in this case."

As Elder was hanged, Andrew Grimes, a burly black sailor from York River, Virginia, was already in the county jail awaiting his trial after being charged with murder. He was accused of killing his messmate, John Martin of Fair Haven, Connecticut, on Christmas 1888. The killing took place on the schooner *Annie S. Carill* while it was anchored in Absecon Inlet that separates Atlantic City from Brigantine. Grimes was convicted in April 1889; Johnson hanged him two months later on June 20, 1889.

The sheriff firmly believed in capital punishment and never hesitated to carry out the jury's verdict. But he always wished he could have interceded beforehand to help prevent the crime in the first place. Johnson considered himself to be a problem solver, a mediator, and an employment agency. He prevented many men from going to jail by offering them a job and workable solutions to their problems. It was a kind gesture that those in trouble respected and readily accepted.

It didn't take long for Nucky to experience Jersey Justice of his own as undersheriff. On December 22, 1906, John Buglio, a native of Italy, was murdered at his Minotola home, just a few miles from Johnson's jail. Buglio, who lived with his wife, Rafella, and their five children, had been bludgeoned to death with a club, and his throat had been savagely slashed, according to police records.

That same evening, police also reported that four shots were fired at Joseph Labriola, a Minotola constable and good-looking dance instructor as he was walking home from the local dance hall; two rounds hit his leg. At first, the attacks seemed to be isolated events; no arrests had yet been made in either case, but Nucky thought there might be a connection. He hoped that his father would assign him to the investigation team.

The sheriff knew that whoever murdered Buglio was likely to be sentenced to death by hanging. The state was supposed to take over all executions for any death penalty crimes committed after March 1, 1907, at which time, convicted criminals were to be executed using the new electric chair at the Trenton State Prison. Johnson was relieved hearing this news since it was finally going to put him "out of the hanging business" after the Buglio case was resolved.

Nucky was intensely interested in this murder case. The sheriff told Nucky to go with the county detectives and check on the details of the murder and the shooting. The friendly, law-abiding Italian community of Minotola was home to about 2,000 immigrants, most of whom were related by blood or marriage and from the same village in Italy.

As one of the first steps, Nucky and the county detectives to interviewed the five Buglio children. Michael "Mick" Raymond, the widow's brother, was also living in the family house, since Nucky thought he might be helpful in providing background information. When Nucky went to the Buglio residence with Detective Frank Lore and his team, Buglio's widow was not at home, but the children were. Three of the five children who were present on the night of the murder recited the same story: Nothing unusual happened on Saturday, December 22, and they did not hear their father leave the house.

But it didn't take long until the children's story began to unravel. Tilly, then 3½ years old, burst into tears, and Lore took her into an adjoining room where she told him her version of the events on the night of the murder. Frightened Maggie, age 7, provided more details and took the detective to the kitchen and on the garden walk to show him a few blood spots. She then told him about the wheelbarrow that had carried her father's body to the backyard and the whereabouts of her mother's bloody skirt buried in the yard.

At first, Raymond, then 24, refused to talk to the detectives, but then he decided to offer more information about his brother-in-law's death. When he was taken to the sheriff's office, he talked about what happened on the night of the murder and asked what the three Buglio children had said. The pieces of the puzzle were starting to fit together. After reading the reports, the prosecutor told Sheriff Johnson that there was more than sufficient evidence to charge Labriola, Rafella, and her brother, Mick Raymond, with Buglio's murder. The prosecutor was planning on seeking the death penalty for whoever savagely bludgeoned Buglio and slashed his throat.

The sheriff, Nucky, and the deputies took all three suspects into custody and placed them in separate cells in the Mays Landing County Jail. About three months later, on April 4, 1907, the process of selecting the jury began before Atlantic County Court of Oyer and Terminer, as the trial court was called at the time. A large number of prospective talismen were present and voiced their opposition to the possibility of another hanging. The special panel of potential jurors was exhausted as the controversy over imposing the death penalty continued. The presiding judge, Supreme Court Justice Thomas Trenchard, who was specially assigned to the case along with Judge Enoch A. Higbee, directed Johnson to round up more potential jurors from the street and bring them to court. This was the first emergency jury roundup in the history of Atlantic County.

The case grew more complicated as more details of the case emerged. Labriola reportedly had a long-term relationship with Rafella that began when he was a boy and she was already married with children. Her husband was apparently aware of his wife's intimate relationship outside the marriage. Their tryst ultimately led to arguments when John Buglio objected to Labriola's visits prior to the murder, according to the *Atlantic City Evening Union* on September 21, 1907. Apparently, the relationship between the Rafella and Labriola was well-known to the Italian community.

"I was at the dance hall all night and when I left, I went straight to my house," Labriola said. "When I reached my house, nature called and I went outside to the outhouse, and when I came out, a figure suddenly appeared out of the darkness. I could not see who he was, but he fired four shots at me, then disappeared as quickly as he first appeared—I was hit twice and called out to my wife to get medical help, which she did." But Labriola's statements in court weren't adding up; there was more to the story than the defendants were saying.

The thoroughness of the prosecutors' investigation and that of the sheriff's office helped the prosecutor's team chisel away at the defendant's credibility. The defendant admitted that when the detective first questioned him on Sunday morning, two days after the murder, he denied being at the victim's home on the night of the murder. He couldn't identify who shot him or how his attacker was dressed, although the shooter was only a foot away from him, according to his own statement.

Members of the matinee audience craned their necks and squirmed in the hard benches as they tried to get a look at Rafella, the grieving widow behind the black veil who weathered the cross-examination unshaken and confident. The final defense witness, who was a surprise to the state, was Rafella's brother, Mick. He was also under indictment for his participation in this crime. He accused one of the detectives of having him sign a false statement that involved his sister and Labriola.

Judge Trenchard charged the jury to apply the facts according to law as they accepted the evidence presented by both sides. The jury began their deliberations at 4 PM and reached a verdict by 9 PM. The courthouse bell rang, and everyone rushed to the crowded courtroom, where the verdict was read. Labriola was found guilty for murder in the first degree; Rafella was found guilty of manslaughter. Labriola's hysterical mother had to be removed from the courtroom after she heard the verdict.

The judge directed the sheriff to bring the two convicted prisoners into the courtroom for sentencing. When Labriola stood before the judge, he insisted that he was innocent, but the judge sentenced him to death by hanging. Both prisoners, along with their attorneys, were seated at the defense table when the justice asked Rafella to stand.

"You have been convicted of manslaughter and the sentence of this court is that you spend ten years in the state prison at hard labor and pay a fine of $1,000 and remain in prison until it is paid," said the judge.

Sheriff Johnson and Nucky led the convicted prisoners back to their cells. Rafella was later transported to Trenton State Prison to serve her time, and Labriola was confined to the Mays Landing jail.

It was common practice to select 12 witnesses to watch the hanging, and Judge Trenchard directed the sheriff to impanel a pool of jurors. The sheriff called out the 12 names of those who would serve on the "death jury," and each selected member walked over to the sheriff and Nucky who were both standing by the jury box. The sheriff told the jurors that they would be told when to report to witness the hanging once the defendant had exhausted his appeals, which would likely be before Thanksgiving.

The appeals process was swift and limited; the applications to the Supreme Court and then to the Court of Errors and Appeals, the highest court, were unsuccessful. A final appeal was taken to the state Board of Pardons, but it refused to commute the sentence of death by hanging. The execution date was set for September 20, 1907, less than a year after the crime took place and five months after the conviction.

Jersey Justice was indeed swift and certain. Labriola never swayed from his story that he was innocent; he swore he didn't commit the crime.

He said he was leaving two notes to be opened after his death with name of Buglio's real killer. Labriola was quick to say that Raymond could have cleared him of the charges, but Raymond lied to protect his sister.

During his nine-month stay at the Mays Landing jail, Labriola grew closer to Nucky since Nucky was responsible for checking on the prisoners each day as undersheriff. Nucky often took a few extra moments to talk to Labriola, but they never discussed the murder.

One day, Labriola asked Nucky to do him a personal favor. He handed Nucky two notes through the prison bars and asked Nucky to keep them in a safe place. It was Labriola wish that Nucky read the two notes publicly after his hanging. Of course, Nucky agreed, but then he realized that he would have to help hang the man he was getting to know and like. Being a man of his word, Nucky reluctantly took the notes and kept them in a safe spot; he dreaded the day he would have to actually read them in public after the hanging.

On September 17, 1907, the sheriff's deputies and four carpenters began building the gallows in the courtyard by the jail out of public view. The sheriff, Nucky, and the deputies anchored two upright cedar posts in the ground, 15' high and 10' apart, and connected them at the top with a cedar crossbeam with a rope and a hangman's noose hanging down from a ring in the center of the crossbeam. The noose had the traditional 13 loops: one for each of the 12 jurors and one for the judge. On the other end of the rope was a 300-pound lead weight that was pulled off the ground near the top of the scaffold and then secured by another rope lashed to a large wooden block firmly embedded in the ground. When the restraining rope was cut, it would release the weight and pull the prisoner by the neck 2' off the ground.

When the scaffold was finished, the sheriff and Nucky tested it. They had cut a cedar log the same height as the condemned man and placed the hangman's noose 2' from the top of the cedar log. The sheriff told Nucky to cut the restraining rope with one fast, hard blow. Johnson wanted to see how high the log rose off the ground.

Nucky swung the cleaver with all his might, cutting through the rope, and the weight hit the ground with a thundering thud. The ground shook, and everyone was silent. With that, the sheriff made a few last-minute adjustments and finalized his calculations for the actual execution.

Just days before the execution, the sheriff let Labriola's family visit him. He had been a model prisoner; he remained calm and courteous to the guards and accepted his fate with remarkable composure. Labriola's mother was permitted to spend time with him, but the sheriff ordered the guards to escort her from the building if she had any emotional outbursts, which would upset the entire prison population. His next-to-last visitors were his wife and two children.

The solemn death watch started on Wednesday in the county jail, and the guards entered Labriola's cell every half-hour to check on him. Labriola vowed to walk slowly to his death with his executioners, the sheriff, and Nucky. At 11 AM on Friday, September 20, 1907, Labriola was to hang by his neck until dead. The sheriff read the death warrant to Labriola at 10:45 AM in his cell as required by law, as the prisoner, wearing his wedding suit, nodded his head slowly and kept repeating that he was innocent.

The death jury of 12 men appointed by the court was standing along the prison walls in the courtyard along with the sheriff deputies in full uniform including white wide-brimmed Western hats. With them were a handful of newspaper reporters and a few other observers who the sheriff had permitted to witness the last hanging. As the sheriff placed the noose around Labriola's neck and tightened the greased rope, the prisoner quietly lowered his head. Then the sheriff pulled the black deathcap over Labriola's face.

With that, the sheriff raised the cleaver and cut the retaining rope with a mighty stroke. Labriola died instantly at 11:08 AM. His body was hanging motionless until the doctor on duty made the official death announcement. A wooden coffin was waiting as the undertaker took the body back to Minotola for a Catholic funeral Mass and burial in Vineland. When everything was quiet, the sheriff asked Nucky to read the two statements that Labriola had given him, which were published in their entirety in the *Atlantic City Evening Union* the next day. The bystanders were hoping it was a confession, but they were wrong.

The first note cast guilt on Rafella Buglio, since "she told me the night she done it." Labriola claimed that he was innocent of the crime and convicted on false evidence. He hoped that "the public will look upon her as a murderess in the world when she gets out of prison." He held on to the hope that he would be vindicated and that "some day I think it will be discovered and the public will know I am right."

When Nucky finished, his father asked him to read Labriola's second letter, which began with the acknowledgment that Labriola "did not get any justice in the court at my trial." He named Detective Lore as the one responsible for coaching the Buglio children to accuse Labriola of murdering their father. "I have a suspicion that Mike Raymond is shielding his sister, Mrs. Buglio, for it is the cause of my death," according to the note. "Mike Raymond's confession is all against me."

There was total silence in the courtyard when Nucky finished the readings. The sheriff announced that he was heading across the street to Norcross's Saloon to have a drink or two since his work was now done. But the exhausted Nucky went home and sat down on a rocking chair on his front porch. He sat with the warm sun on his face and counted his blessings. Mabel came out and sat in the rocking chair beside him; she reached over and held his hand. She knew Nucky had his doubts that Labriola committed the murder and tried to comfort Nucky by saying that he had carried out his assigned duties as undersheriff in a professional manner. Although he did everything with dignity, Nucky still found it hard to be consoled.

The Labriola ordeal was a turning point for Nucky. In those moments after the hanging, Nucky reassessed his life. Having tried a career as a law clerk and as an undersheriff, he was still unfilled and restless. He told his wife that he wanted a change; he said he was going into politics. After all, he saw the respect his father received as sheriff, and he liked the recognition that came with the job compared to those locals who worked long, hard hours in the fields or lived off the sea. And after seeing mansions such as Sugar Hill, State Senator William Moore's estate in Mays Landing, Nucky realized how a career as a public official could provide the good life that Moore and the Commodore enjoyed. And that's just what he wanted. But the reality of what he was to accomplish in his lifetime exceeded even his wildest dreams.

CHAPTER 3

ESTABLISHING A POLITICAL BASE

As part of the coastal plains of southeastern New Jersey, Atlantic County extends from the Mullica River along the edge of Burlington County on the north to the Great Egg Harbor River along Cape May County on the south. In between, there are 14 miles of sandy beaches and Pinelands chock-full of indigenous pine and sturdy oaks. At the heart of this stretch of sandy soil was the state's crown jewel: Absecon Island, home to Atlantic City and three neighboring communities of Ventnor City, Margate City, and the Borough of Longport, all of which were once called South Atlantic City. This was Nucky's home and playground.

The Lenni-Lenape Indians were the first to discover the rich bounty on Absecon Island, covered with scrub pines and sand dunes, and home to seagulls and sand crabs. By 1854, other developers were beginning to see the potential in this stretch of beachfront real estate. Richard B. Osborne defined a portion of Absecon Island and named it Atlantic City, a designation that stood out on the map in gold letters, and a city was born. Osborne, a young engineer who worked for the Camden and Atlantic Railroad, devised special railroad routes in New Jersey between Camden and Atlantic City, a venture that spurred the rapid growth of the burgeoning shore community.

And as the city grew, it didn't take Philadelphia vacationers long to discover the joys of the self-proclaimed City by the Sea and sample its wares firsthand. Atlantic City, with its year-round population of 40,000, had become an exciting metropolitan resort that soared to 300,000 residents when the "shoobies" (a local term for summer visitors who carried their lunches in shoeboxes) arrived in the early 1900s.

Within a few years, Atlantic City had the best railroad service serving any resort in the world for good reason. There were more than 1 million potential passengers within 200 miles of Atlantic City, and the ground was flat. When the railroads were in full operation, as many as 92 daily trains ran in and out of the city. After all, with only about 8,000 total vehicles in the entire U.S., automobiles were not a popular mode of transportation in 1902. There were still too few paved roads for vehicles adhering to a speed limit of 10 mph.

Atlantic City was 18 miles "over the meadows" and growing at a faster rate than rural Mays Landing. The developing shore metropolis was quickly becoming a playground for the mainland and a welcome market for its abundant local farm produce. Atlantic City embodied a special place without governmental interference and without laws that prohibited pleasure-seeking, entertainment, and recreation. It was an isolated island in more ways than one. It developed its own standards regardless of what statutes were on the New Jersey law books. Law enforcement in South Jersey simply looked the other way: The times were good, and Atlantic City wanted to keep its reputation as a popular destination, drawing vacationers nationwide.

Islanders, as the residents of Absecon Island were called, were blossoming into members of a growing cosmopolitan community; they considered everyone who lived "off shore" to be living in the woods. Since Atlantic City had become the hub of all business and recreational activity at the turn of the century in South Jersey, clusters of exclusive international boutiques sprang up along the world-famous Boardwalk and beach with entertaining nightlife and plenty of gambling. Islanders couldn't understand why anyone would ever want to leave.

When Nucky was growing up in nearby Mays Landing, the rural town was a thriving commerce center and the county seat of Atlantic County with a courthouse and county jail. Nucky's view of the offshore communities was different than that of the locals; he was part of it. Like his father before him, Nucky's name as sheriff was familiar to the residents of the Pinelands, aka Pineys. Nucky's father had personally introduced him to local farmers, baymen, hunters, and seamen, and then helped Nucky build a career that rested on the family's reputation of service and public life. In 1908, the 25-year-old Nucky was the youngest sheriff ever to be elected in New Jersey.

Most of the 23 municipalities in rural Atlantic County didn't have police officers, and there were no state police at the time. This vacuum of authority positioned the sheriff as the county's chief law enforcement. And as sheriff, Nucky knew the true character of the residents of southern New Jersey, and many came to him for help. In his official role, he helped many locals in need and treated everyone with respect. When he traveled around the county on official business to serve legal papers or to arrest someone, he was welcomed with a handshake and a cup of coffee. The community didn't fear him; instead, members of the community opened their doors willingly to him. After serving a civil summons or a legal complaint, Nucky often stayed to offer guidance and to counsel the family member over a second cup of coffee. He was ready to help with a family dispute, find jobs for the unemployed, or supply food when a family was hungry. When a disrespectful son or daughter proved too much for a parent to handle, the sheriff was there with a lecture and a view inside a prison cell to instill a little fear and some perspective.

When Nucky traveled through the county to rally voting interest in an election for his post or for that of a friend, his word was golden. He raked in a bumper crop of votes for a candidate with just a nod. Clubs were formed in his name including the Nucky Johnson Boosters in Egg Harbor City, a place where he often discussed the candidates he liked. But more importantly, he talked to members and helped them with their problems. Although he was not always successful, he sure tried, which was exactly what most people wanted anyway. The meeting room in Aurora Hall, a popular German tavern in Egg Harbor City, was the scene of many social events and election rallies where Nucky preached to the crowds and received a standing ovation in return.

As his three-year term as sheriff of Atlantic County ended in 1911, his zest for politics was just beginning. He expanded his political base countywide, gathering a cadre of trusted friends who stayed by his side for the rest of his political life. He often drove around in his open touring car from farm to farm just to say hello to his constituents. He loved politics.

The black community, with its own ward leaders, precinct captains, and poll workers, liked Nucky's frankness and his ability to deliver on promises. To demonstrate their support, they established the Enoch L. Johnson Standpatters in his honor. On one of his many visits to the club-house at 1605 Arctic Avenue, Nucky discovered that black musicians were prohibited from joining the all-white musicians' union. Nucky stepped in with a solution: In the 1930s, he circumvented the problem by arranging a separate union for blacks so they could play at union houses. After that, any time Nucky stopped by the clubhouse, there was always a bottle of bourbon tucked away in the back room safe just for him.

Nucky continued to cultivate Atlantic City's growing collection of ethnic, religious, and business voting blocks as County Collector (Treasurer) and when he became the leader of the Republican Party in 1914. He knew he could count on them to deliver votes on Election Day, and he even provided financial encouragement along the way. He worked out a system directly with the leaders of each group to control their membership vote.

The Italian block vote issued strong support for Nucky's candidates with the formation of the Nucky Johnson Italian American Club. Nucky sat down at many seven-course home-cooked meals and listened as families asked for help getting a promotion or a raise. In turn, Nucky doled out rewards for those who were loyal and politically active. The club leader Joseph A. Corio, a distinguished lawyer, was appointed to the bench, and many Italian members of the beach patrol and the police and fire departments were promoted regardless of seniority.

Nucky concentrated his efforts on the Italian section at St. Michael's Catholic Church and the adjoining school on Mississippi Avenue. This tight-knit Italian community included residents from all over Atlantic County, and many of them sent their children to school at St. Michael's. The schoolteachers, who were nuns of the Salesian Order, came directly from Italy and eventually learned English; the founding pastor was The Reverend John Quaremba who celebrated Mass in Latin but delivered his sermon in Italian. When mainland farmers set up an open market near the bay at the end of Mississippi Avenue, the bounty of fresh produce and poultry lent the name of Ducktown to the Italian section, which is still the center of the Italian community today.

Likewise, if some of the prominent residents in the Jewish community in Atlantic City's Inlet section wanted to hold public office, Nucky always made sure he included one of the local Jewish businessmen on the ticket. Even the citywide Republican Organization in Atlantic City called itself The Enoch L. Johnson Republican Club.

Nucky's affiliation to the Republican Party originally took root with one of his father's friends when the elder Johnson was state assemblyman and sheriff. Commodore Louis Kuehnle took the political reins in the early 1900s as the Republican political leader in Atlantic County and stepped in to replace Republican Congressman John J. Gardner, former mayor of Atlantic City, state senator, and congressman.

As Atlantic City grew rapidly, the Commodore took on more politically active roles, partially to protect his diversified investments around town, which included a heating plant, a brewery, a hotel, local telephone company, and an interest in the United Paving Company. He also was an unpaid member of the Atlantic City municipal water company. Since the first yacht club was founded in Atlantic City with his assistance, he was given the honorary title of Commodore. The Commodore's father, a Democrat who was also named Louis Kuehnle, was a former mayor of Egg Harbor City and made the first family investment in Atlantic City: a hotel.

The elder Kuehnle built the Kuehnle Hotel in Atlantic City in 1875, a property that the younger Commodore eventually inherited. The hotel was across the street from the West Jersey and Seashore Railroad Depot at the corner of South Carolina and Atlantic Avenues. The hotel's pub called the Corner was the hangout for politicians and political hopefuls. As head of the Republican Party, the Commodore controlled many jobs related to his investments, which he disbursed only to the Republican Party faithful.

When a gala celebration was planned for Atlantic City's Semi-Centennial Celebration in 1904, the Commodore led the Golden Anniversary initiative and served on the finance committee along with a host of up-and-coming Republicans, including Harry Bacharach, Lewis R. Scott, and Walter E. Edge. The Commodore was selected the chief marshal in the Marine Parade during the gala celebration, festivities in which all craft started from the Atlantic City Yacht Club. After circling the island, the nautical parade returned to the yacht club with the

Commodore, dressed in full-fleet regalia, leading the flotilla aboard the flagship *Katherine K,* named in honor of his mother.

When Nucky's father visited the Commodore to catch up on the political scuttlebutt in Atlantic City in early 1900, Nucky usually came along for the ride. With the Commodore on the island side and Nucky and his father on the mainland, all the political bases were covered for the Republicans, from sand to soil. Nucky once asked his father and the Commodore how the Republican Party became such a stronghold in the area, and the Commodore explained that most people in South Jersey were just born Republicans, just as they were born Baptist, Methodist, or Catholic. It worked for their parents, so it must be okay for them.

But the Commodore was the exception to the rule since his father was originally one of the few Democrats in Egg Harbor. As with all the Germans who first settled there, the young Commodore came to Atlantic City and decided to register as a Republican to avoid being an outcast. He knew that people in Atlantic City had always taken their Republican politics very seriously, and he wanted to be part of the power structure.

In the past, Congressman William Moore from Mays Landing attended the first Republican National Convention in 1856 at the Musical Fund Hall at Eighth and Locust streets in Philadelphia, when the country was in turmoil over the slave issue. Moore was considered to be one of the founders of the national Republican Party. The newly formed Republican Party wanted to return to the original principles upon which the country was founded and strongly opposed the extension of slavery. General John C. Fremont was nominated the first Republican presidential candidate in 1856, and former U.S. Senator William L. Dayton of New Jersey was the first Republican vice presidential candidate.

Although Abraham Lincoln sought the Republican presidential nod in Philadelphia in 1856, he never received enough votes. Four years later, Lincoln returned and won the nomination to become the first Republican President of the United States, edging out opponent Stephen Douglas.

Moore, who brought the Republican Party to South Jersey, built his home called Sugar Hill in Mays Landing. His political affiliations were legendary. Those who wanted to work for him in the coastal trade aboard his fleet of commercial ships had to be registered Republicans. Those not lucky enough to be born a Republican could join the party in order to get hired.

Moore's business and influence spread throughout the county as he doled out jobs during his four-year term as congressman in 1867, and then he offered state jobs for four years during his time as state senator. Between his business interests and his public offices, he was the man to see for a job.

When Moore retired from public life, John J. Gardner took over. As a popular war veteran from the Civil War as well as a lawyer, Gardner served as a corporal with the Sixth Regiment of the New Jersey Volunteers for four years until the end of the Civil War in 1865. When he settled down, he built a large manor house south of Egg Harbor City; his family owned waterfront land in Atlantic City called Gardner's Basin. Once Gardner entered public life, he stayed in the limelight as mayor of Atlantic City, county coroner, and finally, Atlantic County state senator, a position he held for fifteen years. In fact, he served in Congress until 1893.

With this backdrop of solid Republican power, Nucky joined organizations and expanded his network of friends and colleagues. Nucky was readily accepted into a politically active group called the Morris Guards since he served as sheriff as his father had before him. When he first joined the Morris Guards, he became friends with local movers and shakers who played a pivotal role in his political life and who were instrumental in growth of Atlantic County.

Civil War veteran Colonel Daniel Morris started the Morris Guards, a military and social club in 1887. When Irish immigrant Morris began working on the new Camden and Atlantic Railroad in 1852, he surveyed the right-of-way for the railroad company and then focused on developing the land that would eventually become Atlantic City. Morris, the first surveyor for Atlantic City, was responsible for naming Atlantic City streets after most of the states, state capitals and oceans. The engineer for the railroad, Richard Osborn, is credited with naming the resort "Atlantic City" in 1853. With his love of real estate, the Colonel purchased most of the land between North Carolina and Michigan Avenues as an investment, which later proved to be a very profitable venture.

Morris also established a citizen solider guard that distinguished itself in several wars. The 113 members, who volunteered as a unit for the Spanish-American War, were federalized as Company F, Fourth Regiment of New Jersey U.S. Volunteer Infantry. On July 12, 1898, the company attended a gala banquet at the Hotel Dennis on the Boardwalk with a reception on the then-new Steel Pier overlooking the Atlantic Ocean before they marched off to the Spanish-American War. Walter E. Edge was one of the commanding officers who later soared to political heights in the state and nation.

By the early 1900s, Morris had built a large red-brick armory in the center of Atlantic City on South New York Avenue, just two blocks away from city hall. Morris insisted that every member under the age of 18 practice rifle and marching drills every other week to retain membership and practice target shooting at the top-floor range. It became a popular meeting place for political figures and a mecca for the city's social life before the era of ocean amusement piers, motion picture theaters, and public dance halls.

Several members of the Morris Guards went on to become Atlantic City mayors: Edward Bader, Anthony M. Ruffu Jr., Harry Bacharach, and Joseph Altman. Other members made the who's-who list: William A. Blair became county clerk; Armand T. Nichols became deputy Atlantic City mayor; Walter E. Edge became assemblyman, state senator, governor, and ambassador to France; Allen B. Endicott Jr. became county collector from 1883 to 1897, Atlantic City solicitor, and president of the N.J. Bar Association; James Carmack became sheriff of Atlantic County, and his brother, Mark, became president of Wilson Dairies; Charles Lafferty was added as the U.S. Collector of Customs and Democratic leader; William S. Cuthbert was elected Atlantic City commissioner; Russell "Whitey" LeVan became the Morris Guards historian; and Frank S. "Hap" Farley eventually became Republican Party chairman, succeeding Nucky. Farley's legislative record credits Farley, who also served in the N.J. legislature as an assemblyman and senator for 34 years and as five-time acting governor, as the most productive legislator in the history of New Jersey.

Others in the Farley family were also members of the Morris Guards, including Paul J. Farley, Hap's brother, who also served in World War I and II. Paul, who retired as a full colonel, joined the law firm that became Farley, Fredericks & Ferry. Hap's nephew, Rex Farley, also served in World War II and was killed in active duty. William Graham Ferry, a prominent hotel owner, became the journal clerk in the N.J. Senate and director of Civil Defense for Atlantic County during World War II. Even I was accepted into the Guard when I turned 14 years old.

Nucky was at home with these "big boys" and soon became the most popular of them all during his 30 years at the political helm. The network of statesmen in the Morris Guards created a solid foundation for Nucky's grand entrance into the world of politics.

Nucky's political base was neither confined to Atlantic County nor was it confined to Republican Party loyalists. At the zenith of his political power in 1926, Nucky teamed up with his northern Jersey counterpart Frank Hague to change the election law to favor professional politicians. Hague, the Democratic mayor of Jersey City, was a powerhouse in the state and national Democratic Party. Under the reform, a voter only needed to renew his registration every 20 years, as long as he remained in one community. As a result, a ward leader could easily "honor" the deceased by voting with their names long after they passed on. Nucky was fond of saying that the Lord looks favorably on those who remember the dead, an attribute that leaders of the Republican and Democratic parties readily accepted as virtuous each Election Day.

Nucky quickly became acquainted with the inner workings of the political landscape as County Treasurer and as head of the Republican Party in the early 1900s. Charles Lafferty, the local Democratic leader, and Nucky made sure the Lafferty Democrats received their fair share of public jobs. Nucky didn't want an upstart Democrat to rally against his Republican ticket, which would make the election expensive and leave the outcome in doubt. Lafferty, who was happy with this arrangement, often said, "My Democrats got more jobs working with Nucky than they would have gotten if they opposed him." Nucky figured out how to work the system; he simply cut everyone in on the action.

The vibrant Republican Party that Nucky inherited from Moore became stronger and gained more strength under Gardner and the Commodore in 1914. Nucky always kept in contact with the business and social leaders of the county, but he knew elections were won in the trenches by the constant efforts of his precinct captains and ward leaders addressing the daily concerns of the voters. The ward clubs were engaged all year-round, and those who attended did so for the camaraderie of the members and an opportunity to advance in their jobs if they were on the public payroll. Those who were active politically naturally advanced over someone who was not, regardless of seniority.

During an election year, Nucky unleashed his organization and scheduled weekly appearances for his candidates in every part of the county. No meeting was too small; candidates were sent to sauerkraut suppers at the German churches, spaghetti dinners at the Italian churches, oyster suppers in church basements, celebrations on Washington's birthday, and pancake breakfasts for the volunteer fire company; they dined at roast pork dinners and chicken potpie suppers; and they officiated at strawberry and cranberry festivals, block parties, minstrel shows, 4-H clubs, and beach parties. Likewise, elected officeholders in Atlantic County kept active by contacting their supporters and friends, often going door-to-door to support the Republican Party. Many of the churches welcomed the candidates, letting them greet parishioners after the services with a firm handshake and a friendly smile.

Nucky had his own Republican Club that represented a cross section of the communities that professed a deep personal loyalty to him. Blacks in Atlantic City had their Nucky Johnson Standpatters Republican Club, and each ward had an Enoch L. Johnson Club for the men and a Ladies' Auxiliary for the women. Even Nucky's mother sponsored The Virginia Johnson Republican Club in Mays Landing that held social events year-round. The Johnson All-Stars baseball team was active politically, supporting Nucky in appreciation of him supporting the baseball program.

Each club and ward club provided an election agenda that was then given to Nucky at his Atlantic county treasurer's office at Suite 723. Next door in Suite 722, Jimmy Boyd, Nucky's right-hand man, worked with the clubs to prepare a master list for the candidates, from opening day through Election Day. The coordination was thorough and constant: Nucky checked in with Boyd every day, sometimes twice a day, and often attended the events himself to introduce the candidates, much to the delight of the audiences. Getting people out to vote was a personal obligation of each precinct worker and a job that was taken very seriously. After all, their jobs often depended upon it and they knew it.

Election victories were expected; second place didn't count. The Johnson Machine ran smoothly, well-oiled with cash from Nucky to everyone who worked for the party along with "street money" to get the voters out. Potential voters who didn't want to leave their homes were likely to suddenly change their minds when the precinct captain pulled out a "finsky" (a $5 bill) for each voter.

People-friendly organizations continued to bolster Nucky's political strength during his rise to power. Later, in 1935, when Atlantic City's Irish residents wanted to have their political voices heard, they formed the Friendly Sons of St. Patrick of South Jersey, a chapter of the national organization that dates from 1771 in Philadelphia. The first meeting of the Friendly Sons was at the Graham Hotel at States and Pacific Avenues in Atlantic City at the invitation of the owner, William Graham Ferry. From its inception, the society was nondenominational and welcomed members from all religious backgrounds.

The membership, which was limited to 135, quickly filled to capacity, and others added their names to the waiting list. The bylaws called for three religious leaders for the society: a Protestant minister, a rabbi, and a Catholic priest. When asked why the Friendly Sons needed three religious leaders, Nucky, who was proud of his Irish ancestry, was quick to say, "Every Irish organization should have three chaplains on St. Patrick's Day to help keep the peace."

Nucky arranged for a prominent speaker to address the membership at each banquet; it was usually someone in a high public office who Nucky had helped to elect and was undoubtedly eager to repay the favor. The Friendly Sons' first banquet was held at the Ambassador Hotel on March 16, 1935, with all the members formally attired in tuxedos.

The Friendly Sons were intensely patriotic. Many members, past and present, had served in the Armed Forces, including Commodore John Barry, father of the U.S. Navy. One of the earliest members was General George Washington who accepted membership in Philadelphia on January 1, 1782.

Nucky, who traced his Irish ancestry from 1756, was full of pride on St. Patrick's Day and attended every banquet to share stories with his fellow Irishmen. He reminded them to vote "early and often" for his candidates at upcoming elections. The society still remains the oldest continual meeting organization in the U.S. today, dating from 1771 to the present.

Nucky was readily accepted into the Atlantic City Elks, which enabled him to have personal contact with the leading citizens of Atlantic

City as well as to portray himself as a concerned community leader who used his political power in the best interest of Atlantic City.

Atlantic City Elks Lodge 276 boasted of its charitable activities that included the Betty Bacharach Home for Crippled Children in Longport, New Jersey and its prominent business leaders. They included Harry Bacharach, a mayor of Atlantic City, and Isaac Bacharach, his brother, who served in Congress six terms and, of course, the man who got them all elected to public office, Nucky Johnson. Nucky was given the singular honor to serve as Master of Ceremonies for their Anniversary Banquet in 1932.

Since Nucky's father opened the door to the rural community for his son, Nucky advanced his own image with membership in the Morris Guards, the Elk's Lodge, the Friendly Sons of St. Patrick, and the many political clubs that honored his name. The political and business leaders of Atlantic County dominated these organizations. With his natural charm, Nucky skyrocketed to the top of the political scene in Atlantic County, buoyed by his passion for politics and a growing base of loyal Republican supporters from all walks of life.

HIS HOME TURF

CHAPTER 4

THE ARISTOCRACY
OF THE SHORE

While Nucky was busy building his empire, Philadelphia's high society was busy trading the stifling mainland heat for the cool ocean
breezes of Atlantic City. People began to spend their well-earned summer
retreats at the grand hotels along the resort's oceanfront or at the yacht
clubs along the bay.

Nucky enjoyed Atlantic City's sights and sounds just as much as the visitors who flocked to the shore for fun and its touted health benefits. First,
the saltwater surrounding the island prevented any drinking water from
being contaminated by nearby mainland streams. Second, artesian wells
and the seven miles of conduits over the meadows to a reservoir provided
a continuous source of clear, pure drinking water. In fact, many of the
oceanfront hotels built their own artesian wells and electric generating
plants while promoting the benefits of clean water in their advertisements.
Since Atlantic City was promoted as a health resort, the Philadelphia physi-
cians endorsed the curative effects of salt air. Many wealthy families who
once journeyed to southern resort destinations began to prefer the shorter
trip of 60 miles from Philadelphia to Atlantic City.

Camden and Atlantic's first steam-powered passenger train in 1854
almost made the two-and-a-half-hour trip bearable. The train slowly
chugged along to the shore as the crew tossed a steady supply of wood
into the firebox, generating a cloud of black smoke in its wake along the
way. Passengers sat in plush parlor cars with comfortable reclining seats
and attentive porters. To encourage more vacationers interested in

Atlantic City, the promoters of the Camden and Atlantic Railroad Land Company took a gamble and invited 600 influential residents of Camden, Philadelphia, and New York for a day at the shore to consider the island for future development. And the gamble paid off.

Before the advent of the railroad in 1854, travel to the seaside was a long ordeal. Stagecoaches left at 4 AM from Philadelphia's Market Street to the Delaware River port, and then the passengers took a ferry across the Delaware River to Camden. The Camden-to-Atlantic-City-trip usually took about 10 hours, while passengers suffered on less-than-forgiving wooden benches on rustic Jersey wagons. Travel grew more comfortable when newer coaches adopted shock-absorbing elliptical springs in padded seats.

With the periodic development of direct rail lines to Atlantic City resorts from New York, Washington, Baltimore, Pittsburgh, and Philadelphia, travel turned civilized. The train was fast, comfortable, and direct. Once guests arrived in Atlantic City, they looked for the smartly attired chauffeurs from the hotels holding signs for their respective hotels, so guests could easily hop on board the horse-drawn carriages that ferried them to their hotel of choice.

The hotels along the Boardwalk competed for guests with unique amenities. By 1902, Quaker Josiah White, III had built a luxury hotel next to the City Park on Park Place: the Marlborough Hotel on the beachfront. Four years later, he connected the Blenheim Hotel with an enclosed bridge (the first ever in Atlantic City) across the street with the political help of State Senator Emerson Richards. Thomas Edison, New Jersey's white-haired genius who invented the light bulb, supervised the construction of the hotels. Both hotels catered to quiet but wealthy clientele; afternoon high tea in full traditional British style was served at both hotels. Dinner was always a formal occasion. On weekends, men were required to wear tuxedos; ladies were decked out in evening gowns.

Though the Marlborough and Blenheim hotels were on separate oceanfront blocks, a fully enclosed elevated bridge connected the two over Ohio Avenue. The bridge walkway, which was a showcase where women in pastel-ruffled finery and wide-brimmed hats sashayed from one hotel to the other, became a fashion promenade of the latest fashions known as Peacock Alley.

Quakers Henry W. Leeds and J. Haines Lippincott also owned and operated the Chalfonte-Haddon Hall Hotel with nearly 1,000 rooms in true Quaker-style: excellent dining but no liquor allowed. The hotel actually consisted of two separate buildings connected by a tunnel under North Carolina Avenue. The hotel was so popular that it actually had its own convention bureau to schedule bookings. For years, music was the resort's drawing card; the hotel's Vernon Room featured March Musicales with leading singers from the Metropolitan and Chicago Opera companies. The Chalfonte-Haddon Hall eventually became Atlantic City's first casino in 1978.

The Hotel Dennis, a cottage-turned-hotel in 1860, was later purchased by the enterprising Buzby family in 1900. The new owners added a grand lobby that overlooked the property's green lawns, the beach, and the Boardwalk, so guests could enjoy all the health benefits of the sun and salt air. The only amenity that the Quaker hotels didn't offer was alcohol: No one could get a drink in any of these establishments before, during, or after Prohibition.

Unique luxuries, from telephones in the bedrooms to invigorating hot-and-cold saltwater baths pumped directly from the Atlantic Ocean, guaranteed a market share of the incoming elite clientele. Other landmark hotels offered other enticements. The lounge at Brighton Hotel at Park Place along the Boardwalk became the toast of the town with its fortified Brighton Punch (before Prohibition). The President Hotel at Albany Avenue and the Boardwalk offered residential apartments and a popular Grill Room. The Rudolph Hotel at New Jersey Avenue and the Boardwalk catered to social and political events during the winter where guests enjoyed steam heat in a magnificent sun parlor. The Royal Palace Hotel at the end of Pacific Avenue on the Inlet channel offered rides in the spacious steamship *Mermaid* that sailed hourly from the hotel dock. The Traymore Hotel, known as the Castle by the Sea, was fully illuminated by electric lights on the exterior making it look like a magical castle at night. The Claridge Hotel, at Indiana Avenue and the Boardwalk, was named the Skyscraper-by-the Sea, with views of the ocean and sunsets on the bay from each of its 24 floors. The Steamer Deck overlooked the Park Place gardens with its 10' cascading fountain aglow with colorful lights each night.

For those who couldn't afford top dollar for such luxuries, there were still plenty of accommodations to choose from. Hotels on the side avenues found ways to cater to tourists who could not afford the luxury hotels on the Boardwalk. In 1839, Aunt Millie Leeds first opened a boarding house and tavern on the beach that launched a booming family boarding house industry that grew at the same rate as cottages for the wealthy. And more people began to pursue the excitement of Atlantic City, from gambling to the all-night clubs to other amusements, all of which were tolerated and encouraged by the city fathers.

For those who wanted to see and be seen, the yacht club was the place. The Chelsea Yacht Club at Aberdeen Place and the Bay hosted supper dances as winter entertainment for its patrons at the stately Hotel Rittenhouse and lunches at the Hotel Adelphia in Philadelphia. At the other end of the island, the Atlantic City Yacht Club at New Hampshire Avenue and the Inlet, held joint social functions with its sister facility, the Chelsea Club. While the Bay View Fishing and Gunning Club in Longport was a gentlemen-only club for Philadelphians, the Yachtsmen's Pier and Pavilion was open to the general public at Pacific Avenue eastward from States Avenue.

During the summer, the yacht clubs kept members entertained with a range of activities: bridge, pool, billiards tournaments, dances, get-acquainted luncheons, and regatta events. Other members tried a challenging game of cricket at the Chelsea Sea Cricket Club or hunting at the Gun Club on North Sovereign Avenue or at the Rod and Reel Club in Gardner's Basin. The twin sports of fin and feather attracted avid sportsmen from the East Coast all year-round.

In the early morning as the sun was rising, sports fishermen in bright-yellow hip boots cast their lines into the ocean surf. Locals knew spring had arrived when the piping plovers and laughing gulls scoured the shoreline for horseshoe crab eggs. White sails of the trim sloops and three- and four-mast schooners dotted the distant blue horizon. On board were fishermen determined to pursue their quest for bluefish, weakfish, white perch, and flounder in the spring, and sea bass and codfish in the fall.

The shore's bounty extended far and wide. As families returned from horseback riding on the beach or a trip aboard a donkey-driven beach chariot along the water's edge, they looked forward to fresh seafood in the restaurants lining the fishing piers along the Boardwalk. The catch-of-the-day was a featured entree on every hotel menu.

For seafood lovers, a trip to the shore was not complete without dinner at Hackney's Lobster Restaurant at the end of the Boardwalk at Maine Avenue where diners fished for their own lobsters in a large tank. Not far from Hackney's was Captain Starn's Restaurant and Yacht Bar with a seating capacity of 500 at the end of the Boardwalk. While the captain's fishing fleet assured the freshest seafood for his hungry guests, couples hopped aboard a sightseeing boat from Starn's for a romantic view of the Atlantic City coastline. Starn's also had an ocean pen right next to the docks where children could feed the seals. When the seals popped their heads out of the water, children ran over to a nearby vendor to buy some fish tidbits to feed them.

The city even promoted its healthy lifestyle with two full-time fitness drill instructors: One was assigned to the Atlantic City Beach Patrol Headquarters at South Carolina Avenue and the beach, and the other was stationed at the States Avenue beach on the other side of Steel Pier. The instructors stood on an elevated platform and put the willing participants through a rigorous calisthenics program. Crowds of all ages, shapes, and sizes gathered in front of the platform on the beach as if it was the first day of boot camp, though some cautious spectators preferred to watch on the sidelines along the Boardwalk. The beach turned into such a popular hot spot that the city installed floodlights in the center of town for night swimming.

For the less adventurous, one of the Shill Company's many popular two-passenger hand-pushed wicker rolling chairs provided a relaxing ride along the Boardwalk. The rolling chair's roof and clear side curtains shielded riders from the wind and provided a window onto the world around them.

The pavilions on the wooden way also offered a venue for band concerts, especially America's great John Philip Sousa, who played his military marches each summer, including "The Stars and Stripes Forever." His wife, Jennie Bellis, was raised in Atlantic City and returned each summer. Her father was a Boardwalk photographer, and she was fond of boasting that she always had "sand in her shoes." In the evening, the curtains were raised for musical productions at the Grand Opera House on the Boardwalk, the Nixon's Apollo Theater at New York Avenue and the Boardwalk, the Keith Theater on the Garden Pier, and the Savoy Theatre at the Ocean and the Boardwalk.

Atlantic City's seven-mile wooden Boardwalk, which was built in 1870 for a sum of $5,000, was originally designed to keep the beach sand out of hotels and shops. But it didn't take long for the Boardwalk to develop a life of its own. Bright incandescent lamps illuminated the Boardwalk every evening. The Boardwalk actually turned into world's greatest stage, offering one of the most spectacular outdoor events each spring. When it was time for the Easter Parade, the Pennsylvania Railroad added extra Boardwalk Special passenger cars to transport the expected 70,000 visitors to the shore. The boats at the Market and Chestnut streets in Philadelphia ferried passengers across the Delaware River, where they then took the train to Atlantic City to join in the spring classic that started at the turn of the century.

The parade of people and Easter bonnets varied in style and sophistication, from feathered hats tilted at bewitching angles to cloche bell-shaped caps. Women added high-button shoes, padded bustles, and pastel parasols for a stunning fashion show that extended from one end of the Boardwalk to the other. The men sported their own finery, wearing Homburg's, the Chaplin-type fur felt hat with a grosgrain band; Bowler's, Derby hats with a bound edge and a colorful feather on the side; and straw Skimmers, also known as Boaters, the signature hats worn by gondoliers in Venice.

Proper gentlemen celebrated the spring event by buying new suits from Jacob Reed & Sons in Philadelphia, accessorized with gloves and a walking stick. Young boys topped off their attire with newsboys' flattop woolen caps. The Boardwalk hotels even filled their lobbies with colorful floral arrangements that doubled as backdrops so visitors could stop and have their pictures taken. A steady stream of people strolled along the Boardwalk, stopping to chat with friends for only a moment before moving on with the current of the crowd.

Even Nucky had his own rolling chair that he usually shared with some national celebrity for the Easter promenade, such as Jimmy Walker, the mayor of New York City, or a glamorous actress from a stage show appearing in Atlantic City. Throughout the day, he willingly shook hands with everyone who approached his rolling chair while thanking them for being part of that year's Easter celebration.

The Boardwalk, which could easily accommodate 100,000 visitors, became a rendezvous for friends at other times of the year, too. Visitors liked window-shopping along the Boardwalk with its assortment of shops showcasing merchandise from all over the world. Auction parlors enticed passers-by for estate merchandise that was sold to the highest bidder. Each had a full-time shill, an employee posing as a customer who invited visitors to take a seat and encouraged bidding on a great bargain. The Harold A. Brand store cultivated an exclusive clientele at its auction gallery near the Apollo Theatre with high-end merchandise that ranged from imported china, crystal, and sterling silver to works of art from exquisite collections.

But fashion and goods weren't the only delights along the Boardwalk. Ice cream parlors served generous scoops of frozen confections on sugar cones, and Hires Root Beer offered all-you-could-drink refreshments for 5 cents. The hungry beach-goers grabbed a 5-cent hot dog from a stand and a soft drink from the latest coin-operated machine. Visitors gathered around James's store window and watched as hand-pulled, saltwater taffy was cut into mouth-size pieces.

Nearby, the aroma of almond and coconut macaroons wafted from the A.L. Roth and the G. Carl Tripician stores. Souvenir shops sold seashells and turtles with the words "Atlantic City" painted by hand on them. Some merchants offered cranberry-colored glass mugs customized with the buyer's name etched on the back and the words "Atlantic City" on the front.

Mr. Peanut, the suave mascot for Planter's Peanut, extended a warm welcome with a gloved hand to young and old. As the Boardwalk's official greeter, Mr. Peanut, dressed to the nines with a cane, monocle, and black top hat, was a walking advertisement for Planter's store. After visitors posed for a souvenir picture with Mr. Peanut, they received a sample of fresh roasted peanuts and a friendly escort to the store's open door to purchase a goodie or two.

Atlantic City's proximity to the Gulf Stream made the surf warmer than most resorts for the thousands of bathers who dug their toes into its fine white sand. The guards from the Atlantic City Beach Patrol, the most experienced beach patrol in the world, kept a watchful eye on the swimmers, who gathered to watch the life-saving drills at the Absecon Lighthouse and the U.S. Coast Guard station. Some of the less venturous beach-goers preferred to stay on their beach blankets and enjoy a day under an umbrella watching swimmers tumbling in the surf or the children moving sand from place to place with tiny shovels. In the winter, when the snow arrived, Atlantic City had a work crew assigned to promptly remove any snow that accumulated. As one Atlantic City sign said, "No snow on the Boardwalk."

Families in search of entertainment of all kinds could take their pick of five ocean amusement piers along the Boardwalk: Steel Pier, Young's Million Dollar Pier, the Garden Pier, the Heinz Pier, and the Steeplechase Pier. Atlantic City's Steel Pier, built in 1898 at Virginia Avenue and the Boardwalk, was undoubtedly the most popular spot known as the "Showplace of the Nation." It was so named because it was the first pier constructed on steel pilings driven deep into the ocean bed, rather than traditional treated lumber. For one general admission ticket, a family could spend morning to night enjoying the events: stage shows, a relaxing nap on a comfortable steamer deck chair, amusement rides, circus acts, the world-famous diving horse on the end of the pier, or at the aquarium with fish from all over the East Coast. And then in the evening, couples enjoyed memorable romantic moonlight dancing in the Ocean Ballroom near the end of the pier surrounded by the Atlantic Ocean.

One of the longtime attractions at the Steel Pier was the world-famous diving horse. Sonora Webster Carver, the first woman to ride the legendary diving horse, took the plunge off a 40-foot-high platform into a water tank at the end of the pier. Carver began her career at the age 20, a story that inspired the 1991 movie *Wild Hearts Can't Be Broken*. Amazingly enough, although Carver was blinded after a bad fall off the platform with a horse, she continued to perform the stunt for another 11 years and lived to the age of 99.

The Steel Pier's ever-changing novelty acts were another draw: Shipwreck Kelly sat on top of a flagpole for 49 days; Primo Camera, the heavyweight champion of the world, fought boxing cats and a boxing kangaroo in an exhibition match; movie-goers flocked to the Criterion

Theatre with 10 reels of "moving pictures," a two-hour show that featured a soundtrack with organ music.

For children, the clown-faced gateway to the George G. Tilyous' Steeplechase Pier just a block from Steel Pier let kids step through the mouth of a clown leading into a magical world of amusement rides, games, and thrilling adventure.

Young's Million Dollar Pier, built in 1906, drew crowds for its dance marathons that lasted for days in Young's Hippodrome. Dancers competed in weekly tango dance contests on Friday nights in the ballroom on the pier, "The Home of the Cake Walk," where the then-latest cake walk dance craze was in full swing. In the 1930s, comedian Richard "Red" Skelton orchestrated dance marathons on the Million Dollar Pier that made national news. Skelton later became a beloved comedian on television for the characters he created, the most popular of which were Clem Kadiddlehopper, Freddie the Freeloader, and Cauliflower McPugg. When the ballroom was not staging dancing contests, it was used for roller-skating during the day.

The Garden Pier, built in 1913, was situated in the uptown section of the Boardwalk that attracted an upscale crowd with its more formal Spanish Renaissance-style buildings, old mission red tile, and a formal landscaped multicolor garden. The centerpiece was the B.F. Keith Theatre, which rivaled anything on Broadway with its 2,200-seating capacity and its megaphone plan that ensured perfect acoustics.

The Heinz Pier was the signature national marketing site for the Heinz Manufacturing Company, one of the major national businesses that understood the value and drawing power of this growing cosmopolitan hub. Heinz saw Atlantic City as a prime location to advertise its products with its large "57 Varieties" electric sign that was readable for miles on land and from sea. Guests to the exhibit on the pier received a little green pickle pin as a token of their visit.

The pursuit of healthy outdoor activities opened a host of other venues in or near Atlantic City as well. In 1897, a group of enterprising Atlantic City hotelmen introduced the game of golf to the area. J. Haines Lippincott and Harry W. Leeds of the Chalfonte-Haddon Hall, along with Warren Somers whose family founded Somers Point, joined the "resort golf" craze. Philadelphia Quakers quickly signed up to guarantee a tee time for a fashionable game of golf. The Country Club of Atlantic City, which was organized in 1897, staked its claim to a large tract of land overlooking the bay meadows in Northfield, a few miles offshore. For golfers, the club was a quick ride via the Shore Fast Line, an electric trolley from the Boardwalk hotels to neighboring Somers Point and Ocean City.

One of the first players in 1903, Abner "Ab" Smith from Philadelphia, hit a great shot down the 12th fairway that landed within inches from the hole, allowing an easy putt and a one under-par. His brother who was playing with him shouted, "That was a bird of a shot!" And the term "birdie" was born at the Atlantic City Country Club, a word referring to a shot that entered the cup one under-par or one less than the number of shots allowed for that hole.

But golf was not the only sideline for visitors. A group of prominent Quakers from Philadelphia started the Ozone Club in 1901, for an afternoon of golf each month. Most of the men attended Moorestown Academy or Westtown School for Friends and then went on to Swarthmore or Haverford College. As Quakers, they didn't drink alcohol and preferred relaxing with other Quakers who shared their same beliefs. The club included notables such as Charles Francis Jenkins, vice president of Swarthmore College; Arthur N. Leeds, overseer of William Penn Charter School; Daniel S. White, president of the Traymore Hotel; and Walter J. Buzby, owner of the Hotel Dennis.

At the Ozone Club, men dressed in wool knickers with heavy cotton knee-high socks, topped off with a jacket and tie and a flat top cap, despite the heat. Meetings were held once a month for fellowship and a round of golf at the Northfield Country Club, a short distance from Atlantic City. The members stayed at Haddon Hall as guests of Henry W. Leeds the night before their day on the course. Their game revolved around a competition for the Ozone Handicap Cup. Usually members were fined $1 if they caused a delay in teeing off by transporting his clubs on the wrong railroad line, which happened often.

By 1914, golf had become so popular that Clarence H. Geist, a flamboyant utility tycoon from Villanova, built a self-contained full-serve resort called the Seaview Country Club in nearby Galloway Township. Acclaimed sports architect Donald Ross designed the course after the links layout in his native Scotland. Most players favored the Pine Course because the other Bay Course was infested with biting greenheads. The Richard Stockton College of New Jersey later acquired this facility in 2011 and established an affiliation with Cornell University as part of their joint hotel management programs.

When automobiles were a novelty starting in 1904, Atlantic City sponsored automobile racing on the beach at low tide when the sand was hard and smooth. Contestants arrived from all parts of the country to compete in front of cheering spectators along the Boardwalk, some even wagered on their favorite racers. One of the early racers was Henry Ford alongside Gaston Chevrolet, who later founded his own automobile company, and later Eddie Rickenbacker, the legendary World War I American fighter pilot hero. Many of the drivers later started competing in the early Indianapolis 500 in 1911.

Atlantic City was also known for its thrills in the air. The Aeromarine seaplane, with double wings and pontoons, offered a breathtaking aerial view of the island, a favorite for those who wanted to take their first airplane ride. By 1910, the talk of the Boardwalk focused on the aeroplane, as admiring spectators lined the Boardwalk along Young's Million Dollar Pier for a view from the Atlantic City Air Carnival.

The amenities of the shore lured many prominent East Coast families to nearby Ventnor City. Incorporated in 1903 and named after a resort in England, Ventnor City possessed an aura of exclusivity. In fact, an eight-block area designated Saint Leonard's Tract in the city had deed restrictions limiting it to single-family use. The streets were named after British dukes, which added to its noble ambience. A few prominent families gave their official seal of approval and settled in Ventnor City: Charles M. Schwab, the steel magnate and president of Carnegie Steel Co.; T. M. Daly, president of Centennial Equitable Trust of Philadelphia; the Roebling family who founded the N.J. town of Roebling as well as John A. Roebling's Sons Company of Trenton that manufactured wire rope for suspension bridges; glamorous Lillian Russell, the toast of Broadway; the Wanamaker family who owned Philadelphia's leading department store and built a mansion at Dorset and Atlantic Avenues; and Charlemagne Tower, the U.S. ambassador to Germany. Others notables settled in neighboring Atlantic City instead: Rodman Wanamaker; the Luden family, manufacturers of Ludens Cough Drops; and Dr. Charles Penrose, brother of U.S. Senator Boies Penrose.

A home at the shore was a must for the elite. Some prominent families were actually dropped from the Philadelphia Main Line's Social Register—which tied every stately mansion to financial success—when they gave up their shore homes. Its residents didn't have to impress others about their wealth; everyone simply knew it.

With the opening of Longport's exclusive Winchester School for Boys in 1911, many affluent families and hotel owners began to send their sons to school on the island instead of shipping them back to the mainland. At the time, there was no private school for girls, who were often sent to boarding schools on the Main Line. The students at the Winchester school, under headmaster Douglas Howe Adams, included the sons of the prestigious Wanamaker and DuPont families. With a school up to grade 12 for students on the island, there was no rush after Labor Day to return to the mainland. Chauffeurs simply arrived at the front door in the morning to drive the wealthier island children to and from school.

Those seasonal vacationers who left the island at summer's end didn't leave empty handed. They took a box of James' Original or Fralinger's saltwater taffy, a colorful pennant with the Atlantic City skyline, and a healthy glow to show off their stay at the shore. In fact, when Charles Darrow visited Atlantic City in 1934, he was so inspired by the excitement and wild land speculation that he created the game of Monopoly and named the streets on the board game for those in Atlantic City. Parker Brothers soon began reaping revenues from the game based on this prime batch of real estate; Monopoly became the best-selling board game in the world and is still a testimony to the pinnacle of Atlantic City's growth and prosperity.

As Nucky ventured into the world of politics and launched his mission of accumulating wealth and power in earnest, he made Atlantic City his political base. Building his empire on the Boardwalk wasn't a game of chance; it was his oyster, and he was ready to roll the dice and let fate be his destiny.

CHAPTER 5

FUN CITY:
THEY SHALL COME

A tlantic City's popularity grew by the day. The resort's summer charm continued to enchant more visitors from all walks of life. By the turn of the century, electric trolleys began running along Atlantic Avenue, ferrying visitors to their destinations.

In 1899, gambling was in full swing on Absecon Island. There was Monte Carlo in an old Victorian mansion in South Atlantic City (Margate), and Philadelphia crowds enjoyed roulette and faro, the top two games of choice. In Cape May, people flocked to the popular Blue Pig gambling parlor near the Congress Hotel, where bandleader John Philip Sousa often performed in concert. In fact, his *Congress Hall March* was a tribute for his first concert on the green. The hotel was also an occasional summer hideaway for past U.S. presidents Benjamin Harrison, Ulysses S. Grant, Franklin Pierce, and James Buchanan who vacationed at the Congress Hotel.

Gambling brought in the guests, and cash began to flow. Blackjack, roulette, craps, baccarat, and poker were attracting crowds from the coal-mining districts of Pennsylvania, city dwellers from New York, locals from Philadelphia, and folks from the nation's capital. But once summer was over, the visitors returned home for the winter and returned to the shore each spring. Gambling was not solely played indoors. Wagers even placed bets on fleet-footed canines at the greyhound track at North Carolina Avenue and Absecon Boulevard.

Gamblers who arrived at the shore used Lucy the Elephant as a landmark for the casinos. The six-story, 90-ton wooden hotel in the shape of a pachyderm stood in a feeding position with bright-red eyes, white ivory tusks, and a colorful Maharajah's Howdah on top. At 65 feet tall, Lucy was covered with gray tin (her skin), a manmade frame molded into the shape of an elephant with her massive feet firmly planted in the Jersey sand since 1881. On a clear day, visitors can still see Lucy from five miles away at sea. In fact, sailors on watch aboard their ships were known to stare in disbelief as they passed by, some even swearing off their rum rations for days.

Lucy was the architectural folly of James V. Lafferty, a Philadelphia land developer who wanted to woo prospective buyers to his beach houses in South Atlantic City (Margate). This desolate area of sand and dunes, bayberry bushes, and scattered pine trees was a peaceful spot for summer cottages sprouting up on the island. At the time, the Borough of Longport next to Margate was still totally uninhabited except for the U.S. Life Saving Station and Frye Farm where cows grazed in the open fields. The south side of the borough consisted of sand dunes, and the rest was meadowland. By 1908, more summer cottages were built when the Church of the Redeemer was built in Longport, creating an anchor for the incoming residents.

The Victorian era had not disappeared completely from the shore. Although gambling was tolerated, Atlantic City strictly enforced other laws, including the Mackintosh Law that required everyone to wear an outer garment over a bathing suit in public. Violators who attempted to stroll across the Boardwalk to the beach wearing only a bathing suit were promptly arrested by the vigilant Boardwalk police patrol.

Atlantic City cultivated its reputation for the good life, and sunseekers sampled a variety of pleasures in addition to gambling. Before Prohibition, outdoor beer gardens served as gathering places where likeminded folks could relax. One of the most popular beer gardens in Atlantic City was Schauflers at North Carolina and Railroad Avenues in the heart of the city. The hotel even had its own liberty bell, which rang to summon the thirsty. Often, the bell tolled when a new keg of beer had been tapped from one of the six breweries in the city ready to roll out their barrels: The Atlantic City Brewing Co., the Ballantine Co., Louis Bergdoll Co., Bergner and Engel Co., Christian Moerlein Co., and Weisbrod and Hess Brewing Co.

For tourists seeking good fortune, Professor Alf E. Seward, a self-proclaimed astrologer, opened his Temple of Knowledge at 1541 Boardwalk, near Kentucky Avenue. For a small fee, he offered predictions to the curious on how the heavenly bodies would bring good fortune. Of course, the larger the fee, the bigger the fortune predicted.

To keep rhinestone cowboys entertained, Buffalo Bill's Wild West Show partnered with Pawnee Bill's Far East Show at the City Show Grounds off of the Boardwalk at Albany and Atlantic Avenues. All the performers paraded into the arena on horseback carrying colorful flags at the opening before the bull riding and traditional rodeo roping events began.

Industrialist Charles M. Schwab, a car enthusiast who had a summer home in Ventnor, built a speedway to rival the Indianapolis Speedway in Amatol, a former wartime boomtown 20 miles west of Atlantic City that was once a WWI munitions depot and ordinance plant. The Atlantic City Speedway was built on a 6,000-acre tract on the White Horse Pike where record crowds and outstanding drivers from all over the world came to try out "the fastest oval track in the world." The grandstand held 60,000 fans with standing room for 250,000 more to watch as many as 75 cars competed in a single race. About 80,000 people turned out for the first race on May 1, 1926. Harry Hartz, hero of the Indianapolis Speedway, won the epic 500-mile event. Among the racing cars in the initial race were a Dusenberg Special, a Dode, a Buick Marmon, and a Whippet. But one of the biggest draws for the event was the official: Captain Eddie Rickenbacker, a national hero and the top American ace in World War I. Many fans came just to see the legendary pilot who shot down 26 German fighter planes in dogfights over France.

But on the Boardwalk in Atlantic City, nickelodeons drew visitors for a peek at one of the dozen or more shows each day. Some operators originally called them "penny arcades" and "peep shows," terms that were later changed to "kinetoscope parlors." Patrons sat for hours watching the moving pictures called "the flickers," later known as "talkies" and "movies."

One of the stars of the early flickers was Charlie Chaplin, the short man with the little black mustache, the cane, and funny walk, who became an international star. Years later, the movie premiere of *Gold Rush* in 1925, featuring the mustached actor opened at the Bijou on the Boardwalk in Atlantic City.

Moving pictures even brought sports events to life. On March 17, 1897, sports fans in Atlantic City witnessed the first moving pictures at the State Opera House at States Avenue and the Boardwalk, with the James J. Corbett versus Bob Fitzsimmons Heavyweight Championship of the World in Carson City, Nevada. Fitzsimmons KO'd Corbett in the 14th round to win the title.

Nucky once said, "More stars appeared in Atlantic City, than in heaven." Top performers came to local clubs and theaters to entertain tourist and folks heading for one of the national conventions in town. Nucky never missed an opening night of any headliner. He often invited the star to a post-show party and sometimes invited the entire cast. He told producer Earl Carroll that he considered entertaining the performers as part of his job to promote Atlantic City. "I like to mix business with pleasure," Nucky said. "If they have a good time at the shore, they will spread the word and become goodwill ambassadors for Atlantic City."

During the 1920s, Atlantic City was where the action was. It was the nation's premiere tryout town for new stage shows that were headed to Broadway. Not only did the cast and stars come to Atlantic City to perform, but they also came here on vacation to be with their fellow celebrities and to co-mingle with other show-business people, including directors and producers who they solicited for bookings or parts in upcoming productions.

An opening night of a musical production was a gala occasion. Many of the audience dressed in formal attire arrived by Shill rolling chairs for the premiere performance at Nixon's Apollo Theater at New York Avenue and the Boardwalk, which was former spot of the Academy of Music. The other popular venue was the Keith Theater on the Garden Pier. Even the full *George White's Scandals* production appeared on the Boardwalk the first night it opened. Many shows, after earning a favorable review in Atlantic City, went on to become Broadway legends.

Very few stars escaped Atlantic City without being inducted into the Atlantic City Detective Bureau Celebrity Squad. Nucky usually accompanied the star to Atlantic City's City Hall and introduced the performer to the mayor as people crowded around. As a tradition, the mayor swore in the honoree and then pinned a gold Atlantic City detective badge on the honorary member of the world's elite detective squad. The squad was a who's-who of show business and sports including Joe Louis, Joe DiMaggio, John Wayne, Bing Crosby, Bob Hope, Jack Benny, Roy Rogers, Frank Sinatra, Lucille Ball, and Ronald Reagan. When the official ceremony was over, Nucky often left with the new detective and headed to a gala evening at the Silver Slipper, his club at Illinois Avenue and the Boardwalk.

Paul Whiteman, also known as the King of Jazz, and his orchestra appeared at the Grille Room at the Boardwalk's Ambassador Hotel, playing his theme songs, Gershwin's "Rhapsody in Blue" and "Japanese Sandman." His vocal group included the Rhythm Boys and a young Irish singer by the name of Bing Crosby, who later left Whiteman for a legendary career on stage and screen.

Celebrities such as crooner Rudy Vallee, the original bobbysoxer idol, and Lillian Russell, known as The American Beauty, were regulars on the Boardwalk. Russell, who became the first lady of the American stage for 35 years and often performed at the Boardwalk clubs, liked the shore so much that she built a big home at Atlantic and Wissahickon Avenues in Ventnor. Her home attracted constant attention from the public with its sunken garden and everything "lily" related. The garden was decorated with floating lily pads, pink and royal purple hydrangeas served as a border on the inside wall, and the grounds had formal box hedges with lily-of-the-valley, day lilies, lavender, edelweiss, and angel trumpets.

Atlantic City had its share of scandals, too. The popular Hollywood film *The Girl on the Red Velvet Swing* featured actress Joan Collins as Evelyn Nesbit, who weathered one of Atlantic City's biggest sex scandals. When she was 16 years old, Nesbit met Stanford White, the country's leading architect who eventually seduced her. Years later, Nesbit married Harry Thaw, an eccentric millionaire and heir to a railroad fortune who decided to avenge his wife's lost innocence. On June 25, 1906, Thaw shot White three times in the face at a Manhattan restaurant.

While White's murder shocked New Yorkers, the trial of his killer captivated the nation. This was the gilded age; the 20th century was emerging, and the nation was building monuments to its newfound wealth. White had designed spectacular Fifth Avenue mansions for the Astors, the Vanderbilts, and other high-society families. He also designed and built many of the private clubs including The Players Club, The

Lambs Club, and the Brooks Club in Manhattan. But White's darker side succeeded in luring Nesbit and other young girls to a red-velvet swing in his apartment for an evening that was anything but innocent.

When the trial started in New York, reports noted that Thaw entered his plead as not guilty by reason of insanity. The prosecutor produced witnesses who testified seeing Thaw shoot White and then rested its case. The defense produced a parade of doctors who described Thaw's irrational behavior; then the star of Broadway was called to the witness stand. Nesbit recounted her relationship with White and how he showered her with expensive gifts and then stole her innocence.

After hearing the testimony, the jury was deadlocked, and the judge declared a mistrial. Nine months later, Thaw was re-tried, and this time, the jury found him "not guilty by reason of insanity." However, the trial judge directed that he be incarcerated in an asylum in Matteawan in New York. The verdict made the national headlines.

Harry Katz, an Atlantic City nightclub owner, encouraged Nesbit to return to Atlantic City, offering her 50 percent of the cover charges from the shows at his club as well as her hotel accommodations. She accepted and was a huge hit with her song, "I'm a Broad-Minded Broad from Broadway."

Will Ferry, also known as Ferry the Frog, was a star in the legendary Ringling, Barnum & Bailey Circus and later became known as the most sensational contortionist in theatrical history. (Ferry is actually my paternal great-uncle.) A native of Philadelphia, he devised his novel stage act after watching frogs in a pond on South Christian Street in Philadelphia. On stage, Ferry dressed as a frog, jumped in the lily pond, hopped up on an urn, and wrapped his legs around his neck, forming a bowtie shape, all while maintaining perfect balance.

His wife, Ann "Hattie" Ferry, an accomplished classical pianist, provided the music backstage. For a half-century, Ferry and his wife took their act on a worldwide tour including an appearance at the Centennial Dinner at New York's Waldorf-Astoria in 1935. The fete was in honor of Mark Twain, author of *The Notorious Jumping Frog of Calaveras County*.

Vaudeville and burlesque shows were also in full swing at the shore when many of rising stars honed their acts and launched their careers in show business. Pat Rooney was one of the best dancers; Buster Keaton

became an outstanding comic; Jimmy "I got a million of 'em!" Durante
starred as part of the comic trio, Clayton, Jackson, and Durante, and later
soloed at the 500 Club; Al Jolson, the singer best known for his song
"Mammy," starred in the first musical talking movie *The Jazz Singer*, with
a score composed by Irving Berlin in 1927; and bandleader Ted Lewis
opened his act with, "Is everybody happy?" and directed the members of
his band, including Benny Goodman, long before he was known as the
King of Swing.

Lily Langtry, better known as the Jersey Lily, insisted on having a
red carpet rolled out from her dressing room to the stage to keep the
hems of her dresses clean. She was the first to set the precedent for the
expression "roll out the red carpet." Among the other big draws were
Sophie Tucker, known as the last of the Red Hot Mamas, and Mae West,
the shimmy dancer famous for her quip, *Why don't cha come up and see
me sometime?*

The marquee also lit up for headliners including banjo-eyed Eddie
Cantor, the handclapping, prancing star of the Ziegfeld Follies; the popular Harmonica Rascals and lead conductor, Borrah Minevitch, a
Russian immigrant who starred in *Dreamland* with Eddie Cantor. Then
longtime vaudeville star Milton Berle switched from stage to small screen
as Mr. Television; comedian Jack Benny became the master of good timing; and Bob "Thanks for the Memories" Hope took his place as
America's greatest entertainer in the 20th century.

Composer Irving Berlin penned the lyrics for "God Bless America"
while he was living in his Ventnor Boardwalk home overlooking the
Atlantic Ocean. It was a property that he rented from N.J. Governor
Walter E. Edge for many summers. The words in the song, "from sea to
shining sea" came to him while he was sitting on the Boardwalk watching the ocean and the sun reflecting on the water. He eventually collabo-
rated with Kate Smith, his neighbor at The Oxford, who made the song
the second national anthem.

W.C. Fields—comedian, actor, writer, and juggler who starred in the
Ziegfeld Follies and motion pictures—said in his comedy routine that he
hated Philadelphia so much that he vowed to etch the following words on
his tombstone: "All in all, I'd rather be here than in Philadelphia." But he
never did.

Fields loved Atlantic City, particularly the members of the Atlantic City Beach Patrol, who helped launch his career. With the aid of an Atlantic City lifeguard, Alex Miller, Fields attracted crowds on demand. He often waded unnoticed into the ocean and pretended that he was drowning by bobbing up and down and shouting for help. On cue, Miller and his lifeguard partner blew their shrill whistles to attract a crowd and launched their clinker-built lifeboat through the breaking waves. Once the onlookers assembled to witness the daring rescue, the rescuers rushed him safely to the shore. Fields sat up and started talking to his fans about his show times on the Steel Pier. Fields told reporters that he drowned twice a day in Atlantic City.

Even international magician and escape artist Harry Houdini was a key attraction on the Steel Pier, where he escaped from a straightjacket and handcuffs while hanging upside down on a pole high above the crowd on the Boardwalk.

For entertainment other than family-style fun, burlesque also had its heyday in Atlantic City. The sensational Gypsy Rose Lee danced with only two strategically positioned ostrich feathers while at the Globe Theater on the Boardwalk. Sally Rand, a name given to her by the legendary Cecil B. deMille, was known for her dance of the shedding veils at the Steel Pier.

Black entertainers flourished in Atlantic City at the 900-seat Club Harlem on South Kentucky Avenue, a landmark venue that first opened in 1932. Sammy Davis Jr. appeared with the Will Mastin Trio, which also included his uncle and his father. This was long before he went solo and joined the Rat Pack with Frank Sinatra, Dean Martin, Joey Bishop, Peter Lawford, and Shirley MacLaine.

Duke Ellington and his jazz band launched their 50-year international career in 1923 at Club Harlem; Count Basie's band featured the outstanding jazz vocalist of the era, Billy Eckstine, Sarah Vaughn, Billy Daniels, and Ray Charles and his soul music were also often booked.

When the Big Bands played to crowds in Atlantic City, some listened, but most danced to the swing music. Artie Shaw, the great clarinetist and bandleader, turned Cole Porter's song "Begin the Beguine" into a hit, topping the charts for six weeks in 1938 and making Shaw famous at age 28.

All the big names of the Big Band era appeared along the Boardwalk:

Benny Goodman, Tommy Dorset with his Pied Pipers, and Jimmy Dorsey, Xavier Cugat with the "cuchi-cuchi" vocalist, Charo, Harry James, with his trumpet, Swing and Sway with Sammy Kaye with his College of Musical Knowledge, Guy Lombardo, the legendary "Mr. New Year's," Eddy Duchin, whose band featured "sweet music," and Glenn Miller with his group, The Modernaires. Tragically, Miller was killed in a plane crash over the English Channel while serving in World War II. Then, Lionel Hampton took jazz to a new level using the vibraphone; Gene Krupa gained worldwide fame as a great jazz drummer after he appeared at the Steel Pier.

Accomplished jazz clarinetist Billy Krechmer, who retired to the Borough of Longport, had a successful career as a sideman for such jazz greats as Red Nicholas, Russ Columbo, and the great drummer Krupa. He organized the Ranstead Street Club, an after-hours gathering place for jazz stars including Benny Goodman, Artie Shaw, and Tommy and Jimmy Dorsey.

The beach and ocean were traditionally opened to the public on Decoration Day on May 30, better known now as Memorial Day. That was when King Neptune, (the God of the Sea) with his long gray beard and a flowing robe, wore a crown and carried a trident. Surrounded by bathing beauties, he ceremoniously "unlocked" the Atlantic Ocean from a lifeguard boat with a giant key to open the ocean for the swimming season. King Neptune was accompanied by a national celebrity of the hour who was usually appearing at the Steel Pier, along with the mayor and lifeguards who set sail aboard an Atlantic City lifeguard clinker-built boat. Then the star threw a traditional wreath from the stern into the ocean as the guards steadied the lifeguard boat.

The national press corps loved the event. The photographers with their cameras flashing rolled up their pant legs and waded into the ocean to get a close-up shot of the traditional wreath toss. Of course, the beauties struck poses for the photographers and their newspapers.

Amid this backdrop of fun and folly in Atlantic City, Nucky was getting ready to step into the footlights of the political stage to "Let the good times roll!" His heyday was just beginning.

LEARNING THE ART OF POLITICS

CHAPTER 6

TEACHING A PRINCETON PROFESSOR A LESSON

Atlantic County was growing. From 1900 to 1910, the population had nearly doubled from 46,402 to 71,894, and the county was beginning to emerge as a statewide political force. Nucky was already the county sheriff in 1908, but the time was right for him to start leveraging his political power. So in 1909, he was elected to the post of secretary of the Atlantic County Republican Party, giving him greater political muscle to elect candidates statewide.

In 1910, the timing of the governor's upcoming election offered Nucky a challenging political battle. Nucky wanted no part of Woodrow Wilson being elected to the governor's office and pushed his Republican platform for four reasons: First, Nucky was a staunch Republican; second, Woodrow Wilson, then president of Princeton University, was a liberal Democrat; third, Wilson was from North Jersey and not a true Jersey native; and fourth, Wilson came from an Ivory Tower environment and not from the workingman's world.

Nucky also thought Wilson lacked the necessary political experience to become governor. Locals in the Princeton area knew that Wilson was contemplating higher political ambitions; they knew he was looking at the U.S. presidency. In fact, Wilson's goals were so well-known that in spring 1907, the students at Princeton University included a verse about Wilson in their *Faculty Song* written for a Senior Singing event:

> *Here's to Woodrow Divine,*
> *Who rules this place along fine,*
> *We hear he wants to leave the town,*
> *And try for Teddy Roosevelt's crown.*

Nucky considered Wilson to be a "Georgia Cracker" since he had been born in Georgia and was later raised in South Carolina during the Civil War. While Wilson advocated a centralized government, locals in the rural communities firmly believed in home rule. To Nucky, Wilson was cold, aloof, and removed from the issues that concerned the workingman, especially those who lived in South Jersey. Most of Wilson's life was actually spent in the classroom or as a professor at Pennsylvania's Bryn Mawr College and Connecticut's Wesleyan University. He had only been a New Jersey resident for the past 20 years.

Wilson's views were just plain different from those of rural South Jersey residents; they were a self-reliant people. For them, the less government they had, the better. Farmers, fishermen, hunters, trappers, baymen, clammers, and those who lived off the land made up the bulk of the community. They inherently disliked regulations mandated by any authority, especially anyone from northern New Jersey. Most towns in the area did not have a police force, so the sheriff was responsible for protecting all residents of Atlantic County, a place where justice was known to be dispensed quickly and firmly. That's the way the residents liked it.

The majority of residents in nearby Egg Harbor City were German immigrants who still conducted their town meetings in German and resented any interference from the outside. And for them, everyone who was not German was considered an outsider. In this tight-knit community, there were two weekly German newspapers, *Der Pilot* and *Der Beobacter,* which were widely read by the Germans in and outside of Egg Harbor City. Atlantic City even had its own German weekly paper: *The Freie Presse.* Likewise, the Quakers also had a sizable foothold in the community. In Atlantic County from the Mullica to the Tuckahoe rivers, the Quakers of Burlington County owned 10,000 acres of land. Their passion for independence was legendary; their motto was "Mind Thine Own Business."

With Wilson on the campaign trail, Nucky devised his own political strategy. He decided to campaign for Vivian W. Lewis, the Republican candidate for governor, from Paterson, New Jersey. During the campaign in 1910, Nucky spoke in all parts of Atlantic County and in the neighboring Cape May, Salem, Cumberland, and Camden counties. Nucky's "fiery stump" campaigning in true William Jennings Bryan-style made him a speaker in constant demand. He told the crowds, "Wilson was a failure as a lawyer. His 'daddy' had to support him the one year he practiced in Atlanta, Georgia, and he would also be a failure if elected governor! According to his dismal voting record, he seldom voted in elections, even presidential elections, why should anyone vote for him now?" according to local newspaper accounts.

By September 15, 1910, Atlantic County backed Wilson by a solid margin at the Democratic State Convention at Trenton's Taylor Opera House. Atlantic City lawyer Clarence L. Cole made the compelling nominating speech for Wilson, who won on the first ballot. The political bosses had done their homework and steamrolled his nomination before any opposition surfaced.

On October 20, Wilson resigned as president of Princeton University and began campaigning in earnest. He was actually relieved to get the gubernatorial nomination since he was in danger of losing his presidency at Princeton anyway after challenging the direction of university policy. The day after the convention, Wilson set off on a tour of the state to persuade residents that he intended to meet their needs. He started out in the northern part of the state and worked his way south into Nucky country.

On October 11, Wilson arrived in Paterson, the hometown of Republican opponent Lewis, who was regarded as a man of impeccable personal integrity and progressive political views. Wilson addressed an audience in the Opera House in Paterson, saying: "I have always been an insurgent. By insurgency, I mean the application of knowledge and intelligence to better government. My insurgency is not against government, but it is against the private management of government," as quoted in the *Philadelphia Record*. The audience applauded his stand, and his speech energized his campaign.

On October 12, Wilson traveled to Caldwell, New Jersey, the birthplace of U.S. President Grover Cleveland. Campaign officials expected a gathering of about 300 people at the Cleveland homestead, but a crowd of 3,000 turned out instead. The audience left believing that a fresh wave of reform was sweeping the state, a feeling that reminded them of Cleveland's rise to the presidency in 1888.

But the real test of Wilson's popularity came when he journeyed to Atlantic City, long regarded as the Republican stronghold of the local triumvirate, better known as the Kuehnle Gang: Louis Kuehnle, Sheriff Nucky, and Congressman John J. Gardner. On October 13, Wilson spoke at the Music Theater filled to its 1,200-seat capacity on Steeplechase Pier on the Boardwalk. Wilson's speech focused on establishing a meaningful Public Utilities Commission to regulate rates for railroads, electric, and gas. And he challenged another issue close to their hearts: corruption at the polls. The residents were quite aware of the illegal registration practices that the Kuehnle Gang used. When Wilson spoke of advocating a Corruption Practice Act, it generated cheers from the Democratic audience. The crowd cheered louder when Wilson said, "Anyone who tampers with voting is a public enemy," according to the *Philadelphia Record*.

In late October, Wilson met Lewis, his Republican rival, in Jersey City near the end of the campaign. The candidates were giving their standard messages to large crowds only two blocks apart. Wilson, who was championing his program for an employer liability law to protect the workingman, did not hesitate to challenge the corrupt public officials who rigged elections and large corporations that took advantage of workers. By the end of the campaign tour, Wilson had appeared in all 21 counties in the Garden State with reporter Charles Reade Bacon of the *Philadelphia Record* following his every step.

As residents cast their votes across the state and the election results were tallied, the outcome exceeded all expectations by Wilson's camp. He won 15 of the 21 counties in the state with a plurality of 49,256 votes. As expected, the electorate in the South Jersey counties of Atlantic, Cape May, Cumberland, and Camden voted Republican for Lewis.

Nucky overwhelmingly carried Atlantic City's black northside with the help of Ike Nutter, one of the few black lawyers in the county, and his other loyal black supporters. In the resort, Lewis defeated Wilson. Lewis received 7,502 votes to Wilson's 2,778 votes. In Atlantic County, Lewis also won; he received 9,926 votes to Wilson's 5,253. Wilson wondered about the legitimacy of the numbers, since he didn't think he could be disliked that much with all the Republicans in Atlantic County.

But the northern counties delivered enough of a plurality for Wilson, who was elected the first Democratic governor of New Jersey in 15 years.

Wilson received a total of 233,682 votes to Republican Lewis' 184,426. On January 17, 1911, Wilson took the oath of office in the old Taylor Opera Hall in Trenton.

Since Wilson won the governorship with the backing of North Jersey's well-oiled Democratic political machines, one of his first reforms was to turn on his supporters and denounce back-room politics. He also targeted big railroads that he claimed didn't pay their fair share of taxes as well as giant corporations that controlled many legislatures through their lobbyists. Democratic class warfare that pitted the poor against the rich was born and became embedded in the DNA of the Democratic Party for the next 100 years.

The Democrats also reaped other benefits that election year: Seven of the 10 congressmen were Democrats, a reversal of the state's previous congressional makeup. Plus, there was a Democratic majority in the legislature, which meant that the Democrats would select a successor to replace U.S. Senator John Kean.

In 1911, the New Jersey Legislature could select a U.S. Senator since there was no popular vote by the people for the candidate. However, this changed in 1913 when the 17th Amendment to the U.S. Constitution was ratified, providing a direct vote by the people. James Smith, Jr., who had served in the Senate in the 1890s and wanted to return, recruited Wilson to be the Democratic candidate. But Wilson's support of James E. Martine carried the day. Smith lost and never forgave Wilson for his ingratitude. Both Democrats and Republicans knew that Wilson had his own personal agenda and was quick to disavow party loyalty.

Early in Wilson's first year in office, he soured many Democratic leaders on his patronizing leadership style. He didn't consult them on appointments for political jobs, there were difficulties communicating, and he failed to recognize them on legislative proposals. In his mind, he had become the self-anointed leader of the Democratic Party and governor of all the people of New Jersey by divine right.

His passion for election reform became the Democrat leaders' worst nightmare. As governor and party leader, Wilson went directly to the people to force his reform programs through the legislature. He signed a bill that allowed voters to select candidates in primary elections rather than having the legislature and party bosses doing the selecting. In years past, the northern Democratic leaders had an experienced political machine that left nothing to chance. It wasn't a question of whether their candidate would win; the results were just about guaranteed. These leaders could deliver enough votes to carry the day, even after the polls were closed.

Long before the advent of the electronic voting booths, election officials counted paper ballots manually. With this time-consuming process, sometimes the count wasn't completed until two days after the polls were officially closed. The Democratic-controlled election judges in a county counted the votes, and if they saw their candidate falling behind, the tally process slowed dramatically, and scores of magically misplaced ballots suddenly appeared, most of which boosted the results for the trailing Democratic candidate.

Since South Jersey, and specifically Atlantic County, was such a staunch Republican bastion with strong-arm tactics, there was no fear of reprisal from the Republican sheriff since he was the county's chief law enforcement authority. Wilson knew that and made South Jersey one of his targets for reform. Nucky's remarks about Wilson's failed career as a lawyer didn't help the situation. In fact, Wilson took the comments as a personal offense and decided to make Nucky pay dearly for his harsh words.

To appease his Democratic political backers, Wilson urged the New Jersey Assembly to launch a full-scale investigation into the Republican stronghold in Atlantic County. On January 16, 1911, the assembly adopted a resolution along party lines to appoint five members to investigate Atlantic City. An Atlantic City Citizens Committee also advocated the probe, alleging that there were about 3,000 fraudulent votes cast in the governor's race. This was just the ammunition Wilson needed to challenge the Republican control in South Jersey.

Wilson's primary investigation targeted the present Republican Party leader Commodore Kuehnle, former Sheriff Smith E. Johnson, and Nucky, as presiding sheriff. Wilson believed Nucky wasn't enforcing the state election law or other municipal laws that prohibited all forms of gambling and prostitution in Atlantic City.

A series of 19 hearings, from January 20 through April 7, 1911, recorded the testimonies of disgruntled citizens, precinct workers, investigators, police officers, subpoenaed voters, and homeowners. The hearings culminated with Nucky's statements on February 10, followed by Kuehnle as head of the Republican Party on March 31 of that year.

Wilson was sensitive to the political ill will that South Jersey had toward North Jersey and attempted to infuse local flavor into his investigation by naming a special counsel for the case: Clarence Cole, a popular Democratic Atlantic City lawyer who was perceived locally as more of a prosecutor who sold out to North Jersey politicians. The locals remembered that Cole gave the nominating speech for Wilson at the Democratic Convention. After serving for a brief time as special counsel to the investigating committee, Cole was appointed a circuit court judge as a political reward.

In January 1911, the committee met in Atlantic City's Common Council Chambers and paraded 600 witnesses through testimonies that described incidences of fraudulent voting practices at the polls. The witnesses cited cases where voters were paid to cast votes for a specific candidate; in some precincts, 100 percent of the registered voters voted, some votes were even cast by the deceased. In other precincts, Democratic challengers were physically intimidated, canvass books were lost, affidavits were stolen, election officials were assaulted, whiskey was given in exchange for votes, election workers were kidnapped, and any disloyalty to the Republican Party led to unemployment. City employees were also reportedly expected to make weekly contributions to support the Republican Party.

But on the stand, witnesses often confessed that they had sudden lapses of memory, and hotel registration records were reportedly destroyed accidentally. Dirty tricks were common: Philadelphians loved the shore so much that it had been easy to recruit the unemployed to the ocean resort to cast a vote (or two) in exchange for a day's wages. This was just part of the widespread corruption that the committee unearthed.

The lead witness was Clifton C. Shinn, a well-known local Atlantic City attorney and a member of the Atlantic County Board of Taxation who was serving as a Democratic challenger. He told the committee what he saw while he spent the day in the voting booth at the Sixth Precinct of the First Ward, according to court records of the proceedings:

There was a colored man who claimed to have lived at the address he gave, but could not tell the name of the lady who ran the boarding house—I challenged him, but the Board let him vote. Chester Adams, a white letter carrier came in and voted and later two colored men attempted to vote on his name—I requested they be arrested, but no action was taken.

Q: What was said by the Election Board officials?

A: If they arrested everyone I wanted arrested, the jail wouldn't hold them.

Q: Tell us more what you observed.

A: Harry Payton who voted in the primary had died on October 21, 1910. A colored man came in in the afternoon and said he was Harry Payton and wanted to vote. I requested he be arrested, but no action was taken. On another occasion, a colored man came in for the third time, a triple repeater, and attempted to vote on a different name each time. I did have him placed in custody and taken out of the precinct, then the police officer let him go.

Q: How many persons do you think you challenged their right to vote who didn't vote?

A: I would say forty or fifty. As I challenged someone, a number of men would gather around me, principally colored men, and interfere every way they could with my work.

Q: Tell us what else occurred.

A: A man came in around six o'clock to vote—he didn't know where he lived and didn't know what name he wanted to vote under. I told the Board I wanted this man arrested—they refused.

Q: Are you active in any organizations or political groups?

A: Yes, I am a Democrat. I helped organize the Morris Guards Military organization. I am a member of the Trinity Lodge of Masons and the Elks Club in Atlantic City and Director for the National Bank of Somers Point.

Then John F. Gaffney, a Democratic election officer in the Second Precinct of the Fourth Ward, recalled an incident when a challenger's canvass registration book that William Hoey had been holding was stolen: He said Hoey was standing near the door. A man opened the door, grabbed the book, and ran out. Hoey ran after the man to get his book back.

Q: *Did anyone in the room say anything?*

A: *Yes, Boyle, the judge of elections said Hoey better not go out back, there is a gang waiting for him.*

Q: *Did Hoey come back that day?*

A: *No.*

The Third Session began on February 2, and the chairman announced that the Atlantic County grand jury indicted Stanley Williams, an employee of McDevitt's Co., who was convinced that cash was the motivating factor in the illegal voting. McDevitt's store was directly across the street from the Sixth Precinct of the First Ward at 817 Atlantic Avenue, so Williams had a vantage point to view the activities. The questioning continued:

Q: *Did you notice people coming in and out of the rear of McDevitt's store on Election Day?*

A: *Yes.*

Q: *Were they white or colored?*

A: *Both.*

Q: *Tell the Committee what you saw.*

A: *I take care of the heater in the rear of the store—it has a side entrance. I went into the heater room and saw three or four men sitting around a glass table—he had sort of a ledger—some came in and out twice. They handed him a slip of paper. He would put their name and address in the book and hand them money.*

Q: *What was your impression of what was going on?*

A: *They were getting money for their votes!*

Q: *How many came in that day?*

A: *I heard a gentleman say 308 of them sold their votes.*

Q: *Did you actually see cash pass?*

A: *Well, in the afternoon they were only giving a dollar, they kicked about it, and wanted to know why they were not getting two dollars.*

Witness Frank Bowman told the committee that he was the day manager of the Hotel Dunlap at Ocean Avenue and the Boardwalk, and he worked under the General Manager Robert E. Delaney. When counsel for the committee read a long list of names of those who were registered at the hotel and voted from the hotel, Bowman testified that he did not know whether they lived there or were employed by the hotel. He claimed they had more than 100 waiters during the summer season alone. Some of them worked for a few weeks; others worked the entire summer season. When he was asked to produce the hotel's books to substantiate these facts, he replied: "We have no records, the first of the year all of our books that have accumulated, they are no good to us, we destroy [them] on the first of the year. They are thrown into the furnace by our porter, William Thomas."

William Middleton, an election officer in the Fifth District in the Second Ward, was asked to explain why so many names in the poll book had a line drawn through them. "I was acting as a clerk," said Middleton. "A person would come in and give me their name and I would write it down. Many cases, they would be entitled to vote and I would scratch their name out as voted."

When Middleton completed his testimony, he was asked to count the number of votes that were actually cast compared to the 533 registered voters. He was recalled and the chairman asked him the following questions:

Q: *I understand you have completed your count of the number of votes cast in your precinct out of the 533 registered voters.*
A: *Yes, sir.*
Q: *How many voted?*
A: *533—100% voted!*

The Democratic Party had hired Albert E. Nichols to watch for any illegal voting activity on Election Day. He told the committee that he saw Frank Majane, owner and operator of Majane's Hotel at the corner of North Carolina and Baltic Avenues in Atlantic City, paying $1 to several people outside the polling both at New Jersey and Atlantic Avenues. His provided more details in his testimony:

Q: *How many did you see him give money to?*
A: *At least twenty.*

Q: Did you speak to him about it?

A: No, sir. Except when I had him arrested and served the warrant on him myself. I went to the squire's office with a man he gave the dollar to get the warrant.

Q: Did this stop Majane?

A: No sir, he made bail immediately and went back to doing the same thing. I had him arrested again. He got out and started all over by buying votes. This time, Tom Elton arrested him for the third time.

Q: Did you see Ben Allen and Mr. Griffin on Election Day engage in an illegal activity?

A: Yes.

Q: Majane was a white man?

A: Yes, sir.

Q: Allen and Griffin colored?

A: Yes, sir. Allen keeps a saloon.

Q: What did Allen and Griffin do that attracted your attention?

A: I saw voters coming out of the poll after they voted and they handed them a little piece of blue paper. They would take the paper over to Allen's Saloon and get it cashed.

Then Alfred Heston, the comptroller for Atlantic City and a local historian, was called to the stand, and the questioning continued.

Q: What is the population in Atlantic City?

A: In 1910—46,150

Q: How many are registered to vote in Atlantic City?

A: 12,654

Q: How many actually voted?

A: 9,980

Q: That's a remarkable high percentage.

A: It sure is.

Q: How did the people of Ventnor vote?

A: Democrat Wilson received 55 and Republican Lewis 120.

Thomas Mahoney, a Republican election officer in the Fifth Precinct of the Third Ward, lived at 4 North Sovereign Avenue with his wife and six children. His home is not actually in the ward where he is an election officer. He told the committee that he retained his legal residence at the Quaker Hotel at 1836 Atlantic Avenue where he is the proprietor under a lease dating from October 1910. The committee began to question him about his political activity to establish a record for later prosecution since he was a close associate of Kuehnle's.

The attorney for the committee had the witness admit that he leased the Quaker Hotel in October 1910 from Kuehnle, who was the actual owner. Mahoney permitted 40 people to register to vote from the hotel. Then he was asked the following questions:

Q: *What is there on the first floor?*
A: *I am not familiar enough to tell you.*
Q: *Did you rent this hotel without going to look over it?*
A: *Yes, I banked on its past reputation and what I saw with my eyes.*
Q: *What did you see with your eyes?*
A: *I saw money going over the bar.*
Q: *Did you care about the rental income?*
A: *Not a bit.*
Q: *Can you tell us how many guests were in the hotel in October when your lease began?*
A: *No, sir.*
Q: *Do you keep a register?*
A: *The old register was destroyed.*
Q: *You were a Republican judge in your election precinct last fall?*
A: *Yes.*
Q: *Tell us who were the legal voters entitled to vote from your Quaker Hotel.*
A: *I am not in a position to tell you.*
Q: *Can you name any?*
A: *Yes, about seven.*
Q: *There were forty and you can only recall about seven?*
A: *Yes, that's all I can think of.*

The committee excused the witness, but members felt that Mahoney was protecting Kuehnle. They also believed that the October lease, which was arranged a month before the election, was a ruse to shield Kuehnle personally from false registration and voting fraud from his hotel. On February 9, the committee began questioning Arthur Heenan, an election officer and investigator for the Democratic Party in the Fourth Precinct of the Third Ward.

Q: *Tell us what you found unusual on November 8, 1910.*

A: *Henry Hughes, who lived at 1725 Pemberton Avenue, claimed to have eight men living in his house and they were registered over my objection. After the election, I met him on the street and he said to me, "I do it every year, I am part of the 'Kuehnle Gang.'" I was always afraid of that man!*

Q: *Did your other Democratic challenger object to these eight men voting?*

A: *No. He was scared—certain threats were made to him—his name was Charles Lafferty.*

Then the investigators recalled Frank Steelman to the witness stand and asked him to explain a notation in the registration book.

Q: *Please explain to the Committee how it came about that some of the names are written in ink and some written in pencil?*

A: *Those written in ink were put in on primary day—the ones in pencil were put on the two register days.*

Q: *Why were the names written in pencil on registration days?*

A: *There wasn't any ink there and no pen.*

Q: *Explain the check marks along side the names.*

A: *That they voted.*

Q: *There are some names with two checks.*

A: *Yes. They voted twice.*

Q: *How did that happen?*

A: *Someone voted under that name and then later in the day, the true voter came in and we had to let them vote.*

Q: *There is another mark beside some registered voters.*

A: *Yes, sir, they were ordered arrested.*

Q: *Were they arrested?*

A: *No, sir. Thomas Mahoney, the Election Judge, paid no attention to our request—there were twenty-four of them.*

Q: *You have a notation in your registration book that a voter's name was entered by Judge Mahoney, explain.*

A: *The man was not registered—we had a violent argument and then Mahoney put his name on and allowed him to vote.*

Q: *I call your attention to the name "H.J. Burke" in ink and afterwards changed to "Bird" in pencil.*

A: *Yes.*

Q: *Was this name changed on registry day?*

A: *No, on Election Day. He was registered under "H.J. Burke" and voted under "H.J. Bird." There was a lot of unpleasantness—I refused to give him a voting ticket.*

Q: *Did he vote?*

A: *Yes.*

Q: *Were you threatened with violence by Judge of Elections?*

A: *Yes, all day long.*

Q: *Who put the vote in the ballot box?*

A: *The Judge.*

Q: *How many of the Board objected?*

A: *Two and the other didn't say anything.*

The committee quickly learned that its investigators, who were serving people with subpoenas to appear before the committee in Atlantic City, were being followed. Kuehnle's Gang was unaccustomed to being challenged and had one of their workers follow the process server to find out who the committee wanted to talk to next. Kuehnle's worker told the subpoenaed property owners to write a memorandum listing everyone who was registered in their homes or boarding homes so it would be consistent with the official registration book.

The committee was intent on getting more information about the Republican leadership in Atlantic City. The next person on the list was Emanuel C. Shaner, the surrogate of Atlantic County, secretary of the Atlantic County Republican Committee, and editor and proprietor of the *Mays Landing Record* dating from 1877. When he was called before the committee, he was asked to explain what efforts the Republican leadership made to hold a fair election in Atlantic City. He told the committee that he didn't keep any minutes, but assistant secretary Nucky Johnson, sheriff of Atlantic County, kept them. Shaner fielded several questions from investigators.

Q: *I understand you are active with the Volunteer Fire Company in Mays Landing.*

A: *Yes. I was the President of Hope Fire Company in Mays Landing that was formed in 1895. I was part of the bucket brigade and hand pump team for a number of years.*

Q: *How long have you been Secretary of the Atlantic County Republican Committee?*

A: *Seventeen years—started in 1884.*

Q: *Who was the Chairman during the last election of 1910?*

A: *Lewis H. Barrett—he served two years and I am the Chairman now, starting this past January.*

Q: *Who represents the Committee on the state level?*

A: *Commodore Kuehnle.*

Q: *Tell us about the County Committee Meeting before the election, on November 7, 1910 and who was present?*

A: *The meeting was at the Bartlett Building, at the corner of North Carolina and Atlantic Avenues, in the Young Republican League Room. Present were Sheriff Johnson, State Senator Walter Edge, Mr. Barrett, Commodore Kuehnle, Thomas Mahoney, Alfred Gilson, Samuel English, James H. Hayes and myself—all members of the County Committee.*

Q: *Was a Resolution passed?*

A: *Yes. Senator Walter Edge, who was a Republican candidate for the New Jersey Assembly, prepared a Resolution and introduced it to the Committee, which was unanimously adopted. I sent it to all the local newspapers—the Atlantic City Review, the Gazette, the Atlantic City Press and to my paper, The Mays Landing Record which I bought in 1886.*

Q: *What did it say?*

A: *The newspapers, prior to the election, were claiming massive false registration and the election process would be fraudulent on Election Day. Our Resolution expressed the Republican Party's intent to run an open and fair election and that only legally registered voters would be permitted to vote.*

Q: *Were there any efforts by the Committee to purge illegal regis-*
   tration?
A: *Not to my knowledge. If individuals, through their enthusiasm*
   or foolishness do things that the Resolution taboos, it is not
   something the Committee can stop. We published the
   Resolution hoping it would signal that the Committee wanted a
   fair election without any debauchery of the ballot.
Q: *Do you think there was a fair election in Atlantic City?*
A: *There have been some irregularities which I understand occurs*
   all over the State of New Jersey.

After the committee discovered that several voters were registered
from some of the leading Boardwalk hotels, the owners were questioned
about the incidents. After talking to Jacob Weikel of the Shelburne Hotel,
Frank L. Allen of the Chalfonte Hotel, and Walter J. Buzby of the Hotel
Dennis, the committee learned that it was customary for some employees to live on the premises all year. However, the hotel owners and the
committee were surprised to discover that many other nonemployees
were also voting from their hotels.

Leading into the investigation, the committee was also quite interested in Nucky's electioneering activity on Election Day. The committee
wanted to develop a list of credible witnesses and was hearing of Nucky's
participation in what seemed to be massive vote fraud at every level.

Thomas C. Stewart, the Atlantic County clerk, was recalled to the
witness stand and was questioned about the security of the voter registration books in the county clerk's office. The committee investigator asked
the following questions:

Q: *Did you see Sheriff Johnson take the registration books out of*
   your office since the first of the year—January 1911?
A: *Yes.*
Q: *What did you say to him?*
A: *You will be sure to bring those books back, won't you? He said*
   that he would have them back in the morning and he returned
   them the next morning at 8:45 am.
Q: *Please fix the date as near as you can.*
A: *It was during the week the Grand Jury was in session—that*

started on January 10th.

Q: *Was that before or after the newspapers published a statement that Mr. Bowman, a member of the Grand Jury had voted twice?*

A: *Afterwards, one of the books contained Frank Bowman's name and another book had him listed as F.F. Bowman.*

As the hearing continued, the committee became more concerned that Kuehnle's Gang was contacting many people who were subpoenaed to destroy records and to show up with a memo listing all the people who voted from their property—legal or not.

Malcolm B. Woodruff, the chief of police of Atlantic City, was called to explain the action, or more appropriately the lack of action, of his 112-member police force to enforce the election laws on November 8, 1910. The chief, a surprisingly candid witness, answered each question when he was asked.

Q: *What effort have you made to ferret out the crimes perpetuated at the recent election of November 8, 1910, the past registration day and the last primary day?*

A: *Haven't made any.*

Q: *Why?*

A: *Nobody made a complaint.*

Q: *Have you been instructed to remain inactive?*

A: *No, sir.*

Q: *Did you ever hear, by the people who manipulate the elections, boast they are immune from prosecution—they control the Grand Jury?*

A: *I never heard anything like that.*

Q: *What instruction did you give to your police department on Election Day to ensure there would be a fair election?*

A: *To obey the law. I have a copy of election law and I always revisit it a few days before an election. I personally visited every poll on Election Day and every officer was carrying out his duties. They were obligated to make an arrest if the Election Board Judge signed an order along with the Clerk. The officer would take the person into custody and deliver him to the city jail.*

Q: *Who appoints men to the police department?*

A: *The Mayor, Franklin R. Stoy, he appoints.*

Q: *Upon whose recommendation?*

A: *I don't know.*

Q: *Do you know if the endorsement of a political leader is necessary to get on the force?*

A: *All applications go through me. There are many people who endorse a candidate—they are sent to the Mayor's office—some have most everyone's name who lives in Atlantic City!*

Q: *Chief, is there an assessment levied upon the salary of police officers for election purposes?*

A: *There was a request for 2% of a police officer's salary.*

Q: *Where did the money go?*

A: *I. A. Adams—the Treasurer of the fund for the Republican County Committee.*

Q: *This "request"—did it go to all members regardless of their political party?*

A: *Yes. It also included the fire department.*

Q: *How long has this practice been going on?*

A: *Years.*

Q: *Who is the leader of the Republican Party in Atlantic County?*

A: *Louis Kuehnle, according to the newspaper—he is the leader.*

Q: *And has been the leader for some years?*

A: *I guess so.*

Q: *Has the Grand Jury asked you for assistance to ferret out election law violations?*

A: *No.*

Other Republican tactics were noted in the election process, as City Engineer Lincoln Van Gilder was asked to explain the policy of the Board of Water Commissioners. The board excused employees from work, with pay, to work as election officers.

Q: *Who is on the Board of Water Commissioners?*

A: *Louis Kuehnle, the President; James Parker, Secretary; and the third member, Charles M. Spidel.*

Q: *Who appoints the Board?*

A: *The Mayor.*

Q: *Your department had a number of employees excused with pay to work in the election on registration day, primary day and general Election Day. Who approved this practice?*

A: *The Board of Water Commissioners.*

Q: *What member?*

A: *Either Kuehnle or Parker.*

Some witnesses weren't willing to say too much on the witness stand, such as Charles Vincent, who had lived in Egg Harbor Township since 1888. He was obviously uncomfortable and started squirming in the witness chair. His face became flushed, he began to perspire, and he clearly did not want to be considered as cooperating with the committee. Originally, he was openly defiant to the committee.

Q: *Did you see anything that indicated to you that men were selling their votes?*

A: *I refuse to answer.*

Q: *You can't refuse—you must answer.*

A: *Yes, I saw money—they were going as a group to the water closet and to the back of the fence.*

Q: *Did you see Harry Gensheimer around the polls?*

A: *Yes.*

Harry Gensheimer appeared to give the committee more information on William Sullivan's activities on Election Day. Sullivan was reported to have paid voters to vote on Election Day.

Q: *Did Sullivan say who gave him money to leave town?*

A: *The "Kuehnle Gang" wanted him out of town—he talked too much.*

Q: *Do you know why the Gang wanted him out of town?*

A: *He did a little crooked work in the election—paid people $2.00 to vote.*

Q: *How do you know that?*

A: *I was driving my horse and wagon—carting for him—taking people to the polls. After they voted, they got back in the wagon. I saw him give them $2.00—that was like a whole day's wages for most of them.*

Q: *Tell us what happened with the strangers you carted.*
A: *They were "deadheads"—they didn't belong at the polls. I don't think they were allowed to vote.*

Sigmund Ojserkis, the manager of the Kuehnle Hotel at 1301 Atlantic Avenue, was called to explain why there were many registered voters at his hotel when it was a commercial hotel for travelers. The manager could not recall the names of any permanent residents when he was asked the following questions:

Q: *Wouldn't you know if a prominent person was registered from the hotel?*
A: *Oh, yes the old Sheriff, Smith Johnson had a room, Number 6, and the young Sheriff, Nucky Johnson, has a room, Number 12.*
Q: *Aren't they both married?*
A: *Yes. Nucky has a home in Mays Landing and I think Smith has a property in Atlantic City.*

Simon Faber, a passionate leader of a vocal reform movement in Atlantic City, was quizzed about the 40 people he hired to watch the polls on Election Day:

Q: *What made you become active in Atlantic City Elections?*
A: *It is physically impossible for a town of 46,000 inhabitants to have 13,000 voters. I couldn't stomach it—ten thousand illegal voters—then the "Kuehnle Gang" go around and brag about it.*
Q: *Did you give all the evidence you gathered to the Atlantic County Prosecutor Goldberg?*
A: *No. I don't trust him. If he was here, I would tell him to his face.*
Q: *You realize he is the only man who can prosecute these cases?*
A: *Yes. I have hope there will be a special prosecutor and a new honest Grand Jury takeover.*

Morrell Ingersoll, a resident of Steelmanville in Egg Harbor Township, was questioned about people's names written in the registry book on Election Day when they weren't registered. As one of the clerks for the Democratic Party, he was asked if he canvassed McKee City, deep in the Pinelands, prior to Election Day.

Q: *Did you do a house to house canvass?*
A: *Yes, the best we could. They are not very plentiful. You don't see them until you go through thick bushes, then a house suddenly appears.*
Q: *Who kept the poll book?*
A: *Charles Smith and myself.*
Q: *Did you write some names in the registry book on Election Day?*
A: *Yes.*
Q: *How about Smith?*
A: *I don't know his writing.*
Q: *Was there a Court Order directing their names to be entered in the registry?*
A: *No.*
Q: *What happened to the ballot box at the end of the day?*
A: *I suppose it was taken to the Township Clerk by Charles L. Smith and Mr. Lee.*
Q: *Was the ballot box in Mr. Smith's house after the election?*
A: *I suppose it was there—I hear.*
Q: *How long was it in Smith's house?*
A: *I couldn't rightly tell you.*

William C. Henry, who was a Democratic Election Board member in the Third Precinct of the Second Ward in Atlantic City, worked the entire Election Day. He tried to get the board to agree that any voter who was challenged would not receive a ballot until the dispute was resolved. But the Republican-controlled board would not agree and insisted that each voter should receive a ballot and, if the challenge were upheld, he would not be allowed to vote.

Robert Johnson, the Republican Judge of Elections in the precinct, waited for every opportunity to make sure all potential Republican voters voted whether legally or illegally. The committee asked him the following questions:

Q: *What became of the votes after a challenge was made?*
A: *Unless someone vouched for them, they were not allowed to vote except on several occasions where the votes slipped in the*

box while the controversy was going on. The Board had not taken a vote but the ballot was in the box.

Q: *I call your attention to the name of Lee Butler, 229 North North Carolina Avenue—there are two check marks. Please explain.*

A: *It means he voted twice.*

Q: *On the outside, there is another check mark. Please explain.*

A: *It means a third vote, sir.*

Q: *Three men voted under the name of Lee Butler?*

A: *Yes, someone took an affidavit each time.*

Q: *How many affidavits were taken that day?*

A: *Over one hundred.*

Q: *Did Mr. Johnson attempt to square matters for the double and triple voting?*

A: *Yes, by withholding the next vote that was offered. He took the ballot out of the cartridge and handed the empty cartridge to the Inspector, Mr. Muldoon. The person's ballot was thrown in the trunk.*

Q: *Did the voter know what was happening?*

A: *No, he left thinking he had voted.*

Q: *How often did this happen?*

A: *Only twice.*

Frank Sullivan, an election officer, was recalled to explain what he knew about the missing vouchers, challenger's certificates, and other documents that disappeared on Election Day in the Fifth Precinct of the Third Ward.

Q: *How many vouchers were there on Election Day placed in the Registration book?*

A: *I think about forty.*

Q: *Tell us what happened when Richard McNally came into the polling booth.*

A: *He came in and asked Mr. Conor, who had possession of the book all day, if he could see the book and he said, "Yes." When I later went to check the vouchers, they were all gone.*

Charles Moore, who had lived in Atlantic City for the past 10 years, was a candidate for City Council. He worked the polls on Election Day as a Democratic challenger and told the committee prior to Election Day that he thoroughly canvassed the neighborhood, going door to door to verify who was properly registered. He was concerned about the many illegal registrations since the numbers of potential voters increased. From November 1909 to November 1910, there were 180 new registrations. "I found two hundred names that I could not account for," he told the committee. "There were continued verbal threats against us Democrats, they told me I would be put out of the polling booth next. I stayed in the corner for safety."

The chairman asked what action he and the police took. He said that he asked to have the room cleared—they paid no attention to him—they only listened to Thomas Mahoney. Then David Berner, a local physician who was called as a witness, was asked if he treated Frank Smathers on Election Day.

A: *Yes, I took him to my home, he was very depressed and vomiting—he had symptoms of poisoning. He had been given a drug, which bartenders sometimes use to get rid of people who are causing a problem. They call it "Shoofly"—they use it when they want to shoo an unruly patron out of the bar.*

Q: *Do you give it as your opinion that he was drugged on Election Day in the polling booth?*

A: *Yes—he and Dr. Lock both were poisoned—they had the same symptoms after drinking the water in the precinct.*

Smathers, an attorney who was a Democratic challenger in the Second Precinct of the Third District, then told the committee about his experience on Election Day. He recounted how he became violently sick after drinking water offered to him by the Republican worker. He identified the person who gave him the water as Al Gillison, the tax assessor for Atlantic City.

The chairman wanted corroboration of Edward A. Repp's account of his election books being stolen in the Hygeia Restaurant on Election Day morning and continued the questioning of Charles Lafferty, the other witness.

But the committee refocused their interest in the activities of Sheriff Nucky on Election Day. The counsel for the committee wanted to gather as much information as possible to bring criminal charges against him. This was a golden opportunity that was seldom available to an investigating committee since some witnesses were willing to talk.

John C. Magee, a Democratic precinct challenger in the Fifth Precinct of the Second Ward, had some information about the sheriff's failure to stop the vote fraud, and the chairman asked him the following questions:

Q: *Were you arrested that day?*
A: *Yes, for disorderly conduct. I challenged Harry Lister's right to vote and he was not allowed to vote. I told him to get out. Lister went to the door and a parade of angry men quickly came in. I was looking down and all of a sudden I was punched in the nose. It was Lister. Sheriff Johnson grabbed the man and threw him outside.*
Q: *Did Sheriff Johnson put him under arrest?*
A: *No, sir.*
Q: *Was the Sheriff in and out of your precinct all day?*
A: *Yes, all day long.*
Q: *Does the Sheriff of the County live in the precinct in which he was interested so strongly?*
A: *He is registered from The Kuehnle Hotel at the corner of South Carolina and Atlantic Avenues.*
Q: *That is in this precinct?*
A: *Yes.*
Q: *Is the Sheriff married?*
A: *I believe so.*
Q: *Doesn't the Sheriff have a home in Mays Landing?*
A: *Yes, sir.*

Henry Murtland, a Republican worker, frequently entered the Seventh Precinct of the First Ward, according to Walter S. Leatherberry, a Democratic member of the election board. He drove around in his car and gathered men so they could be registered to vote. Some men came in with their names on a piece of paper, and when they were challenged and asked for an affidavit, the board spontaneously said that it was "not necessary."

On Election Day when it was time to vote, Leatherberry said he continually challenged potential voters; some he was able to stop, some were allowed to vote. When he complained to Election Judge Coll, he was told to stay here and stop them. Otherwise, they were too busy to do much of anything. The witness also complained to the election judge so Murtland would be prevented from going into the polling booth. He was not a challenger or voter, and he did not live in the precinct. The judge refused. "His tone of voice was very frightening to me," said Leatherberry.

Once the votes were finally counted, Leatherberry asked to see the affidavits that the challenged voters had signed so they could vote, but they were missing in a mysterious turn of events. When Leatherberry refused to sign the final vote tally at the end of the day until the vouchers were produced, Coll said, "Well if you don't sign it, you will never get your pay." Leatherberry reluctantly signed the final tally and wrote "Protest" after his name.

Kuehnle and Nucky were prime targets of the committee's investigation along with Robert M. Johnson, (no relation to Nucky), the secretary to the Republican Campaign Committee. Johnson was also a judge on Election Day in the Third Precinct in the Second Ward. Robert M. Johnson was interrogated about Kuehnle's control of the Atlantic County election machinery with the following questions:

Q: *Who is Commodore Kuehnle?*

A: *Commodore Kuehnle is president of the Marine Trust Company, one of the directors of the Second National Bank. He also has a lot of other businesses in Atlantic City.*

Q: *What has that to do with the election?*

A: *I didn't know what they had to do, but as a citizen of Atlantic City he had urged this method.*

Q: *He is, in the common acceptation of the term, the "boss"?*

A: *I recognize none.*

Q: *Then, you deny that he is the boss?*

A: *So far as I am personally concerned I don't know anyone to be the boss; I don't know how many men he bosses; he is in business and …*

Q: *By common repute, will you swear that he is the boss ...*

A: *I am not here to answer that question.*

Q: *... of the Republican Party?*

A: *I have never recognized Commodore Kuehnle as anything else but a friend for twenty-five years.*

Q: *Have you ever heard that he was looked upon and he was called the boss?*

A: *Probably not as often as you have. When he came to Atlantic City back in 1885, his father opened a hotel at South Carolina and Atlantic Avenues which he managed and later his father turned the hotel over to him. He built the Republican Party in our city and started numerous businesses. Some people envy his success and call him "boss" but I call him my friend.*

Q: *Have you ever heard it?*

A: *I don't know as I have heard it.*

Q: *Did you ever read it in the newspapers?*

A: *Oh, yes.*

Q: *Once?*

A: *Oh, hundreds of times.*

On February 24, the committee called William Riddle, the Progressive Republican candidate for Congress, to the stand. He was running against Republican Congressman John J. Gardner. He testified for several weeks that his campaign workers had been preparing 30,000 ballots for distribution on Election Day. The ballots were left in his office in the Bartlett Building at North Carolina and Atlantic Avenues. When his workers returned in the morning after leaving at midnight before the election, all 30,000 ballots were gone. Riddle ran for public office as a Progressive Republican, but basically, he was an independent. The committee's counsel asked him the following questions:

Q: *As a candidate, you went from precinct to precinct on Election Day. Tell us what you observed.*

A: *The election officers in each precinct have a little box and it is traditional for the candidate to drop a dollar or two in the box to buy their lunch—I see no harm in the custom.*

Q: *You have placed your name before the public many times in the* last twenty years. Do you know most of the voters?

A: No, the city has grown very rapidly. No one denies there are a large number of repeaters from Philadelphia.

Q: Not everybody.

A: Well, maybe not everybody. The person who doesn't want to see it closes his eyes. I saw a great number at the train station that arrived from Philadelphia with "grip sacks," small suitcases— they had no legitimate business here and everyone knew it.

Q: How long has this condition existed, in your opinion?

A: I ran in 1892 for the State Senate. There were forty-two people registered in Jesse Foreman's rundown shack on Baltic Avenue. One testified he paid twenty-five cents a month to keep a domed steamer trunk in that shack. Now, that house wouldn't accommodate four people. Domed steamer trunks are only for the rich. They have a dome to accommodate the height of their hats and keep them from being crushed. They are the last trunks to be placed in a ship's cargo hull because the dome prevents stacking. They are the first off so the rich can get their trunks first and be on their way. The old battered domed trunk left in Jesse's shack probably fell off a ship and was rescued by the trash collector.

After Benjamin Allen was sworn in, he testified that he was the owner and operator of the Allen Hotel at 1601 Arctic Avenue in Atlantic City. He explained that there were 35 rooms, and blacks usually stayed at the hotel. There were many people registered from his hotel on Election Day, and the committee quickly learned Allen was part of the Kuehnle Gang.

Q: Who lived in your hotel on November 8th?

A: My wife ran the hotel part and took care of the guest register. I took care of the saloon. She died on October 17th, several weeks before the election, and I have not been able to find any of her records.

Q: Since her death, have any records been kept?

A: No, sir.

Q: What other books do you keep besides the register?

A: My saloon books—but they are all destroyed each year.

Q: *Can you give us the names of anyone who lived in your hotel on November 8th?*

A: *My help—that's all I can remember.*

Q: *Were you working the polls on Election Day and arrested?*

A: *After the election—several days—I was arrested—they say I was paying somebody to vote.*

The committee was concerned about the lack of enforcement by the Atlantic City police department and recalled Chief Malcolm B. Woodruff to explain. The committee was especially interested in the names of the police officers assigned to each precinct since they did nothing to stop any of the alleged illegal activity. The counsel asked Woodruff the following questions:

Q: *You were sent a letter by our Committee asking for the names of all police officers on March 29, 1911 and you did reply the same day.*

A: *Yes, that is correct. I replied that I detailed thirty officers to various precincts and the memo was destroyed after the election— it had served its purpose and was no longer needed.*

Q: *Isn't it possible to give me the names of the officers?*

A: *I can't remember.*

Q: *Chief, there was much disorder at the polls, a challenger's book was stolen at the polls and the police stood by without taking any action. All this was brought to your attention and there was no investigation or anyone arrested. Please explain.*

A: *I have no way of knowing what officers were at a particular precinct. I will have to depend on the honesty of the officers when I ask them at the police line-up each morning. There were three different reliefs at the polling place in a day, they shifted and changed three times.*

Then, Arthur H. Heenan, a staunch Democrat worker, was recalled to explain if he saw money being distributed on Election Day.

Q: *Did you get any money from Lew Mathis?*

A: *I got three dollars for supper and dinner money for the board. We only had twelve dollars and we needed fifteen dollars.*

Q: *Where did the twelve dollars come from?*
A: *It came from the candidates—the councilmen, Sheriff Nucky Johnson and Walter Edge, who was running for Atlantic County State Senator. The candidates did this every year so the board could eat—regardless of the party—it was a long established custom.*

The chairman of the committee then said, "Gentlemen, this has been a long tiring day. We are going to adjourn for the day and resume tomorrow when the first witness will be Sheriff Enoch 'Nucky' Johnson." And as Nucky soon found out, the investigation was far from over.

CHAPTER 7

THE SHERIFF
IN THE SPOTLIGHT

The New Jersey Assembly Investigation Committee had worked dili-gently to reveal the many illegalities of Election Day 1910. Once the Pandora's box was open, committee members wanted to hear from the man who orchestrated the Republican Party's Atlantic County election machinery: Commodore Louis "The Boss" Kuehnle, the head of Kuehnle's Gang.

Counsel for the committee knew that Kuehnle was the leader of the Republican Party in the county stronghold of Atlantic City, according to transcripts of the court records committee hearings. The GOP emerged under the tutelage of State Senator William S. Moore and continued under the patronage system of Republican Congressman John J. Gardner in the early 1900s.

The Commodore was a man of vast influence in Atlantic City who took interest and aggressive action in its development. He not only had a stronghold in the political arena, he held vested interests in several busi-nesses as well, from the Kuehnle Hotel and the Quaker Hotel to the United Paving Company. He also developed the first artesian well in Atlantic City, promoted and assisted in building the Boardwalk, owned the Atlantic City Brewing Company, organized the Atlantic City Telephone Company, was president of Marine Trust Company and the Atlantic City Building & Loan Association, and even owned a heating plant at one time. He also served on the Atlantic City Water Department Board on a volunteer basis, which he considered part of his civic respon-sibilities, but this eventually led to his downfall.

But the committee's findings pointed to such widespread and consis-tent election corruption in every precinct that it was obvious that such

98

practices had to have direction and approval from the leadership at the top. The committee put the Commodore on the judicial hot seat. On March 31, 1911, the committee counsel asked Kuehnle the following questions during the 18th session of the committee hearings:

Q: *How long have you lived in Atlantic City?*

A: *Thirty-five years, I was born on Christmas Day in 1857. Our family was originally from Egg Harbor. My father had a hotel there and then we opened Kuehnle's Hotel at South Carolina and Atlantic Avenues, 1301 Atlantic Avenue, in 1875, to be exact. Years ago, my father was elected on the Democratic ticket as an Atlantic County Freeholder and Mayor of Egg Harbor City, but I never was a candidate for public office.*

Q: *Have you been interested in political affairs for some time?*

A: *Yes. I am looking after the interest of Atlantic City.*

Q: *The interest you have has taken you to all parts of the county?*

A: *Yes, sir.*

Q: *Do you know the workers of the Republican Party?*

A: *I certainly do!*

Q: *Did you read about the padded registration in Atlantic City?*

A: *Yes.*

Q: *What effort did you make to purify the registration?*

A: *All in my power.*

Q: *And what was that?*

A: *My clear instruction to the political workers—we had enough votes to win in Atlantic City and County and did not need any padded registration.*

Q: *Did you make any effort to find out who was responsible for injuries to a Democratic worker?*

A: *Well, I didn't know that was in my power to do that; it wasn't caused by me.*

Q: *You do have control of the police department?*

A: *I do not.*

Q: *Is it not a fact that every person who applies to the police department must have your endorsement?*

A: *No. I have endorsed men for appointments but it is not necessary.*

Q: *You owned the Atlantic City Brewing Company?*

A: Yes.

Q: If a person wants a license in Atlantic City, can he get it without your OK?

A: Certainly he can if the police, the license committee and the members of council are not opposed to him.

Q: Do you dictate to them?

A: No.

Q: Have you heard it said that you do?

A: Yes, but that's not unusual in public life.

Q: You also have an interest in the United Paving Company.

A: Yes. I am the vice president.

Q: And that company is the largest contracting company for public improvements in Atlantic City?

A: I couldn't answer that question; it does a lot of street paving.

Q: Contracts running into hundreds of thousands of dollars?

A: Only lately.

Q: Are you the head of the water department?

A: I am the president—I have been some years.
Q: Have you a financial interest in the heating plant that services Atlantic City?

A: I did, but I sold it.

Q: You are a member of the Atlantic County Republican Committee, the Young Man's Republican League, the Second Ward Republican Club and a delegate to every Republican Party convention for years past, correct?

A: Yes. I was also a delegate to the convention that nominated the Republican candidate for Governor, Vivian M. Lewis, who was defeated by the Democrat Woodrow Wilson, last November.

Q: What majority was guaranteed by you for Atlantic County for the Republican Lewis?

A: Seven thousand.

Q: What did you deliver?

A: Five thousand.

Q: What happened?

A: Mr. Wilson had the best of us. People told us they were for Lewis but voted for Wilson.

Q: *Who is the present chairman of the Atlantic County Republican Committee?*

A: *Lewis H. Barrett—he is in Florida right now.*

Q: *How much money was spent on the election last fall?*

A: *Four to five thousand dollars.*

Q: *Do you know that members of the police and firemen pay a percentage of their salary to the Republican Club?*

A: *I know some of them make voluntary contributions along with the candidate and other public employees.*

Q: *From what you had read and heard, do you admit there was a great deal of illegality in the recent election for Governor?*

A: *Irregularities not illegalities—you have only heard one side of the story.*

Q: *What did you do before the election to stop possible abuses?*

A: *I was a member of the committee that adopted a resolution to encourage a fair and clean election—we had it published in the local paper for all to see including our workers. The Republican majority is too large to stoop to any tactics that weren't on the level.*

Q: *Do you deny that public improvements are throttled by your political machine?*

A: *What has that got to do with the last election?*

Q: *Because you get your power from the machine.*

A: *I don't get any power from any machine. Whatever power people think I have, I get from my investments. I see a bright future in Atlantic City and I am willing to risk my money to make it a great resort.*

Q: *Is it a fact that certain election officers at the recent election for Governor were purchased by the Republican machine?*

A: *No.*

Q: *Have you heard that the influence of the machine is now being used to influence the present grand jury in Mays Landing to prevent anyone from being indicted for vote fraud?*

A: *No, sir. My life is an open book. I have lived here for thirty-five years and intend to stay until the good lord takes me which I hope is not too soon.*

The committee hired private detective Franklin H. Halliday to investigate election irregularities, especially the reported cases of the men from Philadelphia who voted. These men were aptly called "Robins" since they were similar to the birds that suddenly appear in early spring. The committee investigators were ready with their questions for Halliday.

Q: *Tell us about your inquiries in Philadelphia.*

A: *I was able to locate a man by the name of Philip Stinson in Philadelphia. I got him out of bed at 6 am. He told me he had received word to bring as many men as possible to Atlantic City on Election Day. He was able to round up 105. They went by train to Atlantic City the day before the election.*

I took him to his lawyer in the Penn Square Building so he could be aware of his rights. He repeated the whole story and was ready to come back with me to tell the Committee.

We went back to his house to get some clean clothes. It was obvious that the neighborhood was aware that someone had taken Stinson out of his house early in the morning.

After we got to his house, a large group of men suddenly appeared. They forcibly helped me out the front door and Philip out the back—they were less than friendly.

Q: *Did he tell you what the men did that he brought to Atlantic City?*

A: *Yes, they voted at many precincts. He told me the highest one man voted was sixteen and the poorest record was three.*

Q: *Did he tell you who had arranged to bring him and his men to Atlantic City?*

A: *Yes. He told me who had written to him sending the money for the men and the trip.*

Q: *Did you ask how much they were paid?*

A: *They were paid two dollars for each vote.*

Q: *Did he describe to you how they were able to vote?*

A: *Yes, he gave up his guts.*

David Saunders, who voted in the Fourth Precinct of the Fourth Ward, received $1 for his vote. He had given a statement to an investigator, but he was not about to tell the committee anything when he took the witness stand. Then, Howard M. Butler, an Atlantic City police officer, was called to the witness stand to show the influence Kuehnle had over the mayor and police department:

Q: *You were suspended for allegedly talking to our Committee?*

A: *Yes, but I never did and went to the Commodore for help.*

Q: *What did you say to him and what was his response?*

A: *I said, "Commodore, I have been suspended and would like to know what is back of this. I have always been loyal to you and I am a good Republican."*

He said, *"Butler, you have been giving information to those probers," and I said, "It is not true." And he said, "I got it from a good source." And I said, "I would like to know the source."*

Q: *You asked him his source?*

A: *Yes, and he said I was seen with someone in connection with this election probe. He wouldn't tell me his source.*

Q: *Did he decline to help you?*

A: *No, but he did say, "You may as well resign if I find you guilty, you or any other officer, of giving information to the probers."*

Q: *Did you give any information to anyone on our Committee?*

A: *No, sir.*

The chairman said, "Let the record clearly reflect Officer Butler has never been interviewed or given any information to our Committee."

The testimonies were coming closer to the men who were at the core of the investigation. When Governor Wilson appointed special prosecutor Edmund Wilson (no relation to the governor) for the grand jury probe in Atlantic City, it was a learning experience for the Wilsons. Both men did not know how extensively the Republicans controlled the Atlantic County electoral government machinery; however, they learned the hard way.

Nucky knew that it was only a matter of time before members of the Kuehnle Gang were called to the witness stand. One of Nucky's Democratic friends in North Jersey told him that he and the Commodore had been singled out as prime targets in the criminal investigation. So Nucky arranged a meeting with County Clerk Lew Scott and the Commodore in Atlantic City to map out their strategy for the impending political battle.

One of Nucky's responsibilities as sheriff was to select the members to serve on the grand jury. The Commodore first suggested they call their Democratic political friends in North Jersey to "call the bloodhounds off." Nucky had already made the contacts; he heard that Governor Wilson had no friends left among the Democratic leaders, and he would probably go after them next. The Commodore wanted to make sure that postmaster Harry Bacharach was on the grand jury; he knew Bacharach was eager to become mayor of Atlantic City in the upcoming election. With Bacharach as chairman of the grand jury and the other members carefully screened by Nucky, they felt comfortable that no indictments would be issued. They laughed, had a few more drinks, and went home confident they had solved their problem with the hometown advantage.

The Supreme Court assigned Supreme Court Justice Thomas W. Trenchard to preside over the proceedings, and the attorney general was directed to conduct the investigation. Trenchard, a native of South Jersey who was born in Bridgeton about 40 miles from Atlantic City, had served in the New Jersey State Assembly in 1889 as a Republican.

In his official duty as sheriff, Nucky selected his preconditioned 23-man grand jury with Bacharach as a trusted member and jury foreman. Nucky turned the grand jury over to the obviously anxious Attorney General Wilson to present his evidence of election fraud, municipal graft, and gambling throughout Atlantic City.

The grand jury listened attentively to the state's witnesses for several days, and then their attention was directed to the Wilson's compelling argument and that of his assistant B. Nelson Gaskill, a local attorney appointed by the Wilson forces. Under the court rules, the targets of the investigation could not present any defense. However, on June 2, 1911, the grand jury refused to indict anyone and returned a "No Bill." When local Common Pleas Judge Enoch A. Higbee discharged the case, Nucky and the Commodore were overjoyed at the outcome and thought they were unstoppable. The Commodore even threw a victory party at Kuehnle's Corner Saloon with all drinks on the house, celebrating the fact that Jersey Justice had carried the day.

Prosecutor Wilson left town, dreading his impending meeting with the governor where he had to say that he was not welcome in Atlantic County and that he had to leave town quickly for his personal safety. The governor was furious and resented being outfoxed by the South Jersey Pineys. Wilson's national image and election reform program were in jeopardy. After all, he had already tested the Presidential campaign waters with speeches in Missouri, Colorado, California, Oregon, Minnesota, North Carolina, and South Carolina.

According to Wilson's political advisors, the only way to stop the Kuehnle Gang was to get an unfettered grand jury to hear all the evidence. But the jury had to be impartial and that wasn't likely with Nucky as sheriff. The sheriff's legal and constitutional responsibility allowed him to select the grand jury, and all indictments had to be returned by the Atlantic County grand jury.

Wilson gathered his legal staff for a late-night emergency summit meeting in Trenton; they concluded that since Nucky was one of the targets of the investigation, they could try appealing to a friendly judge to temporarily disqualify Nucky as sheriff, and Samuel Kalisch's name was high on the list of "friendly judges." Wilson had just appointed him to a seven-year term on the Supreme Court in April 1911, covering the South Jersey circuit of Atlantic, Cape May, Cumberland, and Salem counties. Kalisch's credentials were impeccable: He was elected president of the New Jersey Bar Association in 1909, and he was also the son of a distinguished rabbi. Well-known as a loyal Democrat, Kalisch had run for Assembly once and for the New Jersey Senate on two occasions but had lost all three elections. As a devoted Democrat, he was ready to repay Wilson for his new Supreme Court appointment.

Kalisch provided an advisory opinion on how to legally impanel an impartial Atlantic County grand jury. He discovered an old statute dating from 100 years ago, specifying that a judge had the authority to appoint an "elisors" jury if the local sheriff was not available, disqualified, or refused to act. The elisors could then select the 23 members to serve as the grand jury from Atlantic County. And that's just what Wilson's legal hit men did. They followed through with Kalisch's game plan without notifying Nucky about his disqualification. On July 7, 1911, the judge appointed two elisors jurors charged with the task of selecting the grand jury in Atlantic County. A special term was set to open on July 18, 1911.

One of the elisor grand jury members was the Reverend Newton W. Caldwell, D.D., an avowed reformer and pastor of the Olivet Presbyterian

Church at Pacific and Tennessee Avenues in Atlantic City. Another was the Reverend Dr. M. E. Snyder of St. Paul's M.E. Church of Atlantic City. Other concerned citizens were added to the jury, especially those who observed the Sabbath, prohibited Sunday baseball, enforced mandatory saloon closings on Sundays, imposed gambling laws, and prosecuted corrupt officials. The Ministerial Union of Atlantic City urged all residents to come forward with information to challenge corruption and to clean up Atlantic City.

For a betting man, the odds didn't seem to be in Nucky's favor. When the Commodore and Nucky opposed the counter move by the state, a series of unsuccessful court appeals ensued. The judges wouldn't oppose the new governor, since they were political appointments and were intent on safeguarding their present and future careers. Nucky hired Louis Hood, a prominent appellate attorney from Newark, New Jersey, to challenge the move that disqualified him. Hood argued that as long as the sheriff remained unimpeached, he could not be removed from carrying out his official constitutional duties. He argued that the court order of disqualification was entered in secrecy without giving Nucky an opportunity to defend himself; therefore, it violated his fundamental constitutional right of due process.

The argument fell on deaf ears, and the appointed elisors jurors were free to select a new grand jury, unleashing a flood of indictments. Attorney Charles S. Moore, a local Democratic activist, and ironically, the son of William Moore, a founder of the Republican National Party. He was appointed as grand jury foreman at the state's urging to make sure the state maintained control inside the grand jury room.

On July 25, 1911, Nucky was indicted for election fraud on the grounds that he removed two registry books from the Atlantic County Clerk's office. Albert Gillison, an Atlantic City building inspector, was also indicted and charged with conspiracy to commit election fraud in bribing William I. Trigler in the Second Precinct of the Third Ward. Gillison was a trusted lieutenant in Nucky and Kuehnle's organization and was targeted to show the public that the grand jury not only intended to clean up Atlantic City, but nobody was above the law.

Eleven others were indicted the same day as Nucky for election fraud violations that ranged from conspiracy to bribe voters and election officers to the kidnapping of an election officer. All were released on bail with their trials scheduled in fall 1911. On September 10, 1911, the grand jury indicted James Scull, city clerk of Somers Point, and other Republican election workers.

Edward L. Bader, a building contractor, and George Profall, an Atlantic City electrician, were jointly indicted for bribing an election official. Bacharach, the foreman of Nucky's earlier grand jury, was indicted for conspiracy "to pervert elections." He denied the charges, claiming that he was indicted by the Democratic grand jury to destroy his chances of becoming mayor of Atlantic City in the upcoming election.

On the same day, Governor Wilson, accompanied by the chairman of the State Democratic Party Edward E. Grosscup from Gloucester County, appeared at the Hotel Chelsea in Atlantic City at a testimonial dinner honoring Judge John J. White. The governor had recently appointed White to the Court of Errors and Appeals. The auditorium was packed with members of the hotel association and local judges, including Judge Enoch Higbee and Judge Samuel Kalisch. The governor praised "the fearless men in public office" and castigated "the cowards in public office" to the applause of the spirited reform crowd, according to the account that appeared in the *Atlantic City Daily Press* the next day.

Nucky pleaded not guilty; George A. Bourgeois, the attorney who Nucky had worked for years ago as a law clerk, was representing him in the criminal proceedings. Bourgeois's very presence took command of the courtroom and instilled confidence in Nucky that he would be victorious. On September 30, Nucky was indicted again for conspiracy along with the Commodore in connection with the Frank Bowman case for voting twice.

In light of the indictments, Nucky realized he was in a political struggle for survival. He continued to carry out his duties as usual and drew the 54 talismen for the October court term, providing Atlantic County with two jury panels. The Commodore commented that Atlantic County was more democratic than any other county in New Jersey since it had both Republican and Democratic grand jury panels.

On October 14, the Commodore was indicted in the final days of the elisors jurors' deliberations and knew he was also in a fight for his political life. He was charged under a conflict of interest state law that had never been tested before in the New Jersey courts. Years before, when the Atlantic City Municipal Water Company awarded a contract for the construction of a water main to F.S. Lockwood, the successful bidder assigned the contract to the United Paving Company. The Commodore was a stockholder with the paving company while serving as a non-salaried member of the Board of the Atlantic City Municipal Water Company. He had invested $5,000 in the company and received 13 percent of the stock in return. This modest investment proved to be his financial and political downfall.

While Governor Wilson's chosen grand jury was grinding out indictments with Democratic Grand Jury Chairman Moore, Wilson jumped into the fight to keep the pressure on the Commodore. Moore worked the inside of the grand jury while the governor worked the outside. Their dual mission was to sway public opinion and to influence the prospective trial jurors in convicting violators in the election cases. Nucky won a temporary legal victory when Bourgeois applied for a Writ of Certiorari (an application to review a lower court ruling) to the Supreme Court, which was granted on October 17, 1912. This allowed all the justices to hear his claim whether the elisor jury had been appointed legally. However, when the case was heard, the court refused to quash the indictments.

Nucky faced a criminal trial. He broke his silence at the county's largest campaign rally in Mays Landing on October 24, 1912. The crowds cheered when Nucky said, "I raise my hand to God and every man here I never committed the crime I am charged with nor any other crime," according to a report in the *Atlantic City Daily Press*.

To keep pressure on the case, the state hired the nationally famous Burns Detective Agency to conduct an undercover investigation to trap Atlantic City public officials who may have accepted a gratuity for public service. Detective William J. Burns had previously made national news for his 1907 investigation resulting in a conviction of a San Francisco official accused of graft. This time around, five of the Atlantic County Freeholders were indicted on September 28, which further weakened the Republican organization.

With attacks emerging on all fronts, the Republican Party went on the offensive. And it did what it did best: It kept winning elections.

To counter the attack, the governor took his crusade to Atlantic City to rally the troops on behalf of the local Democrats and fusion candidates on November 1, 1911 at the Nixon Apollo Theatre on the Boardwalk at New York Avenue. More than 1,400 Democrats listened to the governor challenge the Republicans and praise their candidates in the upcoming election. Wilson charged, "The government of the county (Atlantic) is rotten and disgraceful and managed by crooks. Atlantic City is famous all over the United States for its charm and for—its shame." Then he told the crowd that he "intended to enforce the law," according to an account in the *Atlantic City Daily Press* on November 2, 1911.

On November 4, 1911, the Republicans responded with a mass rally at the courthouse in Mays Landing. Voters from all over the county took the Republican-sponsored train to a rally to hear Gardner and the other candidates blast the Democrats for libel and slander. They hammered the governor for his free trade policy, which would sacrifice jobs of the work-ingman, and the Republicans strongly endorsed a protectionism policy to safeguard local jobs.

On December 18, 1911, one month after Wilson's inflammatory speech, the Commodore went on trial on a conflict of interest charge before Judge Samuel S. Kalisch. The famous "wood-stave waterman pipeline case" began before the largest crowd ever packed into the court-room in Mays Landing. Judge Kalisch had been in the audience at the Chelsea Hotel when Governor Wilson denounced the politicians in Atlantic County on September 11, 1911, which raised doubts in some of the Commodore's supporters that he would get a fair trial.

Details about the case began to emerge as E. W. Shackelford, presi-dent of the United Paving Company, testified that the company books had been burned. The Atlantic City Water Board, where the Commodore had been a member since 1895, awarded the $224,000 contract to F.S. Lockwood, and it was Lockwood who assigned the contract to United Paving Company and the Cherry Company. And it was William J. Cherry who was serving as president of the United Paving Company in 1909 when the contract was awarded.

"I have no absolutely no interest in the award of the water main con-tract except the best interests of Atlantic City," the Commodore told the *Atlantic City Daily Press*. He said he was one of the original founders of

United Paving Company, invested $5,000, and 13 percent of the stock like all the other investors.

Cherry said he needed funds for the job and borrowed the money directly from a creditor of United Paving. He testified, "I am the President of United Paving and have the authority to borrow without the knowledge of the Board of Directors." So Cherry borrowed from United Paving and obtained loans from Marine Trust Company where the Commodore was a director and stockholder. "I never talked to the Commodore about these loans," Cherry said on the witness stand. "It was strictly my project," according to his statements published in the *Atlantic City Daily Press*.

When the case went to the jury on December 22, 1911, Kalisch told the jury that "this case is the first to be tried under the new law that makes it an offense for a public official to award or participating in an award of a contract in which he has a financial interest." He concluded by saying "that if you accept and believe the testimony of the defendant, you should find him 'Not Guilty.'"

The jury began deliberations at 4:30 PM and returned with a verdict shortly before 8 PM: The verdict was guilty as charged with a recommendation of mercy. Judgment day had arrived for the Commodore. Three newspapers in the state urged the court to send the Commodore to prison through its flurry of editorials and cartoons. But scores of well-wishers, hotel owners, banking officials, office holders, and men of the cloth descended upon the Mays Landing Courthouse to show their support for the Commodore at his sentencing on January 24, 1912.

Judge Kalisch addressed the crowded courtroom, saying that he intended to make an example of the Commodore for the voting community. The purpose of this new law, he said, is to act as a deterrent to prevent crime and uphold the high ethical standards of public office. With that, he sentenced the Commodore to one year of hard labor at the state prison and a fine of $1,000 and to stand committed until the costs of prosecution are paid. The judge ignored the jury's recommendation of mercy along with the flood of good character letters he received from a cross section of the county.

While the Commodore's counsel filed an immediate appeal, the Young Men's Republican League planned a large testimonial dinner in the Atlantic City's Hotel Rudolf ballroom on New Jersey Avenue on March 21, 1912, to show their confidence in the Commodore. The committee had no trouble attracting a large crowd to support and honor the Commodore who had just returned from a pre-incarceration vacation in Bermuda.

"It's good to be home again!" said the Commodore, according to reports from the *Atlantic City Daily Press* on March 22, 1912. He didn't waste time in working his magic. "I think it is time for the Atlantic County Republicans to express their preference for our next President of the United States," he said. "I move the League endorse William Howard Taft." A unanimous standing vote, followed by loud cheers, carried the motion. The Commodore returned to his seat; he had not lost his touch.

Finally, on November 26, 1913, the Court of Errors and Appeals affirmed the Commodore's conviction and under the advisement of attorney Bourgeois, he decided to "take my medicine like a man." The Commodore insisted he was an innocent victim of circumstances. He told the press, "Wilson tried to tie me into the 'Boardwalk Graft Case,' the Concrete Ocean Walk Graft Case, election fraud—all without success—and the Republican leadership will continue and rise to new heights under Nucky." When he surrendered at Trenton State Prison on December 10, 1913, his faithful supporters began a drive to gather 30,000 signatures to petition the Board of Pardons for his early release. But that didn't happen; he was not paroled until June 1, 1914.

After the three-year legal ordeal, most of the officials and politicians in Trenton were joyful, and the governor said he had defeated a corrupt Republican organization as part of his platform in his renewed national presidential bid. Other election indictments were released including one for contractor Edward Bader, a close political ally of Nucky's who became mayor of Atlantic City, and Frank Majane.

Nucky's term as sheriff had ended in November 1911. Since he could not succeed himself by law and had no desire to continue as sheriff, he endorsed Republican Robert H. Ingersoll, who was handily elected and took the oath of office on November 15, 1911. Nucky stepped back into the role of undersheriff. Bacharach, who was acquitted on the election charges, was finally elected mayor of Atlantic City on the GOP ticket in 1912.

But as Nucky stayed on as undersheriff, little did he know that a visitor to the sleepy county seat of Mays Landing would dramatically alter his life: U.S. President William Howard Taft was rolling into town by train to campaign for his re-election as President in 1912. Nucky and the Commodore were part of the official welcoming party, as hundreds of residents gathered at the station to greet the president. American flags flew high on every pole and atop porch railings to honor the chief executive on May 28. Even the Water Power Company on the Great Egg Harbor River and Cut Glass Factory closed early to give workers a chance to greet Taft when the train arrived.

Taft, who was winding down his nationwide campaign in Mays Landing, attended a dinner reception at the Marlborough–Blenheim Hotel. Judge Allen Brown Endicott presided as toastmaster at the banquet before the rally at Young's Million Dollar Pier. The president charmed the packed audience of supporters before settling in as John L. Young's guest in his palatial Italian villa adjoining the Million Dollar Pier at No. 1 Atlantic Ocean.

Taft was not only running against the Democratic candidate Governor Wilson, but against former President Teddy Roosevelt, who had been out of office for four years. With an African safari and European tour behind him, Roosevelt had bolted from the regular Republican Party and had formed his own maverick Bull Moose Party to seek an unprecedented third term. This political maneuver fatefully split the Republican Party in two, and the division made Wilson's election victory certain.

Nucky stayed at the president's side, fascinated by the overwhelming attention someone with such power could generate. Nucky realized it was not the person but the power or the perception of power that generated the loyal crowds. And Nucky liked the intoxicating feeling of power. He campaigned for Taft by attacking Wilson at every opportunity and often told crowds, "Wilson was selected in Baltimore at the Democratic Convention on the 46th ballot—that means they had 45 better candidates than Wilson!"

Wilson garnered fewer popular votes than his two Republican opponents combined nationwide, but it was just enough for him to win the election as the 28th President of the United States. He won 435 electoral votes, which was a new record, in spite of winning only a plurality of 42 percent at the polls, which was lower than any candidate since Lincoln in 1860.

Nucky saw the inherent problems with the 1912 Presidential election. Throughout his political career, he was determined to resolve disputes within the party to avoid any similar recurrences. He often referred to Roosevelt as the head of the "Bull Head Party," saying that if Roosevelt had not mortally wounded the Republican Party, Wilson would never have been elected president. Nucky's only consolation was that "at least Wilson is out of New Jersey!"

The state investigation into election fraud and corruption in Atlantic City began to lose momentum as Wilson headed out of the state to the White House. The continued prosecution of the elisor jury indictments was turned over to Special Prosecutor Charles Wolverton, a Democrat from Camden. Wilson just did not trust any attorneys in Atlantic County. The new prosecutor reviewed the charges and decided that most indictments were not provable beyond a reasonable doubt and that they were obtained in the heat of a political battle.

Wolverton applied to dismiss the charges against most of the remaining defendants; the only defendant left to have his fate determined by a jury was Nucky. After three years of appeals and procedural moves by the state and Nucky's lawyer, his case was finally scheduled for trial. Nucky hired a new attorney for his case: former Attorney General Robert H. McCarter, a prominent North Jersey Republican and a skilled trial lawyer who served as Attorney General of New Jersey. Nucky wanted McCarter because he was one of the outstanding lawyers in the state and one of the founders of the New Jersey Bar Association. McCarter was also friends with Kalisch. McCarter moved to have the indictment *nolle prosed* (dismissed) on the grounds that the U.S. Constitution guaranteed every citizen the right to a speedy trial. He considered three years of delays as unreasonable and unconscionable. But Kalisch denied his application, and a trial date was set.

At 10 AM on June 9, 1914, Kalisch ordered Sheriff Ingersoll, Nucky's successor as sheriff, to draw a jury in the Atlantic County Court House in Mays Landing to decide Nucky's fate. The state sent its elite trial team of Attorney General Edmund Wilson as chief counsel, Nelson B. Gaskill, and Charles Wolverton. Nucky did not want to be "out-lawyered" and engaged the local help of former Judge Joseph Thompson and Thomas E. French to assist McCarter. Nucky thought he had all his bases covered.

When Nucky walked into the courthouse, the bailiffs who he had known for years rushed over to greet him and wish him luck. The former sheriff was especially pleased to see David Eberhard, the court crier, who Nucky had come to know when he was sheriff. Eberhard often told Nucky about the days he spent in the Union Army and the hardships the men endured, especially the Southern prisoners. He was only a student in his late teens when he volunteered for military service. It reminded Nucky of his school days in Mays Landing on the front porch with Captain Shepherd Hudson recalling his adventures at sea.

It took more than an hour to select an all-male jury after both sides had exhausted their 10 preemptory challenges. The jury pool was selected from the voting rolls since women were not permitted to vote until 1920 when the 19th Amendment to the U.S. Constitution become law. Finally, both sides agreed in unison that the jury was satisfactory. Nucky sat at the defense table surrounded by his high-priced lawyers and a secret weapon in his briefcase at his side. It was his treasured Irish brick that he knew would bring him good luck.

The state moved to amend the indictment dating from January 14 to January 18, 1911, without objection, which the court routinely granted. It was now time for the state to make its opening statement to the jury. Gaskill, who was selected to address the jury, was the only local lawyer on the prosecutor's team, and the state felt Gaskill would relate better to the locals on the jury. He began by reading the indictments to the jury: "the State will show that on November 9, 1910 a hotly contested election was held in New Jersey for the Governorship and other state wide and local offices which resulted in a massive vote fraud in Atlantic County by individuals and some elected officials." The reading continued:

The Sheriff at that time was the defendant Enoch L. "Nucky" Johnson, the chief law enforcement official of the County who used his position to assist and perpetuate that fraud on the citizens of our county. On January 18, 1911, the then Sheriff Johnson used his political influence as a leading member and Secretary of the Republican Party to intimidate county employees to allow him to remove from the Atlantic County

Clerk's Office two Voter Registration Books with fraudulent intent for the purpose of abetting a fraudulent election in Atlantic County contrary to the law of the State of New Jersey.

The State will produce for you from the witness stand two clerks of the Atlantic County Clerk's Office, Thomas Stewart, and his sister, Jessie Stewart. They will tell you that on January 18, 1911, the defendant came to their office and asked for the registry books for the 4th Precinct of the 4th Ward and the 5th Precinct of the 2nd Ward. Mr. Stewart will tell you he reluctantly gave him the books—the defendant removed them from the Clerk's office and he kept them overnight. His sister will tell you she saw the books on the office desk the next morning.

Gaskill concluded by saying: "Voter Registration Books are sacred to the integrity of the voting process and nobody is allowed to take them from the County Clerk's to indulge in any mischief that may advance his political purposes and to protect individuals who voted fraudulent— especially an individual who voted twice from different precincts!"

As Nucky's lead counsel, McCarter walked over to the jury rail where the 12 jurors were seated and began his opening statement in a low, sincere voice:

Gentlemen of the jury, this case is about credibility. You are going to have to decide who is telling the truth. The State's witness, the two employees of the County Clerk's Office or Nucky Johnson and two officials in the Clerk's Office who were the Supervisors of the state's witnesses.

We will provide for you an Affidavit signed by Thomas Stewart, the State's star witness, that is contrary to what Mr. Gaskill just told you. This statement was taken three years ago, before his superior and supervisor, the Atlantic County Clerk Samuel Kirby, when the events were fresh and crystal clear in his mind which is the best evidence of what occurred, not his present newly discovered recollections. The state's bright shining star will suddenly twinkle and slowly fade right in front of your eyes and be extinguished when he is subject to rigorous cross-examination.

We will also produce for you the former Deputy County Clerk Albert Abbott and his sister, Jessie Stewart, who will tell you the books were never taken out of the Clerk's Office by the defendant.

Mr. Johnson is eager to take the witness stand and firmly and vigorously deny removing the books as charged. The only reason he went to the Clerk's Office to look at the books was to determine if one of the members of the Grand Jury, Frank Bowman, then in session had voted twice as reported in one of the local newspapers—*The Atlantic City Review*. It was the Sheriff's sworn duty to select the members of the Grand Jury and he wanted to be certain that Bowman had not committed any vote fraud.

Sheriff Johnson had a duty to investigate the truthfulness of the newspaper article and the only appropriate way to do it was to look at the registry books. Had he not made an inquiry, the local newspaper would have accused him of dereliction of his duties. There was nothing sinister in his action—he was simply carrying out his sworn constitutional duties.

Enoch is an honorable man and was a distinguished sheriff. He served three years without a black mark on his record. He was proud to serve as sheriff as his respective father did before him. Enoch Johnson decided not to seek another term as Sheriff and on January 8, 1913 he was selected by the Atlantic County Board of Freeholders to serve as Collector of Atlantic County—entrusted with the county treasury. He had to post a surety bond for that position and the bonding company investigation of his background fond him worthy to handle the county's money—your money—you are the taxpayers of this great County.

You can judge his credibility for truth and veracity when he tells you exactly what happened three years ago and I am sure after you balance his clear recollection against the newly awakened recollection of the clerks that you will quickly conclude in your deliberations he is "Not Guilty."

Judge Kalisch thanked McCarter and asked the state to call its first witness, Clerk Thomas Stewart from the Atlantic County Clerk's office. After he was sworn in, he was questioned.

Q: *Did Mr. Johnson, who as the Sheriff, come to your office on January 18, 1910 and request you to give him the Voters Registration Books for the 5th Precinct of the Second Ward and the 4th Precinct of the 4th Ward?*

A: *He did. It was in the morning. I had just finished reading the Atlantic City Review which mentioned one of the members of the sitting Grand Jury, Frank Bowman, had voted twice in the election of November 1910.*

Q: *Did you give him the books he wanted?*

A: *Yes.*

Q: *I show you two registration books. Are these the books you gave Mr. Johnson?*

A: *Yes.*

Once the prosecutor finished his line of questioning, McCarter began his cross-examination. He handed the witness an affidavit and asked if it was his signature. He agreed. Then McCarter asked the clerk to mark the affidavit for identification as D-1.

Q: *This is an affidavit of June 6, 1911 you signed in front of the County Clerk of this court, Samuel Kirby that is now marked D-1.*

A: *Yes.*

Q: *In your affidavit of June 6, 1911, you further stated you gave the books to Mr. Johnson and found them on your desk the next morning and they were the same books I gave him the night before. In your testimony today, a few moments ago, you told the jury you gave him the books in the morning of January 18, 1911. Was it in the morning or was it at night?*

A: *It wasn't at night.*

Q: *You reviewed the affidavit before you signed it, correct?*

A: *Yes, that's what it says.*

Q: *Your affidavit also states you never saw him return the registration books the next morning, correct?*

A: *Yes—it does say that.*

Q: *Then you were mistaken when you signed it?*

A: *I guess so.*

Q: *In your affidavit you further stated you never saw him take the registry books out of the Clerk's Office, correct?*

A: *Yes, that's what is says.*

Q: *The books could have remained in the County Clerk's office all night without your knowledge, correct?*

A: *It's possible, I guess.*

Q: *Are you telling the truth to the jury today or were you stating the truth on June 6, 1911 when you swore, under oath, the books never left the office?*

A: *I am telling the truth today.*

Q: *Your affidavit also states you never saw him return the registration books the next morning, correct?*

A: *Yes—it does say that.*

Q: *Is your recollection today better than it was three years ago when the events occurred and you signed the affidavit?*

A: *I guess so. I didn't review my affidavit since I signed it.*

Q: *Are you telling this jury your recollecting got better over the past three years?*

A: *I guess so.*

Q: *I have no more questions for you, Mr. Stewart.*

The state then called Stewart's sister, Jessie Stewart, who also worked in the clerk's office. Trembling, Jessie took the witness stand after watching her brother crumble and look confused during cross examination. She testified that the former sheriff came to the clerk's office the next morning and dropped off a package for her brother.

She then stated that her brother placed the two books in question on the shelf in the correct order with the other books.

McCarter had only one question for her during her cross examination: "You never saw Mr. Johnson take the Registry Books out of the Clerk's office, did you?" She answered, "No sir."

McCarter promised to produce the defendant, and Nucky took the stand in a courtroom filled with public officials and members of the Atlantic County Board of Freeholders. They all sat on Nucky's side of the courtroom; some were standing against the walls behind Nucky and his defense team showed their steadfast support. McCarter then began his questioning:

Q: *State your full name.*

A: *Enoch L. Johnson.*

Q: *Did you hold public office in the past?*

A: *Yes. I was the Sheriff of Atlantic County for three years.*

Q: *What is your present position?*

A: *I am the Atlantic County Collector (Treasurer) and also Secretary of the Atlantic County Republican Party since 1909.*

Q: *What are your responsibilities as the Atlantic County Collector?*

A: *I manage all the County's money.*

Q: *Going back three years ago, after the election for Governor in 1910, do you recall reading in the local Atlantic City Review newspaper an article in January of 1911 relating to a Grand Jury you had drawn for the January term of 1911?*

A: *Yes. It mentioned that a person serving on my Grand Jury, Frank Bowman, had voted twice—once in the 5th Precinct of the 2nd Ward and once in the 4th Precinct of the 4th Ward.*

Q: *After you read the article, what next did you do?*

A: *I went to the County Clerk's Office where the voting registers are stored to check out the truth of the article. When it comes to election reporting in the newspapers, you can't always believe what you read.*

Q: *What did you do in the County Clerk's Office?*

A: *I examined the books in front of Mr. Abbott and Mr. Stewart and left.*

Q: *Did you remove the books from the County Clerk's Office?*

Nucky looked directly at the jury and said: "No sir—no need to, I had all the information I needed after looking at the books. Bowman's name appeared in both books and there was a checkmark in one—he had voted one time only." McCarter then looked over at the prosecutors and said, "You may inquire of Sheriff Johnson, if you like." Though former Attorney General Wilson was assigned to examine Nucky, he didn't succeed in swaying him from his clear, concise testimony.

Both sides rested and resumed with closing arguments. The court was filled with local lawyers who wanted to see and hear the renowned lawyers in action. According to reports in the *Atlantic City Daily Press*, McCarter began with the following impassioned plea:

The facts are clear. There was a heated election in 1910 and Governor Woodrow Wilson, the Democratic candidate, won statewide but lost in this great County of Atlantic. There is a big difference in South Jersey and North Jersey and I don't have to tell you what the difference is because you are all from South Jersey. South Jersey people just want to be left alone. Candidate Wilson campaigned for more control over everyone's lives, with central power in Trenton, which did not sit well in the South, and they expressed their displeasure by not voting for Wilson—not because of any vote fraud as charged against your former Sheriff, Nucky Johnson.

I told you in my opening statement this case was about credibility—you have heard the State's two pathetic and unreliable witnesses. ...

To believe Thomas Stewart's direct testimony today, you would have to accept the fact that everyone's recollection gets better with age. With everyone I know, including myself, facts fade with time and are not as clear and concise as they were three years ago if I had written them down when the events occurred. The only thing I know that gets better with age is a bottle of wine! I am suggesting to you that his testimony is not credible when weighed against the clear testimony of the defendant and the two supervisors of the County Clerk's Office we produced for you. ...

We urge you to clear the proud name of Enoch "Nucky" Johnson once and for all time and unanimously vote "Not Guilty."

Wilson began his closing remarks. His first impression when he stood in front of the jury rail was that the 12 jurors did not appear to be interested in what he had to say. They were squirming in their hard oak chairs and only occasionally looked at him. Wilson knew he had to say to something to get their attention and he began:

Gentlemen of the Jury, you heard the Judge allude to the newspaper coverage of the trial as the "Battle of the Generals." It is true, Mr. McCarter was the Attorney General of New Jersey from 1903 to 1908 and I took his place when he left that office.

A few years ago, I was introduced to a distinguished member of the bar and he asked me what position I held in the government and I told him, "I am the Attorney General—I took Robert McCarter's place. The lawyer obviously was a close friend of Mr. McCarter and he quickly replied, "You could never take Bob McCarter's place." From that day on I now say, "I succeeded Robert McCarter as Attorney General which eliminates any comparison of us."

Had Robert McCarter been Attorney General when this offense occurred by Mr. Johnson, he would have prosecuted Mr. Johnson with the same vigor he now defends him and I may have been Mr. Johnson's defense attorney. So you see, our background and titles should not be considered in your deliberations. We are both lawyers representing our clients to the best of our abilities.

Gentlemen of the jury, the State of New Jersey thanks you for your public service in accepting to serve on this jury—that was not an easy decision on your part since you know many of the people here that have testified but you took an oath to be impartial even though you know them. If you do not know the defendant, "Nucky" Johnson, personally, you have heard of him by reputation since his family has been around these parts before Atlantic County was carved out of Gloucester County in 1837.

It is true—I am from North Jersey and I was selected by Governor Wilson to prosecute this case. He wants the same things you want—the same thing people in North Jersey want—an honest and clean election. There is no difference in North and South when it comes to honesty—the ballot is sacred—the election registration books are sacred—they must be protected at all times from mischievous politicians or anyone else who wants to tamper with them for political advantages. This defendant intentionally violated the law of this great state!

I think you can imply from the defense testimony that this was a concentrated effort by the political friends of Nucky to cover up his bold behavior of strutting into the Clerk's Office wearing on his chest a five pointed silver Sheriff's badge and demanding the registration books. Tom Stewart knew if he balked, it would probably mean his job—nobody wants to lose their job.

Samuel Kirby, the Atlantic County Clerk, Tom's employer and superior, was aware of the investigation and to protect the head of the Republican Party, had Tom give him an affidavit contrary to the facts Stewart gave to the State investigators—all to protect Nucky and the Republican Party...

The case will be yours to decide in a few minutes. Do you want to see a continuation of corrupt political control over Atlantic County? I urge you to stop it by finding this defendant guilty as charged!

Judge Kalisch slowly turned his highback black leather chair toward the jury box and began his charge to the jury:

Gentlemen of the jury, I want to thank you in advance for your patience and the strict attention you paid to the testimony of the witnesses who testified in this case. This is an important case—important to the defendant since his future is at stake—important to the state since they are trying to make the election process free of corruption so that all the voters in Atlantic County will have confidence in the election process and outcome.

You have listened to very able counsel for both sides present their respective cases—both former Attorney Generals of this great state of ours. Some newspapers have referred to this trial as "The Battle of the Generals." You are not to be concerned about the reputation of the attorneys—your only concern is the facts to the law. Now it is time for you to make a decision and I would like you to listen to the law as I recite it to you and apply the facts as you shall so find them.

The defendant is charged with taking voter registration books out of the County Clerk's Office that is headed by Samuel Kirby. I charge you that it is unlawful for anyone to remove the registration books from the County Clerk's Office. Anyone who does so is charged with evil intent.

The attorneys have argued their positions forcibly and highlighted the facts they feel are important to their respective positions. You should consider what they say and apply the facts, as you find them, in making your final decision. You are the supreme judge of the facts—the Court is the supreme judge of the law. I will not comment on the facts except to make several brief observations for you to consider.

There is a sharp conflict in the testimony—a question of credibility. Mr. Stewart testified the defendant left the Clerk's Office with the registry books—he is corroborated by his sister who told you she found the books the next morning on the desk. The defendant says he looked at the books in the Clerk's Office and did not take them out of the office. His testimony is corroborated by Mr. Abbott and his sister who both stated the books never left this office.

The defendant says that Mr. Stewart should not be believed. He made a sworn affidavit three years ago that the books never were taken out of the Clerk's Office by the former Sheriff.

You can consider the all facts and highly charged political atmosphere surrounding the making of the affidavit. Mr. Stewart was a clerk in the County Clerk's Office. Mr. Abbott was the Deputy Court Clerk and Samuel Kirby was the Court Clerk and both were his superiors. What purpose did they have in having him making an affidavit? Why did they interest themselves? Did Stewart make a statement in the past to the investigating committee of the New Jersey Assembly similar as to what he testified to in this trial—that Johnson took the books out of the Clerk's Office overnight? Was the affidavit sought by Johnson to prepare his defense against future accusations? Mr. Stewart did not appear to me to be a mentally strong person. Did he give this affidavit at the urging of his superiors to protect Johnson and his own job? This has not been explained by either side at this trial. Was the taking of the affidavit at the urging of the defendant? I will not express my opinion on the factual issue—that is for you to decide.

The law presumes Johnson to be innocent and the state must convince you "beyond a reasonable doubt" that he took the books out of the Clerk's Office. If there is a reasonable doubt, you must resolve it in favor of the defendant and find him "Not Guilty."

If you accept the testimony of the state's two witnesses, then you must find the defendant "guilty."

The case was given to the jury to decide, and at 4:45 PM, the bell rang in the belfry after 15 minutes signaling that the jury had reached a verdict. Nucky and the attorneys rushed into the courtroom and took their seats.

After the jury came into the courtroom, the justice asked the foreman to read the verdict. As the words "not guilty" were read, the packed courtroom applauded. The justice shouted, "Order in the Courtroom, Order in the Courtroom!" and the spectators finally quieted down and began leaving the courtroom; the case was over.

Nucky then commented to his lawyers, saying, "You fellows did a great job, but I want to tell each of you a little secret." He then opened his briefcase and showed them his lucky Irish brick, and they all laughed.

In the overall scheme of things, the intense investigation was only a slight detour for the Republican Party. With the Commodore going to jail and Nucky acquitted, the party emerged with a younger, more vigorous leader at the helm who had been tested under fire. He soon brought nationwide attention to Atlantic City.

CHAPTER 8

BOARDWALK COURT IN SESSION

But Nucky's rise to power was a dream that he alone would experience. At the height of the investigation stemming from the alleged voting fraud, Nucky faced tragedy on the home front. On January 17, 1912, Mabel died at age 28 after developing a chronic lung ailment. After six years of marriage to the love of his life, Nucky was devastated. He felt he would never fall in love again. Although he had been a teetotaler before, he began to drink to ease his grief. Nucky carried the pain of losing Mabel at such a young age for the rest of his life.

Nucky remembers his mother saying that although Nucky's marriage lasted only a brief time, they had more happiness than most people had in a lifetime. She told him he should view her death as a sign that the Lord was freeing him to devote his life to his second love—politics. And that he did with gusto.

After Mabel died, Nucky lived the life of a bachelor and eventually moved into a two-story Spanish-style cottage at Iowa and the Boardwalk, and his maid Sarah took care of him. Late one afternoon, Nucky came downstairs for his breakfast. When he didn't see Sarah in the kitchen, he looked out of the window and saw her hanging a multicolored quilt on the clothesline in the backyard.

Nucky called to her to come and fix his breakfast. After all, he had a full day ahead of him and was in a hurry to go to the Boardwalk to meet some ward leaders. But Sarah, a full-framed black lady, didn't like to be rushed, especially by Nucky.

She prepared his usual trenchman's breakfast of a dozen eggs, a rasher of bacon, a half-dozen hot biscuits wrapped in linen with a hot stone to keep them warm, and a pot of fresh-brewed coffee. As Nucky sat down to feast on his breakfast, he asked Sarah about the quilt. She said it was no ordinary quilt. It was a "code quilt." She explained that her grandmother had given her the quilt years ago and not many people knew about code quilts.

These special quilts were hung outside the homes of mainly "God-fearing Quakers and other religious leaders" who helped escaped slaves traveling north before the Civil War, she explained. On each quilt, the patterns woven into the design were directional signals for runaways following the railroad tracks. These signals pointed in the right direction to reach a safe house along the Underground Railroad route.

Since Nucky seemed interested, Sarah continued. She said the code was originally created on the plantations, a secret only told to those slaves who were brave enough to escape from their masters. Since most slaves could not read or write, they had to rely on their memories and the plantation grapevine to pass the code along to other slaves.

As the slaves were working in the fields, they sang a song with a coded message that describing the route from the South to the North following celestial points and the Big Dipper. The words of "Follow the Drinking Gourd" offered a route to freedom following the North Star. More slaves would have escaped, but not everyone was willing to give up their family and friends in the process.

Sarah traced the symbols on the quilts to their African roots and a secret society called the Bush School. Quilters on the plantations passed their secrets by word-of-mouth from generation to generation. Sarah said she still had one of the few copies of one antislavery newspaper, *The North Star*, written by escaped slave Frederick Douglas. Even after the Civil War ended, most blacks considered the code to be so sacred and personal that they would not reveal it to anyone else.

Nucky asked Sarah more about life on the plantations and the tradition of "jumping the broom." Sarah said that was how her grandmother was married. Since there weren't many black preachers who visited the Southern plantations, slaves developed their own marriage ceremony. The ladies gathered flowers from around the main house and tied them to a broom decorated with colorful ribbons. Everyone gathered on the lawn outside to await the arrival of the bride and groom who were decked out in their finest clothes.

After singing spirituals and enjoying a little "holy water" (aka, whiskey), the bride and groom were gently pushed to the center of the circle of friends and family. One of the elders asked the couple if they wanted to be married in the eyes of God and all in attendance. Once the couple said yes, the ladies brought the flower-decorated broom to the center of the circle.

The elder spoke to the couple: "This is a day the Lord has made for you to remember and cherish ... You must remember you will have many hurdles in life to overcome and to start this lifetime journey today, we want you to jump over the broom that is lying on the ground." Of course, when the couple jumped over the broom, they were declared married. Then the elder said: "May that jump over the broom be the highest hurdle you will have to jump and may you have an abundance of health and happiness until distance do you part or the Lord calls you home." As for the phrase "until distance do you part," Sarah explained that since the bride and groom were slaves, most of them were sold several times during their lifetimes and often not as a couple.

Nucky knew New Jersey had slaves at one time; the traders brought them north to Perth Amboy and were given a bounty of land for each slave. "You know, since we are so close to the Mason-Dixon Line, and I can recall stories when I was a boy about some wealthy landholders having slaves in Mays Landing and Bargaintown," he said. "There was an auction block in old Leedsville and a whipping post. That's where the Masonic Lodge is now on the corner of Poplar Avenue and Shore Road in Linwood."

Nucky liked to listen to Sarah's stories, but he liked his breakfast even more. It brought back memories of the leek omelets his mother used to make. When they were hungry, he and his brother used to pick leeks in the field by their old house and carry them back to the kitchen in hopes that their mother put them to good use.

After finishing breakfast, Nucky was ready to start the day's business on the Boardwalk. Weather-permitting, every day at 4 PM, Nucky left his cottage and walked up the wooden ramp to the Boardwalk where he held court with his ward leaders, precinct captains, friends, and office-seekers. Those who were down on their luck or looking for political favor knew that Nucky would listen and often help them out. The crowd consisted of a few of the usual daily "railbirds," who sat on the Boardwalk rail waiting for Nucky. As Nucky strolled closer to his favorite spot, one of the men ceremoniously announced Nucky's arrival: "Here ye! Here ye! The Boardwalk Court overlooking the majestic Atlantic Ocean is now in session. All ye who have business before this Honorable Court, please step forward and be heard, The Honorable 'Nucky' Johnson presiding."

Those waiting for Nucky were well-acquainted with his political power. The crowd greeted Nucky by saying, "Here comes the man … Here comes the man!" Ever cordial, Nucky walked over to the group and shook everyone's hand. As he began to talk to the group, there was an established pecking order he followed: The first were the ward leaders, precinct captains, and officers of the Republican clubs. Deference was always given to the local black group called the Nucky Johnson Standpatters. Everyone took turns waiting for a chance to chat with Nucky, who stayed to talk to everyone. He had a way of making each person feel special.

On one occasion, Nucky saw Napoleon Cummings, one of his most trusted black political leaders who had been a former Negro League baseball player. "Boss, one of the best members of the Standpatters had a heart attack last night," said Cummings, "and there is no insurance or money to bury him. I just left the widow, and she needs your help."

Nucky said he'd take care of everything. He asked Lou Kessel to make arrangements to give Cummings his black Cadillac for the funeral and asked him to have Sarah fill a picnic basket with chicken sandwiches and a pint of gin. Nucky figured the widow needed something to eat on the way home from the cemetery and "a little taste to lighten her load."

Nucky also asked Cummings to make sure the widow saw Pastor Francis Story, a friend of Nucky's at the Baptist Church on North South Carolina Avenue. The widow would make the arrangements and find out the costs, and then Kessel would deliver the cash to the pastor before the services. Cummings walked away a happier man.

Local fundraisers came to see Nucky too, hoping to be on the receiving end of his generosity. Anytime someone was selling raffles for prizes, Nucky often asked Kessel to get his Guerra black collapsible silk top hat from the cottage. Once Kessel returned with the hat, Nucky popped it up with a flick of his hand, saying, "I'll buy as many tickets as you can stuff in my silk hat." A crowd gathered to watch the raffle seller pack the top hat with tickets, and then they applauded when Nucky pulled out a roll of bills to pay for them. Nucky knew he was making a donation to a worthy cause, but the downside was that charities routinely sent their ticket sellers to "lay in wait" for Nucky. No one ever left disappointed.

Nucky also doled out lavish tips at nightclubs and picked up the tab for his guests. He routinely gave any server near his table a sawbuck (aka, $5) just for being there. The Atlantic City Waiters Union No. 508, in recognition of Nucky's generosity, made him an honorary member. Much of his charity helped people he had never met and would never meet. He derived personal satisfaction from sharing his good fortune and considered his responsibility as a leader to lighten the burdens of the less fortunate.

One afternoon, a black ward leader came to see Nucky with three newcomers to Atlantic City, one of whom was Ishman Wallace. Apparently, the men wanted to register to vote because they weren't able to get a job in Atlantic City unless they did. Nucky wanted the newcomers to understand the lay of the land. "That's the way it is in my town boys," said Nucky. "You help us and we'll help you."

The ward leader said he could vouch for all three of the men, since he already knew some their family members from North Carolina and Florida. Nucky had the strategy all worked out: "We should give our Democratic friend, Charlie Lafferty, one, and we should take the other two," he said. "Do any one of you want to be a Democrat?"

Wallace quickly volunteered to be a Johnson Democrat; he said, "but you can count on me to vote for whoever you want." Nucky reached into his pocket and gave each of them a $5 bill so they could have a drink and vote for Republicans on Election Day. After a resounding "Yes sir, yes sir," they left and found the first open bar on Arctic Avenue to celebrate their good fortune.

On another occasion, several black ministers, along with Maggie Alice Collette of the Atlantic County Colored Republican Club, came to see Nucky at his Boardwalk headquarters. Nucky knew something was amiss. "Whenever I see three members of the cloth coming to talk to me, I know you have something serious on your minds," he said.

Apparently, the Ku Klux Klan had been burning crosses and scaring blacks all over the county. One night in Atlantic City, Klansmen appeared in white sheets and hoods after marching in Bargaintown. The black clergy asked Nucky if he could stop them before anyone in Atlantic County was hurt. Nucky's advice was to have as many members of the church register to vote and then have them vote on Election Day. He saw the Klan trying to gain a political foothold in the county and knew that the targets were not only blacks but Catholics, Jews, and all foreigners.

Nucky explained that some Protestant ministers thought the Klan was trying "to save their churches from people like me, you know, the guy who wants to keep Atlantic City an open town where a visitor can get a drink and gamble if he wants to." They called themselves the "Invisible Empire." The Klan built a local headquarters on Fred Boice's farm over in Bargaintown and often met at Eisele's dairy farm, 10 miles from Atlantic City. They had been actively recruiting members from the Mechanics Hall in Pleasantville and registering them to vote. Nucky had been keeping a cautious eye on them for some time.

He personally told the Atlantic City chief of police to run them out of town on sight. There will be no more parades on the island, he said, and if they hurt anyone, Nucky assured the clergy that the Klansmen would also get a taste of swift Jersey Justice.

The Klan recruited members by telling them that blacks and foreigners were taking their jobs in the hotels and in some trades. They encouraged their members to put a restriction in their deeds that only white Protestant Americans can own their land. "We don't want the Klan in Atlantic County," Nucky said. He knew the Klan started in the South after the Civil War. Some confederate soldiers were trying to keep political control and to stop blacks from voting. The more blacks who voted, the less power the Klan had. So Nucky pushed people to the polls and to vote against anyone the Klan supported. He assured the group that none of his Republican candidates were or would be Klansmen.

Nucky said President Wilson indirectly helped recruit for the Klan when he was in the White House. The movie *Birth of a Nation* was written by Thomas Dixon, Wilson's friend and a Baptist minister who glorified the Klan. When Wilson saw the movie in the White House in 1915, he commented to the press, "It is like writing history with lightening and my only regret is it is all terribly true," according to the book *At the Hands of Persons Unknown: The Lynching of Black America* by Philip Dray (Random House, 2002).

The movie and Wilson's remarks triggered violent riots in cities across the country, including Philadelphia. When Wilson ran for governor a few years before, Nucky said he told everyone Wilson was no good. The ministers told Nucky that they pledged their full support and intended to go back to their respective congregations with his message and register to vote for Nucky's candidates.

Nucky was a man of his word. The clergy remembered after World War I when the All Wars Memorial Building was built at States and Pacific Avenues and only white soldiers were permitted to become members. Nucky gave the go-ahead so blacks could have their own building at Kentucky and Adriatic Avenues, which was later used as a temporary hospital for black soldiers during World War I. It turned out to be a fitting memorial to black servicemen.

But curtailing the Klansmen was just one of the problems in Atlantic City. Although Prohibition was still overshadowing the nation, South Jersey had its share of rumrunners who brought in liquor from Canada and the Caribbean Islands. The rumrunners, who stashed their liquor in their high-speed boats safely beyond the 12-mile government jurisdiction off Atlantic City, waited in the dark for the best opportunity to outrun the undermanned Coast Guard gauntlet. At stake was their precious liquid cargo destined for the trucks waiting on the Atlantic City and Cape May beaches.

To keep the flow of alcohol coming into the region, a cottage industry emerged in rural South Jersey before and after Prohibition that sold and produced liquor. Whiskey stills were everywhere: under houses, in chicken coops in the Atlantic City municipal storage yard, and on farms in the densely wooded areas of the Pinelands. Their product, which was usually marketed to the nightclubs and saloons of Atlantic City, Philadelphia, and New York, was in constant demand because it was 180 proof. But the goods were diluted by 50 percent before the public ever tasted it.

Lou Barone, a leading member of a large cartel of underworld figures on the East Coast, had been in the still business for years and wanted to operate a tall column still with a high daily capacity near his Atlantic City market. His group had been supplying the shore from its Central Jersey locations for years, reaching out through political connections statewide. Barone considered South Jersey virgin territory for growth and control, and he wanted a share of the action.

He also knew that he had to get permission from Nucky to move into the area, so he contacted John D'Agostino to set up a meeting. After all, D'Agostino and Nucky were already in business together. D'Agostino operated the Renault Winery in nearby Egg Harbor City, and Nucky had an interest in D'Agostino's Atlantic City Boardwalk nightclub on Illinois Avenue. D'Agostino was close to Johnny Torrio, one-time leader of the Chicago mob before he turned it over to Al Capone. Torrio eventually joined the lucrative whiskey business on the East Coast and became part of the importing syndicate that was called "The Big Seven."

D'Agostino checked out Barone via his New York sources and confirmed he had been in the legal and illegal liquor business for years. He arranged a meeting with Nucky at Iowa Avenue and the Boardwalk, where Barone and his bodyguard met Nucky as planned.

"Mr. Johnson," Barone said, "I am sure Johnny has told you what I have in mind, which could be profitable for both of us. I understand you did give permission for one of your local boys to operate a small whiskey still in the Municipal Yard in Atlantic City, and we will not interfere with their customers."

Nucky never committed anything about himself to a stranger, knowing that it may a set-up by some law enforcement agency, investigative reporter, or political rival. But Nucky was interested in finding out what Barone wanted. Nucky knew that Governor William Moore and Colonel H. Norman Schwartzkopf, superintendent of the state police, had a campaign in North Jersey to put Barone out of business, alleging gang wars and some lead-tainted booze that blinded some people.

Across the river in Philadelphia, a few people had died after drinking contaminated ethyl alcohol at the local cider houses. But Nucky was adamant about maintaining a safe product. "I don't want that down here in South Jersey," he said. Nucky was aware that his group was generating more heat than liquor and that is why Barone wanted to open shop in South Jersey.

Barone admitted that was part of the reason, but he still needed two locations since the shelf life for each still was a year or two before it was raided by the feds. He said the only liquor that was produced for the carriage trade was 180 proof with his column still. It wasn't exactly Jack Daniels Old No. 7 from Tennessee, but it was close.

Nucky was intrigued with Barone's business. In the Pinelands, locals still brewed what was called Jersey Lightening, but the lightening was only sold locally at the corner gas station so the feds never bothered with it. Barone explained that he had a year-round business with about 40 to 50 people, many of whom don't intentionally know each other. Each one did a small job, and then they were gone.

Some women in the operation only bought sugar in small quantities from neighborhood grocery stores all day, which was given to one of Barone's men. The sugar was taken to the storage garage used for the sugar drops. Since a considerable amount of sugar is needed to make mash, the crew could get busted easily if too much sugar was purchased at any one time in any one place. Barone's operation stockpiled about 75 to 100 sugar drops with a total of about 20,000 pounds in hand before a still was even built. When the crew was setting up the actual still, it was a cash-only basis to rent garages from friends, no questions asked.

Barone's group stockpiled five-gallon empty tin cans, large wooden vats, and 50-pound bags of yeast. His trusted friends in the junkyard business set aside five-gallon tin cans and gallon glass jugs for the pick-up men. Once the column still was operating, they had the necessary supplies. He ensured that no supplies were ever purchased in large quantities or by the same people to avoid all appearances of bootlegging.

He looked for a farm deep in the woods and bought the property directly from the owner. Then he moved in the assembly crew who built and operated the still, after guaranteeing a good supply of water, which usually meant drilling a new well and making modifications to the house. The still required a 20' steel column pipe, 18" wide, extending from the basement through the roof in the center of the house.

For fuel to cook the mash, Barone used oil and plenty of it. The crew bought five large oil storage tanks—the biggest possible—from different suppliers, from different parts of the state, and using different names. The serial numbers on the tanks were torched or eroded with acid so the tanks couldn't be traced. Barone's people delivered all the goods to the site, usually in a different rented truck and even made arrangements with five different local oil companies to deliver oil on different days so no one would be suspicious of a large volume of fuel used in a short time.

He kept the electric bills low by using generators and charcoal, but there weren't too many charcoal makers left in the Pinelands. To keep the aroma under control, large piles of apples were piled in front of the still house to give off a mash smell. If anyone stumbled onto the property, they might think they smelled the apples in the yard and not the mash being cooked inside. Often, he even arranged to have a mother and her children stay for a weekend. With the mother sitting on the porch and the kids playing in the yard, any passerby would think a family lives there. When he added a few chickens or pigs around the place, and as he liked to say, "We blend in while we are brewing!"

After the column was working, the assembly crew moved out quickly, since they were too valuable to end up in jail. Many of them already had records, and they were more likely to get sentenced to more serious time in prison than a newcomer. Besides, another location had usually been picked out so they could start the assembly process all over again. Barone's crew usually produced 1,300 gallons of Yak Yak or Red Eye (aka White Lightning or Jersey Lightning) each day.

After six months of smooth operations, the new men on the job (aka "green guys") arrived and stayed until the still was closed or until the Revenue agents put them out of business. Barone explained that the green guys get a business card for one of the operation's lawyers in case there is any trouble. Once the still is raided, the agents will take everything apart and try to trace each part back to the purchaser to make a conspiracy case. "This is their favorite charge—we call it their 'net haul,' and they try to scoop up all the fish including the 'big one,' which is me," Barone said. "I never go into the still once it is in operation and never telephone the still."

The government was aware about of Barone's whiskey business for years, and he was constantly trying to shake the daily tail the feds put on him. Barone had a friend in North Jersey with a car rental agency, and he lent him demonstration cars or sometimes new ones with dealer plates, which usually kept the feds off his tail.

If workers were ever arrested at the still, they couldn't finger any of the people since they never actually met them. If they go to jail, their family gets their full salary, as long as they don't talk. When they go before the court, they usually get probation if they are first-time offenders, since they claimed it was their first day on the job and needed money to support their family. Barone paused. "Any questions, Mr. Johnson?" Nucky smiled. Now he knew it was safe to talk business.

"I always try to avoid bad publicity in South Jersey," said Nucky. "It's bad for business, understand? One incident and out you go! If you are as good as you say you are, you won't need a second chance."

With Barone's new venture approved, he followed his customary plan, opening a large column still on the Ballasteri farm in Absecon, across the bay from Atlantic City. It proved to be a very profitable business for his group and, of course, Nucky as his silent partner.

CHAPTER 9

EDGE FOR GOVERNOR

As sheriff, Nucky often became the powerful voice of the people and came to their aid on many occasions. In fact, on October 10, 1916, The Philadelphia Inquirer published a front-page article titled "Bethlehem Steel to Test Huge Guns on Vast Jersey Sand Tract," a possibility that instilled sheer fright into Weymouth Township residents. The Bethlehem steel plant, which was near Mays Landing, acquired 10,000 acres of swampland that stretched from the far side of Mays Landing to Petersburg. The giant company intended to run roughshod over the community. The site was rumored to be the future munitions plant to supply the Allied forces in Europe during World War I.

Bethlehem Steel had hired local architect Vivian Smith to design and supervise the development of the new town called Belcoville (a derivative of Bethlehem Steel Company), along with a test range for the munitions. When Nucky stepped forward and said the company was not welcome in his county, the steel company quickly abandoned its plans to test-fire munitions. Nucky knew just how to deal with the situation. He didn't have to resort to any threats. After all, Nucky had connections and knew how things operated. The clerk's office could easily lose the company's application to operate. And even if the application was found, there was a good chance that it would never be approved. But when the construction was finally OKd, architect Smith helped develop an instant company town with a school, post office, bank, newspaper, and movie theater. The locals never forgot what Nucky had done to protect their small rural community, and his political endorsements began to carry more weight. Nucky's popularity was growing countywide, and it was time for him to test his political prowess.

In 1916, Walter E. Edge was ready to run for governor of New Jersey. Nucky had initially backed Edge as chairman of the Atlantic City Republican Executive Committee and continued to do so each time Edge ran in a local election. But as Edge's second three-year term in the Senate came to end, along with Democratic Governor James F. Fielder's three-year term in office, a new governor had to be elected in fall 1916.

The 42-year-old Edge desperately wanted to be governor; he felt he had already paid his dues to the Republican Party. He had served as journal clerk in the Senate and secretary to the State Senate, as a delegate to the Republican National Convention that nominated William H. Taft for president, and as part of the New Jersey Assembly in 1910. He had served in the Senate from 1911 to 1916, became acting governor for four weeks in 1915, as well as leader of the Republican Majority, president of the Senate, and delegate-at-large to the Republican National Convention in 1916. Fulfilling his personal aspirations rested on a full-time job in the governor's mansion.

Earlier in his life, in 1904, the idealistic Edge had made a bid for an assembly seat as an independent candidate without the Republican Party backing, but he never made it through the primary. At the time, Louis Kuehnle was the Republican leader. Edge vowed that he would never buck the Republican organization again. He knew he needed Nucky's support to succeed in his campaign for governor; otherwise, he faced the Republican organization's onslaught from the south and the Democrats from the north that could only result in a landslide defeat. Edge knew the political power was Nucky's to dispense, and this was his only chance to get Nucky's full support to win the statewide primary in the 20 other counties. Nucky had the political clout to influence the Republican chairmen of the other counties to secure Edge's nomination. Any gubernatorial candidate from the sparsely populated southern part of the state was also in for an uphill battle against the powerful and densely populated voting block in North Jersey.

Edge owned a palatial Tudor home overlooking the Boardwalk in Ventnor City, the bedroom community for the more affluent residents of Atlantic City. His residence at Oxford and the beach was across the street from the Oxford Apartments where singer Kate Smith stayed when she vacationed at the shore. During some summers, the legendary composer Irving Berlin rented Edge's house as a summer retreat.

Edge, who was born on November 20, 1873 in Philadelphia, traced his ancestry to the Quakers who had resided in the Delaware Valley since the 18th century. He had two great uncles who were members of the Pennsylvania Legislature and another who was the collector for the Port of Philadelphia. When he was two years old, his mother, Mary Evans, died. His father, who worked for the Pennsylvania Railroad, then married Wilhelmina Scull, and the family moved from Philadelphia to Pleasantville, New Jersey, a few miles across the salt meadows from Atlantic City. Walter was four years old when the family moved into his stepgrandmother Elizabeth Scull's hotel in Pleasantville, which was more of a boarding house than a transit hotel. Pleasantville was a typical South Jersey village with nearly 400 inhabitants; its main street was a country road with a few stores, no sidewalks, and no police force.

His formal education in a two-room schoolhouse ended when he graduated eighth grade at the age of 14. But he was industrious by nature and an entrepreneur at heart. He started a newspaper as a teenager and later went to work as a "printers devil," an apprentice for *The Atlantic Review*. For most of the year, the *Review* was a weekly newspaper but switched to a daily during Atlantic City's summer tourist season.

Later, Edge worked for the Dorland Agency, a small advertising firm where he discovered his true calling. Advertising became so much of a passion for him that he acquired the agency two years later. With Nucky's help and a few of his Republican friends, the agency continued to grow as he added work from some of Atlantic City's resort hotels. For starters, his Quaker ancestry helped the local Quaker hotel owners accept him, and his business blossomed. These contacts quickly led to more connections to other hotels in different states that generated even more business. Eventually, the company had branches in New York, London, Berlin, Paris, and other European destinations. His advertising business provided the necessary funding to launch his own newspaper called the *Atlantic City Guest* for summer visitors in 1893, followed by the *Atlantic City Daily Press* in 1895, and then an evening paper called *The Atlantic City Evening Union* in 1905.

His newspapers often endorsed Republican candidates, and those literary efforts were usually promptly rewarded with a few political favors. It didn't take him long to ease into his political career as journal clerk of the New Jersey Senate where he served for two years, then to secretary to the Senate where he served for another four years.

As majority leader in the New Jersey Senate, Edge tried unsuccessfully to repeal the Bishop's Law that required all saloons to close on Saturday. Although his efforts failed, he endeared himself to the local resort businessmen and the Republican organization for his efforts against the opposing ministerial groups. The religious leaders had their new law, but the Atlantic City saloonkeepers ignored it in favor of staying open to serve the thirsty paying public. However, the owners respectfully agreed to close the saloon window blinds on Sundays, out of respect for the clergy.

In New Jersey, the northern urban counties of Bergen, Essex, and Hudson controlled one-third of the Republican votes in the state. Winning the primary was daunting, but then Edge faced an even stronger contest in the general election. The past three governors were Democrats from northern New Jersey, which held the majority of the votes. The Democrats also had the bulging financial campaign war chest to run a full-scale statewide campaign.

Austen Colgate, of the Colgate toothpaste fortune and a popular Republican State Senator from Essex County, had already been organizing a well-financed campaign of his own in spring 1916, backed by some strong state Republican leaders. Edge was concerned that Colgate's supporters had already approached Nucky, and if Nucky had given his word, Edge's dream of winning the election would vaporize. Though he and Colgate were personal friends, Edge was not willing to step aside for his friend.

Edge was relieved to discover that Nucky hadn't pledged his support for Colgate's team. He knew he had to dig deep into his pockets to win a statewide primary election, but he also had to have enough cold cash to make the campaign attractive to Nucky. The state's 21 county Republican chairmen knew Nucky on a first-name basis. In fact, the membership wanted Nucky to lead the state Republican organization, but Nucky declined. Edge banked on having Nucky as his statewide campaign chairman with an opening salvo: Nucky would host a gala party in Atlantic City, South Jersey-style for the state political leaders, elected officials, and celebrities.

Edge had to convince Nucky that his political businessman's message could carry the state. He decided to approach Nucky with the following plan: If his gubernatorial campaign was successful, then Nucky's reign would extend over the entire state, not just Atlantic County. With Nucky's charisma, Edge could jumpstart his campaign in one night. No other state political leader had that magic.

In 1916, Nucky was at the top of his game and welcomed challenges, especially if enough cold cash was involved. He was the man who could make it happen. If he could grease the political leaders' hands with enough cash, the conversation went from the talking stage to actual bonding. This was Nucky's kind of action.

When the two men sat down in Nucky's Iowa Avenue cottage, each had his own agenda and held his cards close to his vest. Nucky could naturally support the local boy, and if he did not, locals might accuse him of selling out to the northern part of the state for personal gain. His decision could affect him politically in his Atlantic County bailiwick. He had to plan his strategy wisely.

These experienced pros knew what hand the other held before they sat down to discuss their route to the governor's mansion. Kessel walked into the room with two drinks since he knew Nucky dealt better when his mind was relaxed. When Kessel asked Edge if he wanted a drink, he looked a bit confused.

"These two are for the boss," said Kessel. "He always takes a double. I'll bring you a double so you both start off the same, but don't try to keep up with the boss or we'll have to pour you in a rolling chair and push you down the Boardwalk to your home in Ventnor."

Nucky opened the bidding. "How much money do you have to run the campaign and when can you make your first payment in cash?" Edge knew the negotiations boiled down to a question of price. He said the race for the governorship was a golden opportunity for both of them. He figured Nucky could guarantee a victory with state jobs for anyone from Atlantic County.

Edge assured Nucky that he wouldn't have to fund the campaign. Colgate was already opening his wallet, and Edge intended to match his rival dollar for dollar. Since South Jersey was growing, Edge was going to make sure that the shore community was not shortchanged as it had been under the last three Democratic governors, that is, if he made it to Trenton.

His military service in the Spanish-American War as a lieutenant colonel had strong voter appeal since talk of war in Europe was brewing across the Atlantic. Edge recounted the day when 120 men of the Morris Guards volunteered as a unit and marched to the train at South Carolina and Atlantic Avenues, cheered on by a crowd that included 62 Civil War veterans and Mayor Franklin P. Stoy.

Nucky wasn't impressed. "The Spanish-American War? It only lasted a little over three months and your unit of the Morris Guards ended up in Greenville, South Carolina," said Nucky. "I wouldn't shout about that from the rooftops in your campaign. You will offend all the real veterans." Edge tried to keep his composure. He assured Nucky that he could take care of public relations and the press. After all, he started the *Atlantic City Press* 20 years ago and was friends with many of the editors of the other papers statewide. He could get the word out as needed.

Then, Edge decided to focus on Nucky's family history. Nucky's grandfather had served in the Civil War and his father served as sheriff for 25 years, plus his terms in the assembly. But Nucky told him that he wasn't interested in public office and never had been. He was comfortable running the campaigns and making things happen; he tried not to step on someone climbing the political ladder in the party. His goal was to kick the Democrats out of office, especially after Wilson was elected governor a few years ago and tried to put Nucky in jail. Nucky muttered about the self-righteous Georgia Cracker who even turned on the Democratic leaders in North Jersey, the guys who made him governor.

Nucky saw the pivotal race as Edge competing against Mayor H. Otto Wittpenn of Jersey City, if Edge was successful in getting the nod from the state Republican Party. In such a strong Democratic county, Wittpenn could walk away with the Democratic primary nomination and put up a strong campaign in the general election. Nucky made it clear that all the cash Edge gave him was being used to get him elected. If anyone asked Nucky later where the money came from, he planned on saying it was his, but he didn't plan on filling out any reports or accounting to anyone else. Edge agreed to the terms and placed an overstuffed manila envelope on the table, calling it his first installment. "Call me when you need more," he said.

Nucky decided to set up two campaign headquarters: one in Trenton and one in Newark at the Robert Treat Hotel. Nucky planned on being the sole South Jersey campaign headquarters open 24/7 and advised Edge to get some of his friends from the *Newark Evening News* and the *Trenton Times* to plant some favorable background stories about him in the northern newspapers.

Under Nucky's tutelage, the local leaders of Mercer and Hudson counties were expected to staff the hotels, select their own workers, and dole out enough cash to pay everyone. He also planned on making sure everyone knew there would be plenty of street money the day before the election and on the day itself.

When Nucky publicly announced his support for Edge for governor, word spread quickly throughout the Garden State and sounded the call for his political troops to take up election arms. Next, Nucky turned his attention to organizing a gala event. For the venue, he selected the ballroom of the Royal Palace Hotel & Casino overlooking the ocean at the end of Pacific Avenue in Atlantic City. On January 1, 1916, Nucky planned on throwing a command performance for the Republican Party faithful to meet Edge. Political leaders came from all parts of the state to offer assistance to campaign for Nucky's candidate. But surprisingly, some of them openly supported Colgate by wearing "Colgate for Governor" buttons.

When Edge entered the ballroom and saw a group of Colgate supporters, he immediately fired away at Nucky. "Why in the hell did you invite Colgate people?" Nucky remained calm; his reasons were solid. These were exactly the men they had to work on, and after they saw all the support for Edge, they just might want to jump on the bandwagon. "No one wants to bet on a dead horse, besides, they all want something," said Nucky. "Maybe we can offer them a better deal than a lifetime supply of Colgate toothpaste."

Nucky worked the room, spending time with each person. "Edge is a sure winner—money is no problem," whispered Nucky. "And when Edge wins, just give me a list of people who want a job." Nucky made needed introductions as he talked to his guests, pairing strong Edge supporters with the tentative Colgate backers. After all, Edge was the only man sure to win against Wittpenn, and this overriding goal was whispered from ear to ear.

When the evening ended, Edge and Nucky went back to Nucky's cottage to discuss their strategy. "We didn't get them all, but I think we got enough," said Nucky. He had made plenty of promises at the party and cautioned Edge to keep the cash flowing. With that, Edge officially threw his hat into the ring for the Republican gubernatorial nomination on January 21, 1916.

Edge campaigned statewide in the latest automobiles called "bone shakers," with rigid seat springs, unreliable tires, and speed limits of 20 mph. Most of the roads were still unpaved, deeply rutted, and covered with dirt, so full-length dusters and bulging eye goggles were the uniform du jour. Since Edge wanted to speak to as many people as possible, he moved around by car and frequently stopped to stretch his legs and chat with voters. He spoke on curbstones to crowds of three, and in barbershops and firehouses, and at church suppers in garage halls, and small hotels along the dusty route. He also renewed friendships with editors at the major newspapers who assigned reporters to cover the campaign. Nucky treated the press like royalty, making sure they ate at the best restaurants and offered them an open dinner tab including all they could drink. In turn, the reporters wrote favorable articles that touched on Edge's human side.

Joe Frelinghuysen, the Republican candidate for U.S. Senator, campaigned often with Edge, and their joint appearances usually attracted crowds. Edge counted on his record of party loyalty and business savvy to reflect his executive ability with campaign slogans that were strong and passionate: "Get rid of the Democrats, three Democratic governors in a row is enough!" and "Three Strikes and You're Out!" and "What did Wilson do for South Jersey except to try to destroy the Republican Party?"

Months of campaigning left Edge physically exhausted. He began to realize that a statewide election took more money and energy than he originally thought and looked forward to the votes being counted, which took two days. When all the primary election votes were in, Edge received a 3,000 plurality out of 149,000 votes cast, and he became the official

Republican candidate for governor of New Jersey to run against Wittpenn. Edge adopted the slogan of "A Businessman with a Business Plan," which resonated with voters since the Democrats were free and easy with state expenditures, a complaint that even today sounds familiar.

Edge's win took the northern Democratic leaders by surprise. When progressive editor Thomas F. Martin of the Hudson County's *Hudson Dispatch* denounced Wittpenn in his editorial columns, Edge's chance of winning the election grew. Democrats respected Martin, who was the former Democratic leader in the New Jersey Assembly and served as Secretary of State. Of course, former governor Wilson supported Wittpenn, which worked to Edge's advantage.

When Nucky and Edge met to discuss the campaign during the final week, Edge was elated over Wittpenn's bad press, but Nucky wasn't. He cautioned Edge. "You are a newspaper guy and think everyone reads the newspapers—even the people who do read the papers don't believe half of it," said Nucky. "It's the vote that count—second place will put you back selling newspapers on the Boardwalk in Atlantic City." Edge could almost taste victory and put his faith in what Nucky had to say.

President Wilson, who was vacationing at Shadow Lawn in Elberon, New Jersey, had kept his silence through most of the election, except for an occasional "porch chat" to his home constituency. But Wittpenn and some of the desperate Democratic leaders persuaded Wilson to go on the attack. Wilson responded, calling Edge an elitist and not a friend of the workingman. Nucky saw Wilson's attack as likely to turn off most Democrats and fire up the Republicans. Wilson was already doing a good job splitting the Democratic Party, which was one of the reasons that Edge became a frontrunner.

On Election Day, Edge settled in at his headquarters to listen to the returns. He won the largest plurality in history for a general state election with almost 70,000 votes, becoming the 29th governor for a three-year term. Nucky, who attended the inauguration ceremony on January 15, 1917, sat quietly in the audience and mused how far he had come in the political world. He had just crowned a governor.

With World War I already in progress, one of the tasks listed high on Edge's agenda was establishing a War Board to enforce the draft. The governor decided to appoint the sheriff and the county clerk in each county to organize the registration and induction of men into the armed services. Before long, Edge earned the moniker of War Governor in support of President Wilson's pursuit of a war against Germany.

Although Edge and Wilson were from different political parties, it didn't take them long to rekindle the relationship that started when Edge was State Senator from Atlantic County and Wilson was governor. Edge quickly forgave Wilson's last-minute attack during his campaign for governor, chalking it off to the rough sport of politics.

On the home front, Edge kept his campaign promise to improve the state's roads and bridges and appointed General George W. Goethals as the state's chief engineer. The general had just completed an engineering marvel: the Panama Canal. Edge's other proposals, including consolidation of state boards, Civil Service reform, greater home rule for municipalities, fiscal reforms, and comprehensive road development, were approved by the legislature one by one.

Another one of Edge's goals included building a bridge across the Delaware River but he realized the Democratic legislature wouldn't approve it since it only benefited South Jersey. He took Nucky's advice and agreed to back a construction project to build a tunnel under the Hudson River into New York from Jersey City; both projects were approved. The Holland Tunnel was eventually named for Clifford Milburn Holland, the chief engineer on the project. Later, the Benjamin Franklin Bridge was built, connecting Philadelphia and Camden, New Jersey.

Edge also delivered on his promise to get Nucky a job, and Nucky readily accepted the prestigious position as clerk of the Supreme Court of New Jersey at an annual salary of $6,000. As the incoming court clerk, Nucky personally requested that Associate Justice Thomas W. Trenchard officiate over the oath of office on February 26, 1918. They spent several hours together reminiscing about the 1907 trial of Joseph Labriola when their paths first crossed. The case still bothered Nucky, who asked the judge if he thought he sent an innocent man to the gallows. Trenchard admitted that every judge may have a moment of doubt, but the final burden rests with the jury that hears the evidence.

As Nucky settled in to his new job as clerk of the Supreme Court, Nucky and Edge often shared the 70-mile commute between Trenton and

Atlantic City. The long commute by rail gave them a chance to talk politics. Edge clearly wasn't satisfied with Trenton as his final destination. He had his sights set on an even higher office in Washington, D.C. And Nucky had his sights set on expanding his own Boardwalk empire and needed to keep his office as Atlantic County Treasurer as his political headquarters.

THE HEYDAY OF ATLANTIC CITY

CHAPTER 10

THE BATTLE OF THE CENTURY

Ladies and gentlemen and all the sports fans in attendance and listening at home on your radios ... 15 rounds of boxing for the heavyweight Championship of the World ... from France, the light heavyweight Champion of the World, weighing 175 ready pounds, with a distinguished record in the ring and a more distinguished record in the service of his native France in World War I, known as the 'Orchid man'—the challenger—Georges Car-PAWN-tee-air! Jersey City's own referee J. Harry Ertie, dressed in white with a black bowtie, shouted out the introduction at the start of the legendary fight between Georges Carpentier and Jack Dempsey in 1921.

"And in the other corner, the pride of the rugged mining camps of the Wild West and the State of Colorado ... weighing 192 solid pounds—the undisputed Heavyweight Champion of the World ... the 'Manassa Mauler' Jaaa-ck Dempsey!"

Months earlier, the fight that became known as the Battle of the Century took root right in Nucky's back yard in Atlantic City. Dempsey's temporary training camp that was set up in Summit, New Jersey, was quickly moved to Atlantic City, about one-quarter mile from the Boardwalk on Albany Avenue.

Jack Kearns, Dempsey's lifetime manager, helped Dempsey train inside at a local boxing club at the National Stadium grounds adjacent to the Atlantic City Airport. The camp was open to guests, onlookers, and even reporters who caught a glimpse at the champ in action. On rainy days, they moved into the nearby airplane hangar. South Jersey-style hospitality is what Nucky knew best, and Dempsey grew to love Atlantic City, developing lifelong friendships with Nucky and then-Mayor Edward Bader.

Nucky never missed an opportunity to celebrate in style. On Dempsey's 26th birthday just a week before the Battle of the Century, his trainer closed camp for one day. After all, the champ had spent nine weeks in intense training. Telegrams from well-wishers began to arrive from all over the country. Reporters who had covered the training camp for the past two months hired a jazz band to show their appreciation for the open camp and free access to the champ. The cake with 26 candles was configured in the shape of a boxing ring with the words piped in frosting on top: "Flash—Jack Dempsey knocks out Carpentier."

When the word "party" was mentioned, Nucky was at the top of the guest list. He was the one who arranged for the daily police control of the crowds, introduced Dempsey's entourage to the community and Atlantic City public officials, and solved problems created by such a high-profile event. Nucky, who was standing next to Dempsey when he sliced the cake, sang a chorus of "Happy Birthday" and enjoyed every minute he spent with the champ in the limelight.

But in the ring, Dempsey loved being the only one in the spotlight. If his opponent was able to stand and walk away, people called it a victory. In fact, Dempsey hit with such power that 60 prizefighters never made it through their first round. This gladiator of the ring, clad in baggy white trunks, ankle-high black boxing shoes, and rolled white socks, constantly bobbed and weaved like a coiled cobra ready to strike. His unshaven granite jaw, high Cherokee cheekbones complemented his deep-set black eyes and blue-black hair. He bared his teeth in such a way that sent instant fear into his opponents even before they entered the ring.

Born June 24, 1895, William Harrison Dempsey grew up in Manassa, a sleepy Mormon mining town on Colorado's southern fringe. As the eighth of 11 children of itinerant Scots-Irish farm worker Hiram Dempsey, young Jack emerged from the West wielding a pair of iron fists. Without any formal boxing training, manager, or trainer, Dempsey found star power at age 24 when he became the greatest gate attraction of the times. As an American superstar, he turned a boxing match into pure theater that captured the imagination of the country and the world.

After Dempsey moved east to Philadelphia, he started building his reputation for ruthlessness after he knocked out Battling Levinsky in three rounds on November 6, 1918. Twelve days later, he KO'd Dan

"Porky" Flynn in one round, and on November 28, he stopped Billy Miske cold in six rounds. After he ran out of opponents in New Jersey and Philadelphia in 1919, he moved into central Pennsylvania where he made four first-round knockouts in less than 30 days.

On August 4, 1919, Dempsey beat Jesse Willard (aka, The Great White Hope) before 19,650 fans in Toledo, Ohio, a victory that earned him the title of the Heavyweight Championship of the World. Willard not only outweighed Dempsey by 70 pounds, he was also 5" taller at 6' 6". He also had a 5.5" advantage with his reach, but Dempsey's unbridled power did not give the champ an opportunity to take advantage of his natural physical attributes.

Just a year later, "Gorgeous Georges" Carpentier, christened "The Orchid Man" by his French fans, made his American debut on October 12, 1920, when he knocked out Battling Levinsky in Jersey City. It took four rounds for him to win the World Light Heavyweight title. Born on July 12, 1894 in Lens, France, Carpentier had plenty of victories under his belt too. He won European titles as a welterweight, middleweight, light heavyweight, and heavyweight. Bill Brady, a Philadelphia boxing promoter, first suggested the fight to Dempsey's manager, saying that Carpentier had worldwide appeal.

Francois Deschamps, Carpentier's manager, wanted $200,000 for a fight between Dempsey and Carpentier, a price that Dempsey's manager agreed to pay; however, Kearns didn't actually have the money. Kearns met with promoter George Lewis "Tex" Rickard, a gambler from Texas with a magnetic personality, to raise the actual funds for the fight.

Rickard, who had recently taken over Madison Square Garden to promote sports events, was always looking for a new opportunity to make a score. Rickard had staged the Dempsey-Willard Championship match the previous year in Ohio as well as other fights all over the country and in Europe, South Africa, and South America. He quickly saw the opportunity for a golden payday for everyone.

When Rickard proposed staging the fight on Boyle's Thirty Acres at the Montgomery Oval in Jersey City, Frank Hague, the mayor of Jersey City and head of New Jersey's Democratic Party, agreed but only on his terms. With the best-oiled political machines in the state and in the country, Hague offered Rickard a deal that was hard to refuse. Though

Jersey City wasn't Rickard's first choice, he wanted the event to be close to New York City to draw a larger crowd.

Hague insisted that the promoters' hire Jersey City police and firemen to control the spectators and to maintain order to and from the fight. The security force had to be paid double time, and the Jersey City chief of police selected the number of policemen and firemen to patrol the area. Hague, who had many friends, public officials, and politicians who would call him for free tickets, so he insisted on getting 1,000 tickets to the best seats in the house for his guests.

The political leader then alerted the promoters about the upcoming election and pointed out how helpful a contribution in the six-figure range could be to the Democratic Party; cash preferred. Hague also agreed that the fight be staged at Boyle's Thirty Acres, since John F. Boyle was one of the chief fundraisers and treasurer for Hague's election campaigns for the past 12 years.

Hague overcame local opposition from the churches to the bout by calling on a close friend, Democrat Governor Edward I. Edwards, a resident of Jersey City and former state senator from Hudson County. Edwards gave his blessing for the fight at a formal dinner at New York's Hotel Commodore. It seems the governor was indebted to Hague since his political machines delivered enough votes to elect Edwards in spite of a nationwide Republican landslide when Republican Harding defeated of Democrat Governor James M. Cox of Ohio for the presidency.

The deal was struck. Both of the fighter's camps decided on a $500,000 purse instead of a percentage split: Win or lose, Carpentier was set to get $200,000, and Dempsey would get $300,000. And with the fight scheduled for July 2, 1921, the promoters began a publicity campaign to lure fans to Jersey City. The hotels in New York City and Philadelphia were quickly booked to capacity. Newspaper headlines announced the event on their front pages in the U.S. and France. As two of France's national treasures, Carpentier and internationally renowned entertainer Maurice Chevalier were photographed together with Dempsey to heighten the demand for tickets. The French newspapers continually reminded their worldwide readers that Carpentier defended France as a flying artillery spotter, while Dempsey sat around in his boxing trunks during World War I.

On some days, more than 1,000 Atlantic City locals turned out at Dempsey's open camp to watch the champ train. He even invited his fans to his sparring sessions for a fee of $1. One of Kearns' toughest jobs was finding sparring partners for Dempsey. Sparring partners traditionally have the most dangerous job in the sport: Kearns hired Leroy Williams as one of Dempsey's sparring partners because he was more durable than most. But when Dempsey knocked him out, even he left, saying, "I had enuff!"

For publicity, Dempsey often sparred with celebrities who were assured they would not be hurt. Vaudeville entertainer Al Jolson even tried once. Though Dempsey was careful to avoid any bodily contact, Jolson ran into a right punch that grazed the top of his forehead, causing a gash that bled profusely. Dempsey apologized, but Jolson was surprisingly pleased. He often proudly displayed his scar at cocktail parties, saying, "Look what Dempsey did to me. I saw fear in Dempsey's eye—fear he was going to kill me!"

Carpentier set up his training camp in an exclusive area of Long Island. He chose the Borough of Manhasset in Gatsby County near a fashionable yacht club and close to exclusive homes where residents played croquet by gaslight at night on their rolling green lawns. But the camp was closed to visitors since the challenger was perfecting his secret weapon, better known as the "frog punch," a maneuver that involved a sudden devastation lunge to knock out the champ and give France its first heavyweight championship of the world.

Prominent Long Island residents who had watched the Frenchman train wanted to witness his final performance, including Ralph Pulitzer, an early aviation enthusiast and son of Joseph Pulitzer, who created the Pulitzer prize for journalism; Harry Payne Whitney, a major figure in breeding thoroughbred race horses and winner of the Kentucky Derby; and J.P. Grace, founder of the Grace international shipping line.

William Randolph Hearst, the publisher of the largest U.S. newspaper chain, realized the market potential of this upcoming bout. Hearst hired George Bernard Shaw, the noted Irish playwright of *Pygmalion* fame, to praise Carpentier in *The New York American*. But *The Tribune*, the paper's daily competitor, ran a rebuttal in favor of Dempsey. This was the beginning of a major newspaper rivalry, causing a buzz that began in earnest and continued long after the fight was over. A cadre of sportswriters kept the typewriter keys in action: Bob Edgren of the *New York Evening World*, Tad Dorgan of the *New York Evening Journal*, and Joe Williams of the *Cleveland Press*, as well as a host of local N.J. sportswriters.

Since most Americans grabbed their news and sports results from daily newspapers, two-dozen newspapers hit the New York City streets daily. The syndicated columns were widely read, and the sportswriters used their talents to create legends. The sportswriters became celebrities in their own right, often better paid than the athletes they wrote about. The radio, which was still in its infancy, had a limited range and not every household had one.

But Rickard recognized a good opportunity when he saw it. He started contacting broadcasters for the rights to carry the Dempsey fight live, the first fight ever to be heard on radio as far west as Buffalo. Radio sales skyrocketed when fight fans heard they could listen to the live fight. To accommodate the radio broadcast, a wooden makeshift "studio" was constructed under the stands. RCA installed telephone lines and a radio transmitter at the Delaware Lackawanna and Western Railroad terminal in Hoboken. The fight eventually reached 300,000 households. The *Atlantic City Press* had a wire direct to its publishing plant for the locals to hear the blow-by-blow broadcast.

After 10 weeks of intense training, Dempsey left Atlantic City. He and his trainer, Teddy Hayes, told the press they were leaving Atlantic City for "an undisclosed private residence in Jersey City" where he would remain in seclusion until fight time. Since Dempsey was in the best physical shape of his life, he wanted to avoid the press to prepare mentally for the fight. Mayor Bader went with the champ and played a game of pool in the estate hideaway of retired General William G. Heppenheimer, the president of New Jersey Trust Co., where they were staying until fight time. The Heppenheimer estate was within walking distance of Boyle's Thirty Acres.

The international event drew boxing's first million-dollar gate and attracted 700 newspaper reporters and 90,000 sports fans from as far away as France, England, Spain, Japan, and South America. For the first time, fashionable members of American high society even made their boxing debut along with scores of public officials.

Tickets went on sale for $5.50 for general admission and up to $50 for ringside seats. Ticket demand was heavy, and scalpers moved in quickly to buy large blocks of seats for resale. Counterfeiters also saw an opportunity for a quick buck, and many were arrested before fight time on Saturday, July 2, 1921, which turned out to be a hot, muggy evening. This was an event that Nucky couldn't miss. Nucky and his entourage took their ringside seats with white linen covers, protected by a team of five burly uniformed Jersey City police officers who were assigned to secure the area when Nucky's group was seated.

In the nation's capital, the U.S. Senate and the House of Representatives had adjourned early so that 90 members of the House and 12 Senators could represent their districts at the fight. Some of the senators did not know the difference between a left hook and a fishing hook, but they wanted to go anyway. U.S. Senator Walter E. Edge from New Jersey was deluged with requests for the coveted pasteboards, which he distributed from the supply Nucky had given him on the floor of the U.S. Senate. He led a delegation of U.S. Senators to the event in his home state.

But the fight also drew politicians and business associates from all corners of the country. Nucky was in his glory and figured he would renew his relationships in the process. Boxing promoter Herman Taylor, known to his close friends as "Muggsy," led Nucky's Atlantic City group to their ringside seats. He knew everyone in boxing's inner circle since he had promoted marquee fights in Philadelphia starting in 1912 at the old Municipal Stadium, Shibe Park, Convention Hall, The Arena, the Baker Bowl, and the legendary Blue Horizon on Broad Street.

Nucky's power group included his friend and investment partner John D'Agostino; Nucky's brother Al; his bodyguard Lou Kessel; Anthony Ruffu, Atlantic City commissioner; Mayor Bader; William S. Cuthbert, director of public safety for Atlantic City; William A. Blair, Atlantic County assemblyman; Charles D. White, Atlantic County state senator; Emerson Richards, deputy attorney general of New Jersey; John Rauffenbart, Nucky's personal criminal attorney; and Walter E. Edge. John Dempsey, the champion's brother, was also seated next to Nucky's group.

When the Atlantic City contingent was seated, Taylor introduced Nucky to John B. Kelly, a brick contractor from Philadelphia who had served in the Army after being stationed in France. A great boxer, Kelly was scheduled by the Army to fight French soldier Carpentier at the Palais de Glass, but Kelly broke his foot two weeks beforehand. It was probably the best break Kelly ever had. When he returned home after the war, Kelly married and had one son and three daughters. One of his daughters was none other than actress Grace Kelly, who later married Prince Rainier Grimaldi and became Princess Grace of Monaco.

For Nucky, the event gave him the chance to renew some old friendships and initiate some new ones. He wanted to get to the ring early to talk business with political leaders from North Jersey and to cement relationships with others who he enjoyed socially, including Jimmy Walker, Democratic leader of the New York Senate. Since Prohibition had been in existence for almost a year, the mob figures who controlled the flow of alcohol had risen to celebrity status with their newfound wealth and social acceptance. Torrio, who was in charge of Chicago, brought his neighborhood "compa," aka Al Capone, from New York's Lower East Side. Torrio, Capone, and a host of their friends from Chicago also had ringside seats. Nucky knew them by reputation but had dealt with them through intermediaries over the years. At ringside, they met for the first time, but it was certainly not the last.

D'Agostino, who ran the Renault Winery, knew Torrio from his contacts in the underworld. He brought Torrio and Capone over to the Atlantic City group to meet Nucky. Capone stood in silence; he knew he was not allowed to participate in the conversation out of deference to his boss Torrio.

Torrio told Nucky to keep South Jersey and do whatever he wanted, assuring him that there was enough to go around and make everyone rich. Nucky even invited Torrio to Atlantic City as his guest to show him what Jersey-style hospitality was like and why Nucky was called "the greatest host on the Jersey coast." Capone knew Nucky liked good cigars and gave him a box of his best Cubans. In turn, Nucky told Kessel to give him a bottle of imported brandy they brought to the fight. The bond between them had been welded, and they were all ready for the fight to begin.

Back in Atlantic City, the *The Press Union* announced that anyone could come to the newspaper office building at Pennsylvania and Atlantic Avenues to hear the blow-by-blow account of the fight as the telegraph came in from ringside. Outside speakers were set up in front of the press building, and the crowd began to congregate for the 3:30 PM broadcast. By fight time, it was a mob scene. Fans were ready for the start of the match. If the champion was still standing at the end of 15 rounds, he remained champion, but the challenger could win a press verdict as a moral victory.

When Carpentier first entered the 18' square ring to the refrains of the French national anthem, he wore a gray silk bathrobe, the smallest challenger to fight for the heavyweight championship in recent years. He moved up in weight class for a big payday, but his trainer was more concerned whether he could take his power with him.

Dempsey followed, wearing a crimson cardigan, and entered the ring amid cheers and a few shouts of "slacker and draft dodger." Dempsey's military record was quite different than Carpentier, a World War I hero, was awarded the Croix de Guerre and the Medaille Militaire. Dempsey, on the other hand, was charged with draft dodging but acquitted by a jury when his mother testified he was the sole support of the family.

Dempsey held his head high as he entered the ring. He dominated the first round. The champion pounded the challenger relentlessly with short, snappy body shots to his liver. The challenger fell through the ropes trying to avoid a punch but quickly climbed back into the ring. Dempsey had been drilled, "Work the body and the head will fall." Dempsey kept his head moving and bobbing to protect him from Carpentier's devastating right hand.

At the end of the first round, Carpentier's nose was broken and his battered belly was glowing pink. Quick off the stool, Carpentier had a plan for victory, and he caught Dempsey flush on the side of his cheek. With that blow, Dempsey's knees buckled. It was a move that brought 90,000 cheering fans to their feet. The hit didn't just hurt Dempsey; the Frenchman fractured his right thumb and sprained his wrist on the champion's granite jaw.

Carpentier followed with a barrage of punches. The pain in his right fist was intense, but he still struck with all the force he had, knowing that each blow made the fracture worse. He was close to sending Dempsey to the canvas when the bell rang ending the second round. The third round was a repeat of the first, except Carpentier was having trouble defending himself against Dempsey's heavy hands. With little strength remaining, Carpentier became a standing hollow shell. He made the mistake of moving straight back, a move that allowed Dempsey to follow him and continue the body blows. The bell sounded, preventing a KO.

The Frenchman sat on his stool waiting for the bell for Round 4. Battered and bleeding, he walked into the center of the ring. The French flag came down in the fourth round when the champion finally pinned his opponent to the ropes and sent him flying onto the canvas with a direct pile-driver shot to his liver, and then to his heart for a nine count. Carpentier slowly staggered to his feet; the champion attacked again, and Carpentier doubled over and collapsed for the final count of 10.

The referee raised Dempsey's arm in victory after 1 minute and 16 seconds in Round 4. The fight was over; it lasted a total of 11 minutes. Dempsey helped Carpentier to his feet and slowly walked him to his corner. After a few minutes, Carpentier walked over to the world heavyweight champion and said, "Well done—you are truly the greatest heavyweight champion of all time. I salute you!" Then he snapped a military salute with his fractured right hand and clicked his heels.

The crowd continued to roar from the opening bell to the 10 count; spectators knew they just witnessed boxing history. In Atlantic City, fans stood in front of *The Press Union* offices in the pouring rain to hear the details of the fight from ringside booming over the megaphone. *The Press Union* started its printing presses to rush out a "Fight Extra" special edition that described the action in each round from wire service reports from ringside. Thirty-thousand copies of the "Fight Extra" hit the stands of Atlantic City 30 minutes after the champion retained his crown, all of which were sold in less than an hour. It was a fight Nucky would never forget and gave him tips for the strategies he would need for the battles that awaited him right around the corner.

CHAPTER 11

GOING TO WASHINGTON UNDER SUBPOENA

Nucky's legendary political prowess and election tactics helped him build a remarkable reputation statewide. However, being in the public eye also included heightened scrutiny by the federal government and his political opponents. On May 16, 1928, the U.S. Senate passed a resolution titled "The Election of a Senator from New Jersey," and Nucky became one of the key targets in the special government investigations.

Nucky soon found himself under subpoena. He needed to explain how he successfully orchestrated Hamilton Fish Kean's Republican nomination for U.S. Senate by defeating a former popular New Jersey governor and a former powerful U.S. Senator of New Jersey. In 1918, Kean made an unsuccessful bid for the senate post but lost to Governor Walter E. Edge. Despite his unsuccessful track record, Kean was determined to carry on his family's heritage of public service that went back generations.

Kean's father, John Kean, was the son of Peter Phillip James Kean and Sarah Sabina Morris, graduated from Princeton University in 1834. He became one of the leading business leaders of his day: He was a stockholder in the Camden & Amboy Railroad, a key to helping to build the Central Railroad of New Jersey, president of the National State Bank of Elizabeth, and president of the Elizabethtown Gas Light Company. As an old-line Whig who later switched to the Republican Party, he became a delegate to the convention that nominated Henry Clay for U.S. President. Kean married Lucy Halsted, daughter of Caleb O. Halsted, one-time president of the Manhattan Trust Company and first president of New York Clearing House.

Kean's grandmother, Sarah Sabina Morris Kean, was a descendent of Lewis Morris who was governor of New Jersey in 1738. Lewis Morris was one of the signers of the Declaration of Independence, member of the New York Provincial Congress, the Continental Congress from 1775–1777, and the N.Y. Senate from 1778–1781 and from 1783–1790.

General George Washington even appointed Kean's great-grandfather to the commission to audit accounts of the Revolutionary Army, and Kean was also a member of the Continental Congress from 1785 to 1787. Washington also appointed him Cashier of the Bank of the United States in Philadelphia, the first national bank of the new government where Kean served until his death in Philadelphia on May 4, 1795. The Kean family lineage ran pure and deep.

Kean's passion for politics and public service extended from his role as chairman of the Union County Republican Committee from 1900 to 1906 and as a member of the New Jersey State Republican Committee. In 1916, he served as a delegate to the Republican National Convention in Chicago, when Charles Evans Hughes, governor of California, was nominated to oppose the re-election of President Woodrow Wilson.

In New Jersey, Kean lived in a historic mansion named Ursino, near Elizabeth. This home in Union County, aka Liberty Hall, had a storied history all its own. It was built by Governor William Livingston in 1772, General Washington held several conferences at this mansion with his officers during the Revolution, and Alexander Hamilton studied law there too. Just before a primary election, Kean traditionally hosted a huge outdoor barbecue on the landscaped grounds to recharge the Republican Party and cement his personal contacts with its leaders.

In 1924, Kean invited Nucky to the family barbecue with the intention of asking Nucky to be his campaign manager for his bid in the U.S. Senate. Although Nucky accepted the invitation to the party, he declined the offer to manage Kean's campaign. He had already pledged his support for Walter E. Edge, but Nucky didn't abandon this potential candidate.

During the next four years, Kean and Nucky kept in contact and developed a strong political and social relationship although their pedigrees were quite different. While Kean's family had substantial banking interests in New York and New Jersey, Nucky's background was the rural

Pinelands. They simply traveled in different social circles, a factor that divided them in many ways but their mutual trust was unshakeable.

After their first meeting in 1924 when Nucky was running Atlantic County elections, Kean hand-delivered a substantial cash donation to Nucky with a note, "Please donate this to your favorite charity." Kean wanted to make sure that Nucky knew he still had political aspirations and valued his support in the future.

In early 1928, Kean and Nucky met again at Liberty Hall to discuss the upcoming Republican primary for the U.S. Senate. Members of the Republican Party couldn't agree on one of the three contenders: Edward Stokes, former governor of New Jersey; Joseph Frelinghuysen, former U.S. Senator; and Hamilton Fish Kean, an active leader and constant contributor to the Grand Old Party.

Kean knew it was going to be a tough and expensive campaign that would likely exceed the New Jersey Corrupt Practice Act's limit of $50,000 in campaign expenditures. But Kean reaffirmed his commitment to have Nucky manage his campaign. Though Nucky agreed, he asked Kean to get someone else to keep the books and file the reports, a job for which he had already appointed John Scott, the three-term county clerk of Essex County. Kean wasn't asking for public contributions; the $50,000 he gave Scott was from his personal funds.

Nucky liked the way Kean operated. He saw Kean as a strong candidate with an undeniably impressive lineage and pledged to spend all he was given on the campaign. As the barbecue and politicking continued among the party faithful that night, Nucky started campaigning on the spot. Since most of the Republican leaders were there, Nucky worked his political magic from table to table. Before the end of the evening, he had the campaign in full swing with a few party chairmen already pledged to support Kean.

Nucky knew that all three primary candidates were after the same registered Republican voters, so his first tactic was to contact Frank Hague, mayor of Jersey City and the undisputed Democratic political head of the state. Hague was one of Nucky's frequent guests in Atlantic City, so when Nucky invited him to a gala party at the Ritz-Carlton Hotel, Hague accepted. Nucky's parties were memorable and leaders of both political parties were always welcome. Hague and Nucky met in Nucky's beach block cottage across the street from the Ritz on Iowa Avenue. After a couple of drinks (Hague only drank ice water), Hague wanted to know what was on Nucky's mind.

"Walter Edge is for Stokes because he is from South Jersey and former State Senator from Cumberland County," explained Nucky, "but I told him I am committed to Kean. Walter beat Kean four years ago and there is some bad blood there. Edge is going to use whatever connections he has in South Jersey and, without me, there are few to none to vote for Stokes. I need more registered Republicans and this is where you can help me."

Hague already knew what Nucky was after. He planned on registering some of his Democrats as Republicans for the primary, which Nucky saw as a win-win situation. "This will be good for both of us," he said. "If your Democratic candidate wins in the fall, you will still have control. And if Kean wins, I'll make sure you get whatever you want." And with that, Nucky gave Hague a hefty envelope and asked that he donate it to his favorite charity.

On May 15, 1928, the outcome of the Republican primary election had been essentially sealed in that one key summit meeting between the two power brokers. Kean won the Republican primary election and then the general election by defeating incumbent Democrat U.S. Senator Edward I. Edwards. However, the defeated Republican senatorial primary candidates, along with the newspapers, cried "foul" and demanded that the U.S. Senate investigate Kean's reportedly excessive election spending to prevent him from stepping into the senate seat.

The U.S. Senate Subcommittee, which later became known as the Reed Committee, was responsible for tracking expenditures in senatorial primaries and general elections. Members of the Special Committee of Five (three members from the majority Republican Party and two members from the minority Democratic Party) were instructed to conduct a thorough investigation and to submit their report to the full Senate. In June 1928, Senators Charles L. McNary of Oregon and William H. King of Utah held formal hearings in Washington, D.C., with James A. Reed from Missouri serving as chairman.

The three Republican primary candidates were called before the committee in the nation's capital along with their campaign managers. The committee wanted detailed reports of campaign finances to see whether the candidates had adhered to the New Jersey law that limited campaign spending to $50,000. Edwards, the successful Democratic primary candidate for the U.S. Senate, wasn't required to appear since there were no reported irregularities in his campaign.

As the first candidate sworn to testify, Kean was questioned about the details of the campaign and the transcript states:

> *A: I went to Newark to see John Scott and asked him if he would take charge of running my campaign. He had just run a successful campaign for himself for County Clerk of Essex—this is the largest county in New Jersey—the largest county for Republicans. I thought this was the key. He gladly consented.*
>
> *Q: How long has John Scott been County Clerk of Essex County?*
>
> *A: He was elected three times.*
>
> *Q: This is the county that includes the City of Newark?*
>
> *A: Yes, in the north of New Jersey.*
>
> *Q: I assume Mr. Scott proceeded to create an organization, did he?*
>
> *A: Yes. The organization went all over the state. The headquarters was a small office in Newark at the corner of Broad and Market Streets. It is the second place in the United States where the largest number of people pass by each day—Forty-second Street, in New York City, being first.*
>
> *About two doors away there was a small office I rented as my headquarters. Mr. Scott worked there and had a staff.*
>
> *Q: In each of the twenty-one counties in New Jersey, did you have an individual or organization to promote your interests?*
>
> *A: Absolutely!*
>
> *Q: Who handled the funds?*
>
> *A: Mr. Scott—I transferred $50,000 from my firm account to the campaign fund in the Federal Trust Company of Newark.*
>
> *Q: How did you give that to him, by check?*
>
> *A: By check.*
>
> *Q: Did he return any of that money to you?*
>
> *A: No.*
>
> *Q: How many weeks did you spend in going around the state yourself?*

A: *I spent nearly every night from the time I started from January 5th to May 15th.*

Q: *When you went over the state, did you make speeches?*

A: *I made speeches, shook hands with people and called on everyone I knew. There were Herbert Hoover for President meetings that were organized by the County Committees—meetings for all the candidates.*

Q: *Were you running with Herbert Hoover or were you just running wild?*

A: *We were running independently but I attended any meeting I could—sometimes six or seven a night.*

The questions then shifted from the campaign activity in North Jersey to the following questions about Kean's activities in South Jersey.

Q: *Do you know a man by the name of Enoch Johnson in Atlantic City?*

A: *Yes.*

Q: *How much did you give him?*

A: *Nothing.*

Q: *Was he engaged to work for you?*

A: *Yes, not engaged working just for me. He was working for the whole Republican ticket.*

Q: *What position did Nucky Johnson have in the Republican Party?*

A: *He is very influential in Atlantic City. He asked me to go down to a meeting in Atlantic City of Orthodox Jews. I went down and there must have been two to three thousand people in the hall—it was jammed packed—wall to wall people!*

I spoke and then they called on other speakers. Each of them got up and started his speech by saying: "I am for God and Enoch Johnson!"

Q: *Do you regard that statement as a great display of intellectual capacity on their part or of devotion to the party?*

A: *I am only showing you the devotion to Enoch Johnson. That is what I am trying to show you.*

Q: *He is the political leader in Atlantic City?*

A: *Yes and has been for some time.*

Q: *Is he in the Edge Group or Anti-Edge?*

A: *In the Edge Group. Some may say United States Senator Walter Edge is in the Johnson Group.*

Q: *Was Senator Edge supporting you?*

A: *No.*

Q: *But the organization in Atlantic City was supporting you?*

A: *Yes.*

Q: *Was Johnson supporting you?*

A: *Yes.*

Q: *Were you asked to make a contribution to the Johnson Group?*

A: *No.*

Q: *You said Mr. Johnson asked you to go down and address a meeting?*

A: *Yes, that is right. It was a meeting for the City Commission for the five-member commission election—they run the government in Atlantic City.*

Q: *Did these speakers, of those who spoke, say they were for God and Johnson or for Johnson and God?*

A: *I quoted what they said. I am only telling you. I never heard anyone get up and start a speech that way and a cheering standing ovation when he finished.*

Q: *Do you know Isaac H. Nutter? [A black Atlantic City attorney]*

A: *Yes. ...*

Q: *Did he maintain a campaign headquarters not only in Newark, but also in Atlantic City?*

A: *No.*

Q: *Were not he and Mrs. H. Blanche Harris connected with and working in headquarters, in some headquarters, or a place in Newark?*

A: *Mrs. Blanche Harris had a headquarters in Newark. She was hired by my manager. ...*

Q: *Was it not common talk, Mr. Kean, that you had contributed $25,000 to the maintenance of those headquarters?*

A: *If it was, it was a lie. ...*

Q: *Is it not a fact that there were a very large number of people*

working there, at the headquarters and other places in Newark
to whom payments were made from $5 to $10 a day?

A: I do not know.

Q: How many times did you visit Atlantic City?

A: Three, four or five times.

Q: Was it not stated repeatedly during the campaign and especially as the campaign approached its climax, and immediately
after the campaign, that you and your representatives were
spending enormous amounts of money, very greatly in excess of
the $50,000 limitation imposed by the State of New Jersey?

The questioning continued focusing on contributions to specific
organizations.

Q: What was the basis of the charge that you had paid Mr. Enoch
Johnson $200,000 or a larger sum of money?

A: $200,000; that was the thing. The charge was that I had paid
Mr. Enoch Johnson $200,000; that I had given each chairman
of the twenty-one county committees a blank check which he
could fill in after the campaign at his inclination. Those were
the charges!

Q: Is it the custom in New Jersey to issue blank checks? [There was
laughter in the courtroom.]

A: Not by me.

Q: I noticed in your statement that you listed the total amount
expended up to May 12, 1928 was $39,143.30—two days before
the primary election. This would leave in John Scott's hands,
roughly $10,856.70.

A: Correct. It is explained in a supplemental statement.

Q: What was the purpose of keeping the $10,000 back? Was it to
be used on Election Day?

A: I suppose the purpose was to distribute it among the county
organization.

Q: For Election Day purposes?

A: Yes.

Nucky then next to take the stand as the featured witness, since he
was one of the targets of the inquiry. And the questioning continued on June 2, 1928:

Q: *State your full name.*
A: *Enoch Lewis Johnson. Most people call me "Nucky."*
Q: *Where do you live?*
A: *Atlantic City, New Jersey.*
Q: *What is your business?*
A: *Real Estate Broker and County Treasurer for Atlantic County.*
Q: *How long have you held that position?*
A: *Twelve years, I think.*
Q: *Are you a Republican?*
A: *Yes, Sir, and very proud of it.*
Q: *Who did you support?*
A: *Hamilton Kean.*
Q: *Have you been connected with his organization in the State of New Jersey?*
A: *Not necessarily.*
Q: *Are you a County Committeeman or connected with the Republican Organization in Atlantic County?*
A: *I am a State Committeeman.*
Q: *How long have you held that office?*
A: *Three years.*
Q: *Did that position bring you in close contact with Mr. Kean in his ambitions and political activities?*
A: *Not necessarily.*
Q: *Did it at all?*
A: *No.*
Q: *Have you been friendly with Mr. Kean for a number of years?*
A: *No Sir, not necessarily.*
Q: *With whom have you worked?*
A: *I don't know much about State politics.*
Q: *You confine yourself to the County?*
A: *Atlantic City, principally.*
Q: *And you are friendly with Senator Edge, I have been told.*
A: *I still am.*
Q: *And you supported Senator Edge in his candidacy for the United States Senate?*
A: *Yes, Sir.*

Q: *Senator Edge supported former Governor Stokes this past election.*

A: *I believe so. Could you speak louder? I am slightly deaf.*

Q: *Did you receive any contributions from Mr. Kean or anyone on his behalf?*

A: *No, I did not.*

Q: *Did you take any part in the campaign outside of supporting Mr. Kean?*

A: *Surely.*

Q: *Well, what did you do?*

A: *We had a commission fight in Atlantic City before the primary. I was actively engaged in that election—five commissioners running for control of Atlantic City.*

Q: *Did you receive any money from Mr. Kean or his treasurer and campaign manager in the Atlantic City fight for control of that city?*

A: *Mr. Bertrand Whitman, the campaign manager for the city candidates may have. He is one of our leading citizens—editor for the Pleasantville Press and President of the Pleasantville National Bank. Governor Edge appointed him to the Atlantic County Board of Taxation and is now the Clerk for Atlantic City.*

Q: *How much did he receive?*

A: *I don't know.*

Q: *You heard he received some money?*

A: *Yes, Sir.*

Q: *Was any of that money spent for Mr. Kean in Atlantic City?*

A: *I do not know.*

Q: *Did the local papers carry any advertisements for Mr. Kean?*

A: *Not that I know.*

Q: *Were you about the voting polls on Election Day?*

A: *No, just to vote the straight Republican ticket.*

Q: *Was there a meeting you attended composed partly of Jewish people during the campaign?*

A: *Several.*

Q: *How many meetings did you attend?*

A: *I don't remember.*

Q: *Did it occur to you that Mr. Kean was receiving the endorsement of people at these meetings?*

A: *Yes, because they were for him.*

Q: *For what reason?*

A: *Because they thought he was a good Republican, I suppose.*

Q: *What brought Mr. Kean into prominence?*

A: *He was a National Republican Committeeman for the past ten years and in 1916, he was a delegate to the Republican National Convention in Chicago.*

Q: *Did they admire him because he was a National Committeeman?*

A: *I do not know about that but his family is very prominent—he did run for United States Senate in 1924—so his name was well known to Republicans.*

Q: *Did you speak at these meetings for Mr. Kean?*

A: *Surely I boosted him at a lot of meetings.*

Q: *You boosted Mr. Kean?*

A: *Yes and Mr. Larson for Governor of New Jersey.*

Q: *What vote did Mr. Kean receive in the County?*

A: *I do not know.*

Q: *Did he carry Atlantic County?*

A: *He sure did.*

Q: *Who paid for the election meeting where Mr. Kean spoke and you spoke?*

A: *They were a ward organization—had been in existence for years—Atlantic City is a well organized Republican Party.*

Q: *Who was in charge of the campaign in Atlantic City?*

A: *B. F. Whitman, City Clerk for Atlantic City.*

Q: *Did he receive any money from Mr. Kean?*

A: *I do not know, Sir.*

Q: *Nearly all the fellows in your group were for Mr. Kean?*

A: *Yes, all of them.*

Q: *Who did the colored people support?*

A: *They supported the organization ticket that included Mr. Kean.*

Q: *How many constituted the inner-circle of your organization?*

A: *Four thousand five hundred office holders?*

Q: *In the State?*

A: *No, in Atlantic County.*

Q: *What is the population of Atlantic County?*

A: *About 160,000.*

Q: *Do a good many politicians gravitate to Atlantic County?*

A: *Yes, sir. It is a seaside resort. [A sudden burst of laughter filled solemn chamber.]*

Q: *You must have an inner-circle who dominates the group?*

A: *All the ward leaders and township leaders.*

Q: *What is your connection with the organization?*

A: *I am part of the organization.*

Q: *Mr. John Scott, Kean's campaign manager and Court Clerk for the powerful Republican organization in Essex County, has told this committee that you, Mr. McCutchendon, David Baird, Jr., George Johnson and George Page of Trenton were the principals running Mr. Kean's campaign—who selected you to represent Atlantic County?*

A: *No one in particular. I was invited because I have been active in Republican politics for a number of years. David Baird, Jr., from Camden County also has been a strong Republican supporter and fundraiser. After he graduated from Princeton University, he took over the family lumber business. His father was elected Sheriff back in 1887, the same year my Pa was elected Sheriff in Atlantic County. We have been close with the Baird's ever since. My Pa and me supported David Baird, Sr. when he successfully ran for U.S. Senate—a very proud day for the Baird Family.*

Q: *What are you doing with 4,500 office holders in a small county?*

A: *You will have to take that up with the people who approved them—I have nothing to do with that.*

Q: *Are they all Republicans?*

A: *No, the Department of Streets and Parks are controlled by the Democrats.*

Q: *Do you recall a meeting where you spoke, 3,000 people present, and Mr. Kean spoke and the people in the audience said "they were for you and God"?*

A: *They say so many things about me, I do not remember.*

Q: *Are you such a dominant figure that they mention you right along in connecting with the Deity?*

A: *I should not think so, but everyone can say what they want in my neck of the woods.*

Q: *Do you know anything about this senatorial primary?*

A: *I lost sight of national and state campaigns—I was fully involved in the fight to control Atlantic City.*

Q: *Did you collect any money?*

A: *No.*

Q: *Did you make a contribution?*

A: *Yes. $100.00.*

Q: *How much was collected for the campaign?*

A: *I do not know.*

Q: *How many persons are employed around the polls in Atlantic City?*

A: *Only what is provided by law.*

Q: *How much are they paid?*

A: *I do not remember.*

Q: *Have you ever been County Chairman?*

A: *No. I am Secretary of the County Committee. I was Sheriff of Atlantic County once and Clerk of the Supreme Court of New Jersey.*

Q: *How many colored voters are there in Atlantic County?*

A: *Seven or eight thousand.*

Q: *Did any particular person handle them?*

A: *No. They have organizations of their own, which clubs are duly chartered and have been in existence for years. I have known many colored people in the County for years—most of them by their first name. I help them and they help me each election. In fact, they named one of their Republican Clubs after me—"The Johnson Standpatters."*

Q: *What is a standpatter?*

A: *Before I came along, the politicians only cared about the colored around Election Day. I take care of them all year around and they stand firm for my candidates when I ask them for a vote— that's a standpatter.*

Q: *Did you go through the State of New Jersey and make any collections of money?*
A: *No, Sir.*
Q: *Did you receive any money from Mr. Scott or from Mr. Kean for your services?*
A: *No, Sir.*

On February 22, 1929 the Special Committee of Investigating Expenditures in Senatorial Primary and General Elections submitted its final report to the U.S. Senate: No further action was to be taken. Kean's wish came true when he was sworn in as U.S. Senator from New Jersey after defeating the incumbent Democrat Senator Edwards with a plurality of 233,129 votes. The newly elected U.S. Senator served one six-year term until 1935.

New Jersey also rallied for Herbert Clark Hoover, the Republican candidate for the presidency who became the 31st U.S. President. It was a good year for the Republicans and a stellar year for Nucky. He went into the nation's capital under a cloud of suspicion, had his mettle tested under fire by the full power of the U.S. Senate, and came out with a political halo that endeared him to the Republican leaders in New Jersey for years to come.

CHAPTER 12

A MONUMENT TO POLITICAL POWER

Although tourists found plenty of excitement in Atlantic City during the summer, they always headed home with a box of saltwater taffy and a suntan at the end of the season, leaving the shore behind to settle in for a long, lonely winter. If Nucky wanted to give the resort staying power and create more local jobs, he needed additional attractions. And he knew that every job he handed out was a guaranteed vote for one of his candidates.

One of the first such attractions was the Miss America Boardwalk Parade, which attracted mostly daytrippers. The Miss America Pageant only extended the summer season briefly until just after Labor Day, but local consensus was that a new and larger venue for the beauty contest could take the event to an all-new level and attract nationwide attention to Atlantic City.

In the aftermath of World War I, the country was trading in its wartime economy for a new consumer economy. Conventions and trade shows generated business, especially when visitors could enjoy a vacation at their boss's expense. Nucky honed in on the idea of building a large convention hall to keep visitors in town longer and spending more money on Atlantic City goods and services.

Nucky first visualized the idea in July 1921, after the Jack Dempsey/Georges Carpentier Heavyweight World Championship Fight in Jersey City. As Jersey City Mayor Frank Hague's guest, Nucky was just one of the estimated 90,000 people who were corralled into a dusty Jersey City field to watch the slugfest.

But in Nucky's eyes, Atlantic City had much more to offer: the world-famous Boardwalk, the most popular beach in the country, top entertainers, and oceanfront hotels. If Atlantic City had a convention hall on the Boardwalk, it could open the doors to a host of sports events, conventions, and a national showcase for the Miss America Pageant.

Creating a sound marketing strategy was nothing new to the resort. Back in 1908, the Atlantic City Publicity Bureau was launched with Walter E. Edge as its first president. The goal was to market Atlantic City as a health resort for the entire family. Hotel owners strongly endorsed this marketing strategy, and some even featured indoor saltwater swimming pools. But Nucky wanted local organizations to shift their focus from health resort to conventions. By 1926, some conventions were already finding Atlantic City to be a good destination, including 12,000 Shriners and nearly 10,000 delegates to the National Electric Light Association.

Although the late 1920s weren't the best economic times, the financial challenge did not deter Nucky. The breadth and depth of his vision were undoubtedly brilliant: He wanted a little city on an island several miles long and a mile wide with 40,000 people to build the largest convention hall in the world. He enlisted the support of Atlantic City Mayor Edward L. Bader. In fact, Nucky was so convincing that Bader later claimed the idea as his own. When Nucky first spoke to Bader about a convention hall, the mayor was skeptical, especially where they would find funding to build the facility.

"From a bond issue, we will have to go to the voters and I'll take care of that," Nucky said. "You know I have never lost a municipal election and we can win this one if we do a selling job. Besides this election is only for Atlantic City, where we are the strongest—with the best ward leaders and precinct captains in the state—they'll get out the vote."

Nucky saw the construction project as a source of jobs for local residents. His goal was to build a seven-acre hall that covered an entire city block. Something that size could guarantee jobs for years. Even when the hall was finished, conventions would start rolling in from all over the country, with more jobs for each show … ushers, guards, maintenance men, and a full-time convention staff.

He also considered the voting potential that such a project would generate. He planned on taking care of the Northside blacks who voted as a block, and he started by meeting with the black ministers. His plan was to increase the money in the Coal Fund (a free coal for the needy), open a warehouse, and stock it with food for the faithful. The message, he said, was clear for those who joined the cause: Every house was warm in winter and a basket of food was there for the asking.

Bader became a vocal cheerleader for the new hall and expanded Nucky's list of advantages for the city and its residents. More hotels would have to be built, small Boardwalk shops would prosper, restaurants would need more help, and the nightclubs would get more action. But overall, the project would create jobs in the winter when the town usually went into forced hibernation. Locals regarded it as, "Three months of hurry and nine months of worry."

Nucky made sure that no roadblocks emerged from the State House in Trenton by contacting the North Jersey Democratic leader Frank "I-am-the-law" Hague. They enjoyed bestowing favors on each other since it gave each of them an opportunity to flex and show off their political muscle. Though Nucky and Hague had their differences (the mayor didn't drink or smoke, wore a Derby hat with a plain suit, and took great pride in running a strong political organization), both men shared the fact that they were constantly under investigation by state and federal authorities. Since Hague selected the Democratic legislators of North Jersey who controlled the New Jersey Senate and Assembly, Nucky extracted a personal commitment from Hague that the legislature would OK the bond issue of about $13.2 million payable over a 40-year period, allowing Atlantic City to build the hall.

Finding the perfect spot for such a massive facility was no easy feat. But as fate would have it, a fire had destroyed Rendezvous Park, a popular amusement center at Georgia and Mississippi Avenues extending between the Boardwalk and Pacific Avenue. This prime patch of ocean-front real estate amounted to seven full acres in the heart of the city. Nucky insisted that the location would be the cheapest and easiest to acquire. It was the perfect Boardwalk site between the two railroads entering the city.

Nucky launched his personal crusade to persuade Atlantic City residents to cast a "yes" vote for the bond issue. He started to contact voters and opinion makers personally to convince them of the many merits of the hall. Every Sunday, he went to a different church where the ministers greeted him in appreciation for all his past favors. Nucky explained that the hall meant new jobs, some all year long. He urged the ministers to talk to their congregations and to encourage everyone to vote for the bonds to build it.

Before he left each session, Nucky reached into his pocket and handed the minister a sealed white envelope with the amount of $1,000 written on the outside. "It was nice of you to listen to me, Reverend," said Nucky, "and I would like to donate $1,000 to your building fund." The ministers were usually quite surprised and replied, "But we don't have a building fund." Nucky just smiled and said, "You do now."

One of the VIPs on Nucky's list was Madame Sara Spencer Washington, the founder of Apex Hair Co. at 1801–1803 Arctic Avenue. She knew jobs would improve the quality of life for the black community. Washington was a self-made millionaire who earned her riches by selling her straight-hair conditioner for black women. Eventually, her business empire included Apex News Services, Apex Laboratories, and Apex Beauty Schools, which expanded to New York City, Washington, D.C., Baltimore, Chicago, Atlantic, and Philadelphia.

Washington was not only a savvy businesswoman, but she had a good grasp of the local political scene. She was one of Nucky's longtime financial supporters, a member of the Atlantic County Republican Committee, president of the Atlantic County Association of Colored Women Club and an alternate to the Republican National Convention in 1944 and 1948. She also founded the Northside Easter Parade that allowed members of the well-dressed black community to parade proudly down Arctic Avenue in the black business district. When Nucky appealed to Washington to rally support in favor of the convention hall, she pledged her full backing.

Nucky gave Mayor Bader the thumbs-up to start acquiring the land. He told Bader, "If you appoint a 'Site Selection Committee' of ten, you will end up with eleven opinions. I prefer a committee of one," Nucky said. "So let's get to work since I don't hear any dissent." He wanted progress, not conversation. Otherwise, the project would be talked off the drawing board if committees started to get involved in site selection.

On November 6, 1923, the referendum election was held in Atlantic

City, and voters approved (by a 2:1 margin) the condemnation of the former Rendezvous site at the beachfront, bounded by Georgia, Mississippi, and Pacific Avenues, as reported in the *Atlantic City Press* on November 7, 1923. On January 31, 1924, condemnation proceedings began, and the land was acquired in September 1924.

Unfortunately, Bader died unexpectedly in 1927, which created a political scramble among the commissioners to take his place. When the dust finally settled, Anthony M. Ruffu became the new mayor. When Nucky first met with Ruffu to discuss the convention hall project, he told him, "I put my political future on the 'chopping block' in building this hall and we need to get the best manager in the country to manage this giant. There is nobody in the county and certainly no one in Atlantic City, including all your relatives, who is going to get the jobs unless I give him my OK. I want you to contact the managers of all the convention halls in the country and get the best. They'll jump at the chance to manage the largest convention hall in the country!"

Ruffu realized that this was an opportunity to thank Nucky for helping him in his bid for mayor and to show him that he could successfully lead the city. So when Ruffu contacted the managers of all the convention halls across the country, he was surprised at how few halls there were and that they were not large in the major cities. After several months, the mayor reported back to Nucky at a meeting in Nucky's cottage. By then, the mayor had spoken to more than 10 managers nationwide and told them about the hall in Atlantic City. Each one confirmed that the convention business was booming. After Ruffu's research, he had more confidence in Nucky's idea of building the largest convention center in the world.

Ruffu selected Lincoln Griffin, the manager of the Cleveland (Ohio) Public Auditorium, to look over the city and to take the job of overseeing the project. Griffin had been the manager of the Public Auditorium in Cleveland since 1922, and before that, he was the business manager of the Cleveland Symphony Orchestra. Best yet, he was a staunch Republican. Griffin accepted the position.

The hall and stage was designed to be the largest in the world with unlimited versatility, from cultural, educational, and sports events to conventions. Freight trains could run right into the hall so exhibitors could easily unload supplies. Nucky insisted on it when he spoke to the architectural planners and designers. This would be the largest hall in the world to be built without roof posts or pillars, with a seating capacity of 41,000 people. The hall could accommodate a standard 13-story building in the center of the auditorium and not even touch the top of the roof. Some engineers said the facility couldn't be built in a beachfront location atop a water table that was just a few feet below the surface. But when it was completed, at a cost of about $13.5 million, the hall was watertight and sitting on 30-foot pilings, all 12,000 of them.

When State Senator Emerson L. Richards heard of Nucky's plan, he was delighted. This was an opportunity he never dreamed he would have in his own hometown. Emerson was an accomplished musician, a master organist, and a leading national authority on design and construction of pipe organs. He had no trouble approaching Nucky with his idea to design and build the largest pipe organ in the world to give life and personality to the planned mammoth hall.

Richards, a trial lawyer, had worked his way up to the political ranks by serving in the New Jersey Assembly in 1911 and now was serving in the New Jersey Senate since his first election in 1916. When he went to see Nucky, he shared his vision for the music. Nucky thought about it briefly and liked the idea. But he asked Richards to run the idea by the mayor without saying that Nucky had already OKd it. Fortunately, Bader took to the idea instantly, and Richards started to work on his design, enlisting the expertise of the world-renowned firm of Midmer-Losa of Merrick, Long Island, to manufacture the organ at a cost of $400,000. The project took four years to complete and was still not operational when the hall was officially dedicated in 1929.

The organ had to have great power, more versatility, and finer musical values than any other in existence. When finished, the organ weighed 150 tons and used more than 250,000 feet of lumber. The controls were designed so the organist could find every stop and control within easy reach on the console on the side of the stage. Using the organ's giant electric brain, an organist could command the tone of any one or all of 33,112 speaking pipes and generate any kind of music from jazz to classical.

The construction of the hall lived up to all of Nucky's expectations: Jobs were available for the party faithful. The general contractor, Markland Co., a local contractor, found a job for anyone Nucky sent over, but if they did not really want to work, Nucky quickly knew about it. When the construction foreman called Nucky about one of his selected workers not carrying his load, Nucky had the work-shy worker delivered to his suite at the Ritz for a meeting. During the time the worker rattled off a standard litany of excuses, Nucky listened quietly and then said, "It's the super's way or the highway. If the construction super calls me again about you, you're through."

Nucky, who always praised loudly and criticized softly, often put his arm around a worker's shoulder and offered him a few words of solace. "Now go back to work and remember, it's a bitter cold winter to be out of a job," cautioned Nucky. "You have a choice—freeze to death or starve to death. Make sure you work the polls for us on Election Day and be sure you get the whole family out to vote Republican."

Every week, Nucky visited the hall during the construction to watch its progress. It also gave him an opportunity to talk to the workers, many he knew on a first-name basis. When they saw him coming, they would shout his name and give him a thumbs-up. "Here comes the Man!" they cheered.

The auditorium also featured a public address system could pick up a whisper from one end of the building and send it clear to the other. The exterior was covered with Indiana limestone and marble, which added visual dignity to the structure. Mellow floodlights, softly tinted with the blue and green of the ocean, bathed the structure in subdued light at night.

At long last, the hall was finished after three years of work. With such Herculean efforts in the design and construction, it only seemed fitting that the grand opening of the hall was just as elaborate. It was Ruffu's job to complete the hall in time to celebrate Atlantic City's Diamond Jubilee Year in 1929; Bader's widow was given the honor of laying the cornerstone at the dedication ceremony.

For the formal dedication of the auditorium, Nucky was busy calling on his many contacts to launch the hall into the national spotlight. He arranged through Edge to have the 31st U.S. Vice President Charles Curtis come to Atlantic City to dedicate the hall on May 31, 1929. Curtis, a staunch Republican from Kansas, served with Edge in the U.S. Senate and readily accepted his invitation.

Mayor Ruffu was Nucky's choice as the master of ceremonies. That way, Nucky could control the program with the decorum it deserved.

He asked U.S. Senator Edge, U.S. Congressman Isaac Bacharach, State Senator Emerson Richards, and Governor Morgan F. Larson to speak at the dedication. Of course, they were all Republicans. A few months later, President Herbert Hoover appointed Edge ambassador to France.

A sea of 30,000 people filled the hall and outside promenade to the delight of the planning committee. The local reception convinced Nucky that he picked a winner. Flags of 75 nations and the seals of all the states accented the Roman Renaissance-style edifice. Even the building supplies were a collaborative effort, drawing from 37 states and 10 foreign countries.

Also in attendance were British Ambassador Esme Howard, Spanish Ambassador Don Alejandro Padilla Y Bell, and Governor Franklin Delano Roosevelt of New York, soon to be the 32nd U.S. President, and Governor John Stuchell Fisher of Pennsylvania.

When the ceremonies were nationally broadcast over a radio hook-up, Atlantic City received its first nationwide publicity. Even the USS *Wyoming*, the flagship battleship of the U.S. fleet, was anchored offshore from the hall and fired a salute from her 16-inch guns to recognize and salute Curtis. This naval salute responded to an army battery on the beach in front of the hall that fired their salvos.

All eyes were riveted skyward to view the USS *Los Angeles*, a dirigible, as it floated over the hall. At just the right moment, the dirigible sent a signal that automatically threw a switch illuminating the front of the hall. The light created an aurora borealis effect to commemorate the 50th anniversary of the invention of incandescent light by New Jersey's own Thomas Edison.

The national and international press covering the gala heralded it as the premier convention hall worldwide. Some newspapers even called it the eighth wonder of the world with an architectural majesty that attracted many national conventions beyond all expectations and revolutionized the convention business for years to come.

All the fanfare of the convention hall showered Atlantic City with national recognition and assured the resort a robust economy for the future. Likewise, the success of the hall changed Nucky's image from political power broker to a visionary civic leader. He had bridged the gap from the unsavory world of politics to the respectability of community leader. In 1929, Nucky was the man of the hour.

THE GOING GETS ROUGH

CHAPTER 13

CAUGHT IN THE CROSSHAIRS

As the man about town, Nucky loved being in the spotlight and was noticed wherever he went. But the attention wasn't always from friends and fans. The IRS also followed his every move, and it wasn't hard to do since he made no effort to avoid them. Nucky's background dossier included confidential reports from secret sources, alleging that he received graft to protect wide-open gambling and bookmaking operations in Atlantic City.

In the Atlantic City region, Nucky controlled the flow of illegal liquor as a member of The Big Seven into South Jersey during the 13-year Prohibition era that ended in 1933. The IRS also had reliable information that public contractors were expected to contribute to the Republican Party to receive their fair share of contracts. The game of pay-to-play was routine at the shore.

Although the IRS's sources were never publicly disclosed, consensus around the Department of Justice credited William Randolph Hearst from the *New York Evening Journal* as the top informant. His team of investigative reporters dug up dirt that would make good copy regardless of its accuracy. Allegations of crime, graft, and corruption made big headlines and sold plenty of newspapers. The federal government accumulated enough information on Nucky and his dealings to open a criminal active case against him in 1936.

Nucky's business deals and personal relationships revolved around an expanding world of celebrities and notables. His relationship with Al Capone first started in 1921, when Nucky met Johnny Torrio and Capone at the Dempsey-Carpentier fight in Jersey City. At the time, Torrio was the undisputed boss, and Capone was his understudy. Capone's reputation for violence was legendary, which he believed would deter others from getting in the way of his driving ambition to be boss. And he had his chance four years later in 1925, when Bugsy Moran and two of his gang members ambushed Torrio and left him for dead outside his Chicago apartment. Amazingly, Torrio survived and finally gave Capone control of the operation. Torrio said he was leaving Chicago and going to New York City for health reasons. Simply put, he didn't want to die from "lead poisoning."

Nucky and Capone met again six years later in Chicago at another celebrated boxing match: the Dempsey-Tunney Heavyweight Championship of the World. George L. "Tex" Rickard, Dempsey's promoter, invited Nucky to the match on September 22, 1927 since they had developed a friendship when Dempsey trained in Atlantic City. A group of Nucky's friends wanted to see the bout because of their fondness for Dempsey and in hopes that he regained the title he lost to Tunney in 1926 in Philadelphia.

Many South Jersey fight fans wanted to join Nucky's entourage since he traveled first class, a style that they could never afford on their own. When Nucky was making the travel plans for the fight in Chicago, he asked Mae Paxson who managed the Atlantic County Treasurer's office to make the arrangements. Mae was married to Bill Paxson, the brother of Atlantic City Commissioner Joseph A. Paxson, and she knew who to call. She reached out to some of Nucky's contacts and called in his IOUs, the first of which were with two local brothers Harry and Isaac Bacharach.

Since transportation was at the top of Paxson's list, Harry helped with that. Harry was past president of Atlantic City Council and once served as mayor of Atlantic City. More importantly, he was a personal friend of the directors of the Pennsylvania Railroad that provided passenger service from Atlantic City to Chicago. The directors also knew that Harry was in line to become a member of the N.J. Public Utility Commission that regulated the industry in New Jersey. Granting any request to a future commissioner would undoubtedly promote goodwill for the company. Harry needed to make arrangements for two coaches from Atlantic City to Chicago on September 21. Within minutes after Paxson called him, Harry reported back to her that the Nucky Johnson Atlantic City Special was set to roll out of Atlantic City on September 21, 1927.

Nucky also told Paxson to contact Isaac Bacharach, who had been serving in Congress since 1915 and had been a delegate to the 1920 Republication National Convention in Chicago. While he was there, Isaac had made influential contacts and knew the best hotels, so he reserved three luxury suites at the Belmont Hotel in a very fashionable district of Chicago.

Capone welcomed Nucky and his entourage to the Windy City and sent three black limousines to the Union Train Station to pick them up and take them to the Belmont Hotel. Illinois Republican State's Attorney Robert E. Crowe was at the station and personally welcomed Nucky's train when it arrived. Crowe was a Republican leader in Cook County who had teamed up with Capone to have Bill Thompson elected mayor of Chicago in 1927. Thompson had a solid working relationship with Capone that was acceptable to everyone except federal law enforcement.

Jack Curley, a wrestling promoter in Chicago, was also part of the welcoming party, but his motives were far from altruistic. As the premier wrestling promoter nationwide, he depended on his personal contacts to launch events all over the country. And after discussions with Nucky, Curley thought Atlantic City was a good destination for some future major attractions.

Capone made sure the limos were at Nucky's disposal for the duration of his stay in Chicago. But for Nucky and Capone, the Tunney fight wasn't the only item on their agenda. Before the event, they wanted to discuss Capone's plan to set up a meeting in Atlantic City with his nationwide business associates to get ready for the end of Prohibition. Torrio, as the elder statesman of the mob, convinced Capone that all the bosses in the country should have a sit-down meeting. Their goal was to keep cash flowing once liquor was legalized, and Nucky's home turf seemed to be a good spot on the East Coast.

Once they finalized plans for the big meeting in Atlantic City, the men settled in to enjoy the Dempsey-Tunney fight that made boxing history. With 105,000 cheering fight fans at Soldiers Field in Chicago, the record-breaking sporting contest exceeded $2.7 million. With Tunney as champion, he received a record $1 million, and Dempsey collected $450,000 with the balance going to the promoters. The event also was also controversial for its legendary long count. When Dempsey knocked

Tunney to the canvas in the seventh round, referee Dave Barry motioned to Dempsey to go to the furthest corner. The referee started the count after seven seconds had already elapsed. Tunney rose to his feet at the count of nine and went on to win a 10-round decision to retain the Heavyweight Championship of the World. Sportswriter Damon Runyan, who was sitting ringside, reported that Tunney was definitely down at least 14 seconds in the seventh round, which fueled the controversy nationwide. In fact, it's still a hot topic in boxing circles to this day.

Almost two years later in spring 1929, Capone and Torrio met again with Nucky in Atlantic City, along with key members of the organized crime syndicates across the nation. The guest list was a who's who of mob figures: Frank Costello, gambling boss of New York, brought Joe Adonis with him; Albert Anastasia; Meyer Lansky, the brains and money man who viewed a syndicate as a sound business practice; Harry "Nig" Rosen and Max "Boo Boo" Huff of Philadelphia who controlled the liquor business in the City of Brotherly Love; Charles "Lucky" Luciano of New York and a rising national crime figure; Arthur Flegenheimer with a street name of "Dutch Schultz" from Cleveland along with Moe Dalitz and Charles Polizzi; and Lou Rothkopf was Boston's King Solomon. Detroit's Purple Gang was represented by Joe Bernstein; Abner Zwillman represented Northern New Jersey and Western Long Island; and of course, Capone, who Torrio brought to Chicago from their old neighborhood on New York's East Side. Representatives from Detroit, Kansas City, and New England also made an appearance.

During Prohibition, Torrio had organized rumrunners and bootleggers into a cartel known as "The Big Seven," including Nucky as the member for South Jersey. He was instrumental in calling together these king pens to halt the bloodshed in Chicago by rival factions because he thought all the bad publicity was bad for business. Torrio had survived an ambush of his own so he was quite familiar with the cutthroat tactics at work. He also wanted to set up territories to avoid future disputes and to develop a hierarchy to enforce decision making.

Moe Annenberg, who started his career in the newspaper circulation business for the *Chicago Tribune*, arrived in Atlantic City, sponsored by his Chicago mob backers. He wanted permission to set up a nationwide wire service to provide racing odds and racing results to every racing horse room in the country. This lucrative control over national gambling was given the highest priority at the meeting.

Nucky was prepared to entertain his guests in style. He reserved the front tables in all the nightclubs and restaurants for his visitors; he arranged for a fleet of black limousines to drive them all over Atlantic City, from sun up to sun down. He rolled out the red carpet for his guests at the President Hotel in Atlantic City.

Capone arrived with the largest delegation that included Jake "Greasy Thumb" Guzik; Frank Nitti, Capone's chief enforcer; and his personal bodyguard, Frank Rio; along with some muscle men who always shadowed Capone everywhere he went. Capone enjoyed riding in a rolling chair on the Boardwalk and going to the local fights at the Waltz Dream Arena at 123 North Ohio Avenue in Atlantic City.

Damon Runyan, who came to Atlantic City to cover the mob convention, was able to interview Capone as they sat on a park bench on the Boardwalk. Runyan had a special relationship with mob figures: They enjoyed seeing their names in print, especially when Runyan glamorized their lives. To celebrate the event, a photo of Al Capone and Nucky walking shoulder to shoulder along the Boardwalk was plastered on the front page of Hearst's *Journal* after the meeting in Atlantic City.

The convention galvanized the mob figures from all parts of the country and created a governing board that the state and federal governments have never managed to stop to this day. Lansky and Luciano's influence dominated the decision to divide up parts of the country; the bosses of each territory were designated and agreed upon. [Annenberg was given an exclusive to operate a national wire service to horse rooms throughout the country.] After Prohibition, the mob later became part of the Mafia when it moved into drug trafficking, union corruption, and extortion.

The timing of the meeting couldn't have come at a better time for Capone. With George "Bugs" Moran's gunmen eager to avenge the St. Valentine's Day Massacre of February 1929, Scarface wanted to get out of Chicago. He had orchestrated the gangland killing of the century. Seven mobsters were gunned down as hit men disguised as police officers lined up all their victims against a brick wall and gunned them down with Thompson submachine guns. This massacre even caused some mob leaders to rethink their images.

Since the Atlantic City convention lasted only a few days, it was still too dangerous for Capone to return to Chicago. So he decided that the only safe place for him was in jail on the East Coast. He took a train from Atlantic City to Philadelphia where he was arrested for toting a gun; of course, the scenario was prearranged. He pleaded guilty and was taken to Philadelphia's Eastern State Penitentiary, where his accommodations were anything but stark. His cell was furnished with an Oriental rug and a portable radio along with a steady supply of his favorite Cuban cigars.

At the end of Prohibition in 1933, the IRS and the Department of Justice continued to follow Nucky's activities and expenditures. The government knew that local municipal and state authorities were not going to investigate Nucky since he had either appointed or elected many of the Republican officials in law enforcement. Nucky's close political and social ties with Democratic state leader Frank Hague also protected him from the Democratic side of law enforcement. With Nucky's indestructible line of defense and local political protection, only outside special agents, prosecutors, and judges could be trusted.

Nucky was a savvy businessman. He dealt strictly in cash, kept no books, had no bank or brokerage accounts, and listed no assets in his name, except for a few minor holdings. He filed his federal income tax returns on time and reported substantial commissions to equal his visible expenditures. He kept his public expenditures to a minimum by having others make cash purchases. His gross receipts consisted of income from the American Oil Company, where he served as a part-time salesperson, and the *Mays Landing Record*, in which he had an ownership interest and served as president of the newspaper. He didn't report his $6,000 annual income as Atlantic County Treasurer since it was not taxable at that time. To build its case against Nucky, the IRS uncovered income from other sources and an amount in excess of his reported commissions. This way, the IRS could establish a track record of willful evasion of income taxes and filing a fraudulent tax return.

An extensive undercover operation traced a steady stream of cash to Nucky from bookmakers, gambling parlors, horserace betting, bingo halls, kickbacks on public contracts, and prostitution houses. If all the operators were identified, the next step was to flip participants and scare them enough to first become government informants and then reluctant witnesses later. This was no easy task. Gambling was deeply entrenched in Atlantic City's DNA, and as its popularity increased, the city began to grow and prosper. Most businessmen were comfortable with open gambling in Atlantic City. After all, these were services that the tourists demanded, just like a hotel room with an ocean view on the Fourth of July.

The Department of Justice sources estimated that Nucky received between $350,000 and $400,000 in illegal gambling protection annually in Atlantic City in the late 1930s. According to federal estimates, there were 20 horse rooms where people bet on horse racing results from tracks all over the country and each paid $200 per week; 16 numbers banks, each paid $100 per week; and eight large bingo halls, mainly on the Boardwalk, paid from $100 to $350 apiece each week. Eight major bordellos paid $100 per week during the 10-week peak summer season and $50 per week for the rest of the year. On top of this cash flow, a minimum of $25,000-plus was paid in kickbacks from public contracts. Of course, employees of the cities and counties were expected to contribute to the Atlantic County Republican Organization, which was called ice money, to keep their jobs and to be considered a worthy candidate for promotions and raises.

When investigators asked locals about Nucky's source of income, the majority defended him. How can Nucky live the lifestyle he enjoys on his county treasurer's salary of $6,000 a year? This was a question that the special agents kept asking to get someone to talk about Nucky, but no one took the bait. In fact, the common response in Atlantic City was, "Why don't you go back to Washington and leave us alone."

On January 20, 1935, another unexpected event turned the national spotlight on Atlantic City, giving the shore the image as a protected retreat for criminals. Alvin Karpis, aka U.S. Public Enemy No. 1, rolled into town and escaped after a daring shoot-out with local police.

Karpis had spent a total of 25 years in Missouri, Kansas, and Oklahoma penitentiaries, became a public enemy when he joined the Kate "Ma Barker Gang." Her son, Arthur "Doc" Barker, led the gang along with her other son, Fred, hijacking mail trucks, robbing banks, and kidnapping wealthy Midwesterners. In 1934, Ma Barker and Fred were killed in a shoot-out with the FBI in Florida, where Doc Barker was taken into custody, but Karpis escaped. In fact, FBI Director J. Edgar Hoover vowed to arrest Karpis personally. His instructed his agents to "shoot to kill."

Karpis and fellow gang member Harry Campbell drove all night from Florida to visit their longtime girlfriends in Atlantic City. The girls (Dolores Delany was Karpis' girlfriend) had arrived by train a week earlier from Florida and had already checked into the Danmor Hotel on South Kentucky Avenue, close to the Boardwalk and beach. Delany, who was eight months pregnant, asked the hotel desk clerk for the name of a doctor who could see her on short notice and gave the clerk a $20 tip. Immediately, the clerk made arrangements for her to see Dr. Carl Surran. Meanwhile, the two fugitives parked their car with Florida license plates in the Coast Garage, an indoor parking garage across from the hotel; they didn't think anyone would see the car.

The next day, Atlantic City foot patrolman Elias Saab discovered the fugitives' car quite by chance. He noticed the Florida license tags and alerted the detective bureau that it may be a stolen vehicle. Detective Witham Mulhern and John Brenner went to the hotel not realizing Karpis was on the FBI Public Enemy list and that he had a submachine gun. At 5 AM, the detectives checked with the office night clerk. The clerk told them the owner of the Florida car was C. Carson who was registered with G. Cameron on the fourth floor. The detectives walked up the stairs to the fourth floor where Mulhern found the hotel door ajar. He poked his service pistol through the door and shouted, "Stick 'em up!"

Always prepared, Karpis pumped his Thompson submachine gun at the doorway and the battle began. Luckily, Mulhern escaped with only a bullet graze on his cheek, and the detectives emptied their service revolvers as they retreated down the stairs. Karpis and Campbell made their way out of the rear of the hotel to Westminster Avenue and circled back to the garage, where they stole a car.

The fugitives not only left their girlfriends in the room across the hall, but one of the stray bullets from Karpis' machine gun hit Dolores Delany in the leg. The fugitives were determined to go back for their girlfriends, so they circled around the block twice in hopes their girlfriends would be waiting outside and ready to jump into the car. But that didn't happen. Karpis was hanging on the outside running board of the car with his machine gun positioned for a police shoot-out. After a police chase along Pacific Avenue, Karpis escaped. The Atlantic City police decided that capturing Karpis was best left to federal authorities who had equal firepower. The *Atlantic City Press* splashed the details of all the events on the front page. Augustus Sandmann, who later became a Catholic priest, lived on Westminster Avenue as a teenager and recalls all the excitement that day and hearing the gunshots between Karpis and the police.

Nucky was furious when the chief of police called him on the phone about the shoot-out with Public Enemy No. 1. Nucky shouted, "How in hell did Karpis get in town without you knowing about it?" The chief told Nucky the other news about Delany's pregnancy. More embarrassing yet, she went to see Dr. Surran who just so happened to be the Atlantic City police surgeon.

Nucky knew what bad publicity Karpis's escape generated and that his name would somehow be tied in with these fugitives. Karpis continued to rob banks for the next two years until Hoover personally took him into custody on April 30, 1936. Karpis was among the first federal prisoners sent to the maximum security Alcatraz Prison in San Francisco Bay. He spent more time at "The Rock" than any other prisoner and was among the last to leave when it was closed in 1963 by Attorney General Robert F. Kennedy.

As the *New York Evening Journal* continued to release a barrage of corruption news about the Johnson Machine in Atlantic City, the once-timid local reform candidates began to surface. Again, questionable voting practices drew attention and cast a shadow over Nucky's operations. In 1936, the feds launched a joint investigation of Nucky authorized by Secretary of the Treasury Henry Morganthau Jr. The federal investigation, which continued for the next four-and-a-half years, was intent on taking Nucky out of circulation.

On May 12, 1936, William B. Shields, a long-time Republican activist opposing Nucky, ran for the Atlantic City Commission along with local reform candidates including independent Republican Daniel S. Bader, the son of Mayor Edward L. Bader. Despite the strong campaign against Nucky's ticket, Bader lost by 7,000 votes. Shields cried foul; he requested a recount and an investigation by the Atlantic County Grand Jury. The county court ordered a recount that gave Bader 3,000 additional votes, but it was still not enough to upset the election results. Nucky's slate won the election amid cries of corruption. If anything, the election just added fuel to the political fire that was already burning brightly.

Shields swore out warrants, and 60 people were summoned before the Atlantic County Grand Jury. Albert D. Osborn, the nationally recognized handwriting expert who testified in New Jersey's Charles Lindbergh kidnapping case in 1932, was consulted about the questionable handwriting on some ballots in the Atlantic City elections. Numerous ballots were deemed fraudulent and later thrown out by the court.

The *New York Evening Journal* mounted daily attacks and began referring to Nucky as the "baldheaded Republican boss," the "Czar of the Boardwalk," the "Overlord Playboy of Atlantic City," and "Henchman of Republican Governor Harold Hoffman." However, the *Journal*'s favorite characterization of Nucky was the "baldheaded Belshazzar," a reference to the last King of Babylon who was warned by God about his impending defeat in a handwritten message on the temple wall. Nucky's machine was vulnerable to attacks because little attention was paid to Election Day "irregularities." It was the results that counted. Nucky often told his precinct captains that "second place only counts in horseshoes—not in elections."

Rabbi Julius Goldstein supplied an affidavit stating that when he went to vote, he received a ballot that was already marked with the appropriate candidates. Even Edmund Kite, a captain of the Atlantic City Beach Patrol and former professional wrestler, was arrested and charged with voting three times. Magistrate Edward Nappen, who was also a precinct captain, was arrested for trying to intimidate witnesses before the grand jury. The background investigation showed his previous Philadelphia criminal record should have disqualified him from ever becoming a magistrate in the first place.

Loyal Republican and County Prosecutor Joseph Altman was accused of "dragging his feet" and asked to get an outside special prosecutor to clean up the city and county. There was also a cry to impanel an Elisor Grand Jury that indicted Nucky in 1911, claiming the entire jury selection process was corrupt, and Nucky controlled it all. The *Journal* charged that Democratic leader Charles I. Lafferty was part of the problem, jumping at any chance to receive some crumbs from the Republicans' bountiful table. Even the grand jury was subject to attack by the *Journal* for trying to create an atmosphere of economic disaster for Atlantic City if Nucky was not removed from power.

The *Journal* described Governor Hoffman's every political move and appointment as having sinister motives. Even Colonel H. Norman Schwarzkopf, head of the N.J. State Police, was removed in favor of the governor's choice of Mark O. Kimberling, who was the warden of the state penitentiary in Trenton.

Before he became governor, Hoffman was Nucky's friend during the 1934 primary for governor when Atlantic County Senator Emerson Richards wanted the nomination. Nucky agreed to remain neutral, which permitted Hoffman to win the nomination and the governorship over the Hague machine-backed Judge William Dill, a judge on the Court of Errors and Appeals. Hague's Hudson County machine turned out 110,000 voters, 107,000 of which went to Dill. However, Hoffman narrowly won the state by only 12,000 votes.

The *Journal*'s daily explosive coverage of the Atlantic City Commission recount concerned Hoffman. The power of repetition was a formidable weapon against the Nucky organization. On June 16, 1936, the urgency of the problem reached the danger zone. The governor quickly left the Republican National Convention in Cleveland for an emergency weekend meeting with Nucky in Trenton.

A Hoffman confidante suggested that a member of Attorney General David I. Wilentz's staff take over the investigation and remove Atlantic County Prosecutor Joseph Altman. This was designed to give credibility to the inquiry since the reform movement in Atlantic County had lost all confidence in Altman.

With the Great Depression engulfing the country and wiping out fortunes, many people filed bankruptcy. The *Journal* seized this as an opportunity to undermine Nucky's political image even more and create the impression that he was personally responsible for the economic downturn in Atlantic City.

When Atlantic County was forced to issue script (a form of county currency to pay its employees' salaries and utility bills), the *Journal* chastised Nucky for not properly managing the county's fiscal affairs as county treasurer amid claims that he didn't go to the county treasurer's office daily and that he left the county's treasury responsibilities to Mae Paxson, his longtime administrative secretary, and Marie Boyd, her assistant.

By 1938, the Federal Grand Jury in Camden, New Jersey, began cranking out indictments. A total of 21 people in Atlantic County were charged with criminal counts of tax evasion from gambling activity. None of them pleaded guilty since Nucky had protected them for years from local and state enforcement agencies, and they expected him to do the same with the federal charges. They considered an indictment a routine business hazard and expected it simply to disappear.

But the following year, Nucky regained the spotlight. On May 10, 1939, the Federal Grand Jury indicted him, along with Joseph A. Corio, Anthony P. Miller, and Janet Garwood, for conspiracy to falsify their 1935 income tax returns. This indictment against the group was the backlash resulting from a public contract to build a new railroad terminal at Arkansas and Arctic Avenues in Atlantic City; Nucky reportedly received a share of the profits as a kickback.

The government expected that once Nucky was indicted, his untouchable persona would vanish, leaving every man for himself. But this didn't happen. In fact, the reverse happened: those who gave statements to the agents actually denied giving such information when summoned before the probing grand jury in Camden. They believed Nucky was "bullet proof," and they expected his political armor to protect them.

On June 9, 1939, a second indictment was returned against Nucky for income tax evasion in 1935, 1936, and 1937. These years covered income that Nucky allegedly received from the numbers gambling syndicate for protection to operate and to keep others from moving into their territories. The three principal witnesses for the government in the upcoming trials were Judge Joseph A. Corio, the attorney for the railroad terminal construction contract in 1935 where Nucky reportedly received a kickback, and Max Weloff and James Towhey who delivered protection money to Nucky from the numbers bankers 1935 and 1937. Strategically, the government decided to move its strongest cases for trial first for the 21 numbers operators who were indicted to gain their cooperation to prevent jail time. The feds adopted a boxer's proven strategy, "If you attack the body, the head will fall."

The first jury was selected for the case against Austin "Dick" Clark since the evidence was so compelling. He reported no income for numbers in 1935 and 1936. For 1937, he reported $20,000 one week before the trial date. A squad of eight U.S. Marshals stormed into Atlantic City and served subpoenas on more than 200 surprised witnesses for the upcoming trials. This heightened the drama that was about to be played out in the federal court in Camden, 60 miles from the shore.

The federal agents had obtained statements from many of the numbers writers who worked for Clark; they provided their best recollections of the amounts of their books given to Austin. Each writer received 25 percent commission of the amount of numbers he wrote. There were "pick-up men" who went to the numbers writers to pick up the numbers slips and the money they collected. They received 10 percent for their collection work and delivery of the cash and slips to the numbers bankers at Atlantic City's Belmont Hotel at 37 North Kentucky Avenue.

On May 22, 1939, Clark's trial began, which resulted in his conviction on June 7. The government produced 60 reluctant witnesses who testified in the federal court in front of intimidating men who sat in the front rows of the courtroom. Clark's sentencing followed on June 16, 1939, when Judge Albert B. Maris gave him three years in the penitentiary. It sent a chilling message to other bankers that they better cooperate or face a stiff jail sentence.

Others began to plead guilty, but on June 30, 1939, the case of numbers writer Benjamin Rubenstein went to trial resulting in his conviction. On July 12, he was sentenced to two-and-a-half years in the penitentiary. William "Willie Wallpaper" Kanowitz and David Fischer, who were horse-room operators, admitted to federal agents they paid $160 a week for protection in 1935, 1936, and 1937, but they gave the protection cash to a person who had since died. When they appeared before the grand jury on August 9, they gave evasive answers but admitted they gave protection money to "Frank" and "Joe." However, they denied it was Frank Molinara and Joe Camarota who worked for Samuel Camarota. The Camarota brothers operated a large gambling parlor at the Hialeah Nightclub at 1917 Atlantic Avenue in Atlantic City. The grand jury chose not to believe them, citing them for contempt of court and intentional obstruction of the grand jury investigation. They were taken into federal custody and placed in the Mays Landing jail, since it was the government's practice then to use local jails for short-term sentences or for prisoners awaiting trial.

Sheriff Al Johnson, Nucky's brother in charge of the Mays Landing jail, allowed the prisoners to have gourmet meals brought in from restaurants of their choice. He also let the manager of their horse room visit them in prison two or three times per week so their bookmaking operation continued to function and prosper seamlessly. When federal agents finally discovered that their plush confinement did not deter their criminal operations, the prisoners were then transferred to the far end of the state in the Hudson County Jail in Jersey City.

The IRS was offering a "get out of jail free" card to anyone who turned on Nucky. But his colleagues didn't cave in. The horse rooms could not operate without immediate racing results, and Moe Annenberg still operated the Nationwide News Services that provided wire service of horse racing results to subscribers nationwide. These initiatives, which had been approved in 1929 at the Atlantic City crime convention, included plans to start a nationwide racing results service that was legal according to the feds.

Arrangements were made to install the race wire service only in horse rooms with permission to operate in Atlantic City. Each horse room was compelled to pay $200 per week, $40 of which went to Annenberg's company and $160 to Nucky. Samuel Camarota was in charge of the entire operation, and his brother Joe and partner Molinara collected the money each week.

The government had compelling testimony about the payoff system, but there still was no proof that Nucky received any of the money. Many of the local bookmakers were called before the Camden federal grand jury, but none cooperated. In fact, they went out of their way to protect Nucky. Even Molinara and Joe Camarota denied receiving the payoff money. Though the government tried to hold the two bookmakers in contempt, officials were compelled to proceed with indictments for perjury just to save face.

The grand jury called Samuel Camarota who invoked his rights under the Fifth Amendment, so he would not incriminate himself. The grand jury cited him for contempt, and federal Judge Guy Laverne Fake, who was hearing some of the gambling cases from the overcrowded Camden criminal docket, sentenced him to six months in jail on September 19, 1939. Nucky was pleased that Fake had stepped in since he was a former Republican from Bergen County before President Calvin Coolidge appointed him to the federal bench in 1929. Having friends and acquaintances in the right places could have its advantages.

The government also focused on the graft paid by the bordello operators. Undersheriff Raymond R. Born was the target of a violation of the Mann Act for transporting females for interstate commerce in prostitution. George Whitlock, an Atlantic City jitney inspector and a staunch member of Born's Third Ward Republican Club, admitted that he collected money from the madams and gave it to Born. James McLaughlin also admitted to being a brothel collector but denied giving the weekly envelopes to Born. He was indicted on August 9 and charged with attempting to evade his income taxes for 1935, 1936, and 1937.

Starting in July 1939, the numbers barons who had been convicted were called before the grand jury. All of them denied paying any protection money and denied they operated as a syndicate. Ralph Weloff was given special attention since he was reputed to be the collector of protection money from the numbers operators for Nucky, similar to the role of Sam Camarota had with the horse parlor operators. They were referred to by the federal agents as "bagmen."

On January 16, 1940, the much anticipated trial of the black numbers banker Leroy B. Williams began. He was represented by Isaac Nutter, a black Atlantic City attorney who was unfamiliar with federal criminal procedure and the proper defense for an income tax evasion charge. The judge, recognizing the inadequacy of defense counsel, tried to guide him through the trial, and the jury became sympathetic to the defenseless defendant. After Nutter's dramatic gospel-like closing statement, the jury returned after nine hours of deliberation and found the "misguided soul" not guilty.

The government was stunned, but Williams had committed an even greater crime: He failed to pay his attorney. This ingratitude turned his attorney into an avowed government informant. An enraged Nutter reportedly supplied the government with the details of the numbers operations and encouraged witnesses to tell the truth. Nutter told the government that from 1935 through 1940, the numbers banks worked together at one headquarters and divided the profits equally among the eight banks. The next formidable challenge to the government was to prove the existence of the operation with protection money being paid directly to Nucky.

Herndon Daniels, a numbers banker who had pleaded guilty in 1939, was sent to Lewisburg Federal Penitentiary. Since becoming a government informant, Nutter told the government that Daniels admitted the syndicate existed and explained how it operated. A writ of habeas corpus was issued, and Daniels was taken from Lewisburg to testify before the federal grand jury in Camden. He described how they formed a syndicate to stop the practice of paying higher percentages to the pick-up men and writers and a system of resolving territorial disputes. The headquarters was set up in the Belmont Hotel in Atlantic City, which Daniels owned. Four men ran the syndicate and divided the profits equally. The headquarters received an average of 50,000 numbers slips per day from the pick-up men. Most importantly, Daniels disclosed that the syndicate paid $1,200 per week for protection.

The government's focus was to show how payments made their way into Nucky's pockets. Three collectors had been convicted: Ray Born, Joe Camarota, and Sam Camarota. Born collected from the bordellos, Joe collected from the horse rooms and had gone to jail without naming Nucky, and Sam appealed his conviction while still refusing to name Nucky.

In the meantime, Nucky's attorney had filed for a Bill of Particulars, and Trenton Federal Judge Phillip Foreman, who was temporarily sitting in Camden, ruled that the government had to furnish the defense with evidence and names of potential witnesses. This was good news for Nucky. Foreman was a Republican. Although he was never an elected official, he was appointed U.S. Attorney by President Herbert Hoover.

Nucky exhausted all political efforts to sidetrack the government, but he was heading on the fast track for trial. He knew it was time to find his good luck charm, that lucky Irish brick. "I don't know how much luck is left in you," he said, "but I hope there is enough left for this case."

CHAPTER 14

CIRCLING THE WAGONS

Several of Nucky's political contacts in Washington and his personal connections in Chicago told him in the early 1930s that the IRS had received special marching orders from the new Democratic government officials in the Department of Justice. They were going to take immediate action to wipe out Nucky and the bastion of the Republican Party in South Jersey. The Roosevelt administration was going to flex its powerful muscle and crush Nucky's political empire.

Nucky found out that Assistant U.S. Attorney General William H. Boyd controlled the investigation through longtime friend John D'Agostino. When Nucky was Atlantic County Treasurer, both D'Agostino and Atlantic City Commissioner William S. Cuthbert signed his surety bond required by the county for the office in 1934. D'Agostino and Nucky had also invested in real estate deals together including the Silver Slipper nightclub at Illinois Avenue and the Boardwalk in Atlantic City in 1925. D'Agostino was always looking for a business opportunity, especially if it had anything to do with the liquor business, whether legal or illegal.

D'Agostino initially invested in the brewery business with Johnny Torrio in Philadelphia after Prohibition ended in 1933. During Prohibition, Torrio had organized rumrunners and bootleggers into a cartel known as "The Big Seven", including Nucky as the member for South Jersey. D'Agostino became a criminal target by IRS Special Agents because of his association with Torrio and what appeared to be a legitimate brewery business in Philadelphia. However, the IRS had reliable information that D'Agostino was fronting for Torrio who was reported to have had an undisclosed million-dollar investment in the venture.

Torrio's relationship with Nucky also caused the government to scruti-
nize all of Nucky's business deals, especially after the IRS learned Nucky
was on the board of directors for D'Agostino's brewery.

While under constant investigation by IRS, Torrio had Assistant U.S.
Attorney General William H. Boyd on his silent payroll. Boyd, who had
18 years of service in the Department of Justice, had complete access to
the field investigation via IRS special agents. On the civil side, there were
fines and penalties; on the criminal side, there was a criminal indictment
and a possible prison sentence. Boyd was the one responsible for making
the life-changing decision whether to proceed with a criminal indictment or seek a civil fine.

The Department of Justice attorney was a treasure chest of information about the ongoing undercover investigations of Nucky, Torrio, and
D'Agostino. But Boyd's superiors were relentless about turning the civil
investigation into criminal cases. Eventually, Boyd was indicted for leak-
ing information, but the distraught career attorney committed suicide
before the case ever went to trial.

D'Agostino had purchased the East Coast's largest brewery in
Philadelphia for $1 million in 1932. The brewery, which had been closed
since the Volstead Act became law in 1920, occupied an entire city block
at 10th Street and Montgomery Avenue. Although the brewery could
produce more than 350,000 barrels of beer annually, D'Agostino intended to double the capacity with new technology. Nucky had a small, undisclosed ownership interest, but Torrio supplied most of the cash to final-
ize the deal and to modernize the brewery. After Prohibition ended in
1933, the Philadelphia brewery was open for business.

The three investors made a special arrangement: Torrio and Nucky
invested, but their names didn't appear on the books; D'Agostino dis-
creetly funneled their profits to them. D'Agostino took a risk getting
involved with Torrio, since any sign of double crossing terminated their
business relationship as well as his life.

The federal investigation of Nucky's affairs in Atlantic City continued
to focus on protection money from bookmakers who took bets on horse
races, from numbers bankers who took bets on a numbers lottery, and
from bingo halls, brothels, and kickbacks from public contracts that were
paid to operate in Atlantic City.

Nucky received confidential information that the numbers bankers had flipped after they were threatened with long prison terms. Word on the street was that they planned on testifying about protection money they gave Nucky each week. The other witness the government was likely to produce at trial was Judge Joseph A. Corio, who reportedly gave Nucky a kickback on the 1934 construction of the new railroad terminal at Arkansas Avenue in Atlantic City.

Whenever political pressures mounted, Nucky found solace in his native Pinelands, away from the constant scrutiny of the IRS and the personal attacks from the *New York Journal*.

One Saturday in the early spring of 1940, Nucky told Lou Kessel to put on some overalls, borrow a pickup from a friend, and throw some old boots into the back of the truck. He also told Kessel to pack some food along with a dozen packs of Beechnut chewing tobacco, which was always a welcome treat for Nucky's Piney friends. Kessel packed two wicker picnic baskets with sandwiches and chewing tobacco, three cases of beer, and a case of top-shelf whiskey that was fresh off a rumrunner's boat.

They drove 40 miles to Waretown, deep in the Pine Barrens of Ocean County, to hear some bluegrass picking, singing, and, if they were lucky, maybe even some yodeling. Nucky used to call bluegrass picking "country music that makes your heart smile." As they entered the village of Waretown on Wells Mill Road, Nucky told Kessel to turn at the only traffic light in town onto a dirt road and drive three-quarters of a mile to a cabin known as the Home Place to Pineys. They drove past a posted sign on a tall pine tree that read: "Trespassers will be shot. Survivors will be prosecuted."

Nucky told Kessel about the two Albert brothers who lived in the cabin. "They are deer hunters and raise Tennessee Walker foxhounds," he said. They came from Sayerville in Middlesex County and moved into the Pines in the early 1930s. When they hunt with a group, they have some of the men fan out in the woods and drive the whitetail deer toward the hunters. They looked for the older bucks with large racks. Bagging a big buck gets bragging rights for the entire hunting season.

Years ago when the Albert Brothers had started playing their guitars, people came from all over to listen and to play and pick with them before the pot-bellied stove in their cabin. Some came with fiddles, banjos, ukes, hognose harps, mandolins, the washtub bass called the "gutbucket," and wooden spoons. Others came with washboards and carried a beat with a sewing thimble on their finger flying over the grooved metal surface of the ribbed washboard. Some just carried a whiskey jug and blew across the top of the open jug opening for a bass beat.

One of Nucky's favorite musicians was "Mr. Spoons" who slapped his legs with flying wooden spoons to get the crowd to their feet. Most of the time, the foot-stomping bluegrass music echoed in the air for miles. For Nucky, the sounds of the Pines were part of the culture of the Pineys; it is a call to their soul, he often said.

When they drove into the driveway past the dog pens, and chicken and bird coops, they parked the truck. The excited dogs began to bark and growl until brothers Joe and George Albert came out of their cabin. They greeted Nucky and told him that the backwoods country boys from the Alleghenies of Pennsylvania were coming to play tonight. These musicians wrote their own music and yodeled better than any of the mountain folks in Switzerland or Austria.

The brothers motioned to the shed where the good-ole boys were tuning up. None of them read music, and often, the first time they heard a song was when they played it. Some of the players just met that evening, but they still played as if they were lifetime friends. Nucky told Joe that he would stay for the music only on two conditions: First, everyone had to polish off all the sandwiches and liquor Kessel put on the picnic table, and the packs of Beechnut chewing tobacco was all theirs. The second condition was that the Pineconers played and sang his favorite song, "Old Rocking Chair."

Joe chided Nucky about having "a fancy for the ladies," especially since he knew Nucky never remarried since he lost Mabel years ago. Nucky told Joe that he had all the long-stem beauties he could handle in Atlantic City, thanks to his friend Earl Carroll. Carroll brought showgirls from his Vanity Productions in New York to the shore for weekends. Nucky considered them all easy on the eyes. "It makes me feel like a kid in a candy store—I don't know which one to pick," said Nucky.

But Joe wanted to find out about what he had been hearing and reading in the papers about Nucky. Joe asked why the Revenue men were out to get him, so Nucky gave him the quick version of the story. It all boiled down to money.

The people of the Pines didn't pay attention to the taxman since they were used to bartering for everything and didn't have cash income. In fact, there wasn't much business in this part of the Pines, except for cultivating cranberries on flooded flats in the fall. Then again, the native Indians in the area had no trouble surviving and made everything they needed. Joe said an old man, who locals said was half-Indian, still made birch bark canoes. Some Pineys were shingle miners who moved heavy cedar logs from the deep swamps in the Pines. They traveled down rutted roads to harvest the logs. If they came across a fallen or rotten tree, they collected the moss and sold it to a local florist for packing plants, since moss holds water like a sponge. But the best money was made in selling oak saplings that were bent into hoops to hold together the frame staves of oak whiskey barrels. Joe said they could never make enough of them for the moonshiners.

Life in the Pines revolved around fishing, trapping, clamming, and hunting. Joe said he remembered one ingenious old-time fisherman who used to take a caged carrier pigeon with him in his Garvey when he went fishing for basic communications. If he needed help, he tied a note to the pigeon that was trained to fly back to another cage on the dock.

In season, one of the local delights was fried herring fishcakes. The local fishermen caught river herring swimming upstream from the ocean to the fresh headwaters of the Mullica River in the early spring. The herring traveled into little freshwater streams to spawn, and so many of them would mass together that the water looked as if it was boiling. Once caught, the herring were soaked in a salt barrel. Then the herring were removed and the process was repeated to remove as much oil as possible from the fish. Then, the dried herring were dropped into a pot of fresh water, where they blew up to full size again. Then, the herring were ready to use in fishcakes.

Everybody in the Pines was a member of some fishing or hunting club. The Marsh Elder Gunning Club was a home away from home on the marshes off Barnegat. The marshes were filled with shanties where hunters and anglers could get out of the wind and rain during a sudden thunderstorm. Others would sit on the front porch and carve duck decoys all day to make a few extra bucks, said Joe. He remembered Harry Shourds as one of the best carvers, especially his replica of the red-breasted Merganser. Kids went to his house in Tuckerton and watched him in action sitting on his grandfather's Schnitzel bunk, a carving bench.

Joe wanted Kessel to try some Jersey Lightning, but Kessel didn't need any moonshine to get him going. Within minutes, he was in full swing, dancing his native Cossack folk dance in a seated position with his legs jutting out in front of him just like the New York Rockettes in a chorus line. While he was going full speed in front of the kicking band and the fiddler, a crowd gathered around him and began clapping, whistling, and yelling.

When his newfound fans made a shrilling sound, Kessel was stunned; he couldn't tell if it was good or bad. Nucky explained that shrilling was the highest compliment an entertainer can get in this part of the country. Kessel was a hit with the Pineys.

On the road back to Atlantic City, Nucky knew that the day of reckoning for him was coming, and it was time to organize a legal game plan. His friend and attorney John Rauffenbart held a summit in his law office at New York and Atlantic Avenues in Atlantic City to map out their strategy for the upcoming criminal federal trial, with Nucky, John Bewley (Nucky's accountant), Johnny D'Agostino, and attorney Emerson Richards.

Nucky started the meeting by lambasting the Democrats for trying to destroy South Jersey's Republican stronghold as a political vendetta for his many years of Republican victories. He said that Congressman William Moore started the Republican Party in Atlantic County and New Jersey just before Lincoln was president, adding that Commodore Louis Kuehnle organized the party in Atlantic City. Both were successful businessmen, and the Democrats always resented their success and personally attacked them at every opportunity.

Rauffenbart, who was a seasoned criminal trial lawyer, figured that the investigation was probably triggered by resentment. But they had to face the reality of what the three witnesses were going to say about handing cash directly to Nucky. Rauffenbart predicted that Corio would say he gave Nucky $28,000 in cash in 1934 as a kickback from Tony Miller for the $2.4 million railroad terminal construction job in Atlantic City.

Weloff and Towhey, the numbers bankers, would testify they paid Nucky $1,200 per week for protection in 1935 and 1936 to operate their numbers syndicate in Atlantic City. After four-and-a-half years of intense investigation, this is the best case the government could fabricate.

Rauffenbart asked Nucky how he planned on explaining what he did with all the money if the IRS wanted to interview him. Nucky replied without hesitation, saying: "I spent it on booze, broads and the rest of it I wasted!" Bewley saw this as an income-tax evasion case, but to prove it, they had to show that Nucky committed other crimes to get the money. That alone could strongly impact the jury's decision. Protection and kickbacks didn't sit well with many church folks. While most people cheat on their tax returns and jurors are sympathetic to anyone who is hauled into court on tax charges, they don't look kindly if the money came from illegal ventures. On Nucky's tax returns each year, there was an income entry for commissions of $60,000, without stipulating a source. That can be attributed to any source Nucky wanted as a cushion for any possible charge from the IRS.

Frank Hague once told Nucky that the Democratic Department of Justice had direct orders to put his case on the "rocket docket." Nucky wasn't going to get any part of the New Deal. In fact, the only deal he going to get was in Lewisburg Federal Penitentiary if he didn't give up the people he put into high office, according to D'Agostino.

Hague was friends with Franklin D. Roosevelt; Nucky remembered that in 1936, FDR came to Jersey City to lay the cornerstone for the highrise Jersey City Medical Center, which was Hague's pet project. The center, which had 2,000 beds, was one of the largest in the country that didn't charge any fees for the poor, said Nucky. But Nucky said the government knew but couldn't prove that Governor Walter Edge, U.S. Senator John Kean, and Governor Harold Hoffman spent more money for their elections than allowed by law and that Nucky could deliver their respective political heads on a silver platter. If Nucky talked, it would be a major blow to the Republican Party in New Jersey for the next 10 years.

D'Agostino realized that Nucky would never flip on his friends, but he wanted to make sure Nucky realized that he was alone. The crew he helped to elect vanished the minute the indictment hit the newspapers. But as captain, Nucky said he would proudly go down with the ship rather than betray his friends. D'Agostino wanted to devise a plan, which included bringing in high-profile legal talent who did similar federal criminal work all the time. He explained that he meant no disrespect to Rauffenbart and Richards, who he considered two of the best criminal trial lawyers in South Jersey.

Richards and Rauffenbart welcomed the suggestions for outside counsel and agreed to assist in any way possible. Since Rauffenbart spent most of his life trying criminal cases, Nucky asked what his options were in defending against these Roosevelt charges. His legal counsel figured Nucky had three options. First, he didn't have to take the stand or say a word, but jurors might think he had something to hide if he didn't tell them his side of the story and then mercilessly attack the credibility of the government's witnesses. The government has the burden of proving Nucky guilty beyond a reasonable doubt, and the defense only has to create reasonable doubts by showing that the witnesses were lying. Second, Nucky could take the stand and say that he received the money as political contributions, and the amount not used for political purposes was reported as commission on his tax returns. Or third, Nucky could take the stand and deny receiving any money, attack the credibility of the three witnesses, then fill the courtroom with outstanding character witnesses for days or as long as the judge will let them.

Rauffenbart turned to Richards for his comments. Richards told Nucky to play up his successful background as sheriff of Atlantic County, clerk of the Supreme Court for four years, as a member of a committee in the assembly, and as county treasurer. If Nucky took any construction kickbacks, he certainly could have done it on the $20 million construction of the convention hall or for the millions he handled each year as county treasurer. Nucky's 30 years of public service were unblemished.

Corio's claim that he gave Nucky $28,000 will look like chump change when the jury was given the total picture, said Richards. Corio brought this indictment on himself when he took the $60,000 from Miller. He was supposed to pay the taxes on the entire amount, give some back to Miller, keep some for himself, and then supposedly give Nucky $28,000. He double-crossed Miller who was also indicted. His only way out was to say he gave Nucky money to save his own hide. That's the deal the government cut with Corio. The feds wanted to make him their star witness.

A jury was more likely to believe Nucky, since no one had much sympathy for Corio. The jury will think Corio kept Nucky's cut just like he squirreled away the tax money, said Richards. They could say that each of the numbers bankers earned $250,000 a year from their illegal numbers syndicate operations and that they obviously paid someone for police protection. The most logical one to get the payoff was a higher-up in the police department of Atlantic City and not the county treasurer, who actually had nothing to do with running the police department. The county treasurer was strictly an administrative job with no supervision of police forces in the county.

"I understand Jack Southern, one of the numbers bankers, told the Special Agents he gave the protection money to Captain Frank Ferretti of the Atlantic City Police Department," said Richards. "The IRS told him that as a ruse to protect you Nucky, since the Captain is now dead. They claim it is an old defense 'the dead man did everything.'"

For Richards, the best defense included Nucky taking the stand, looking the jurors right in the eyes, and turning on his natural charm by telling them about his background and his family. He thought it was better that Nucky deny getting any money and say that the desperate witnesses against him are all testifying to cut a deal with the government to save their own necks.

Rauffenbart added that if Nucky took the stand, he needed to be prepared for tough questions during cross-examination: How could he throw his annual New Year's Party of more than $30,000 on his treasurer's salary of $6,000 per year? How could he afford his fleet of cars, a suite on the ninth floor of the Ritz-Carlton, and still maintain his Iowa Avenue cottage and an apartment in an upscale section of New York with his partying buddy Jimmy Walker on his county salary? Nucky knew where he stood and thanked the men for a great work session and invited them all to The Knife and Fork Restaurant at the corner of Albany and Atlantic Avenues for a drink and a crabcake sandwich.

D'Agostino searched for a top criminal lawyer to represent Nucky and spoke to his contacts in Philadelphia, Pittsburgh, New York, Chicago, and Cicero, Illinois. D'Agostino knew the drill; he had just been indicted on three counts, along with two other men, by the U.S. Grand Jury in New York on February 6, 1939, for plotting to aid Torrio.

D'Agostino retained a local Atlantic City criminal attorney Edward
Feinberg and a nationally renowned New York trial counsel Stuart
Gibboney as his defense counsel. But Nucky needed someone familiar
with New Jersey, especially since Judge Albert B. Maris was recently
appointed as the trial judge.

Maris, who was a member of the Third Circuit Court of Appeals in
Philadelphia, generally did not preside at trials, but he was specially
assigned to serve as Nucky's trial judge in Camden. Maris had only been
on the federal bench since 1936, after his appointment by FDR for his
loyalty as chairman of the Delaware County Democratic Party and as a
member of the Pennsylvania Democratic State Central Council. Nucky
was convinced that Maris would take great personal pleasure in taking
down a Republican leader such as Nucky. This was exactly his role when
he tried to defeat Republicans while serving as the Democratic chairman
of Delaware County in the 1930s. He was the same Democrat but in different clothes.

Nucky's friend Herman "Muggsy" Taylor recommended Billy Gray, a
Republican Party stalwart from Philadelphia, as counsel. Gray handled
high-profile criminal cases and projected an image of a trusted preacher
rather than a calculating Philadelphia lawyer. To see if Gray and Nucky
were a good match, Taylor set up a meeting in Gray's shore cottage in
Brigantine on the adjoining island next to Atlantic City. Nucky and
Taylor attended, along with attorneys Rauffenbart and Richards, and
D'Agostino.

Gray advised Nucky that before he would render legal advice, he
must be officially retained as Nucky's attorney. Being retained is a long-
honored custom among criminal lawyers in Philadelphia, a tradition that
the judges respected. Gray said that if a case was called for trial and the
attorneys had not been paid, they simply requested a continuance by
telling the court that a critical witness by the name of "Mr. Green" could
not be located. The judge understood and granted a continuance until
the attorney's fees had been paid. Gray told Nucky that this was not a
reflection on his trust, but payment created an attorney-client relationship that allowed Nucky to talk to Gray candidly.

Gray decided that the fee for the day's services would be $1, payable
before they proceeded. Nucky reached into his pocket and pulled out a

$5 bill, gave it to Gray, and said, "This is the smallest I have. I don't need any change." So Gray pulled out four $1 bills from his own pocket, gave them to Nucky, and said, "I never overcharge my clients. Let's get to business."

Gray told Nucky that he was entitled to a jury of his peers, and this created a serious hurdle from the start. The dictionary defines a "peer" as someone who is an equal, and Gray assured Nucky that he didn't have any equals. "Nobody on that jury lives like you, dresses like you, entertains like you, or enjoys the same lavish lifestyle as you do," said Gray. "The jury will be evaluating you from the moment they lay eyes on you; therefore, you have to be well-schooled on how to behave and, especially now, to dress."

Gray cautioned Nucky to dress as a dignified banker and the respected defender of the county treasury. "You do have a definite dignifying bearing about you and with a new conservative tailor, you will project an image of credibility the moment you walk into the courtroom without saying a word," said Gray. He also detected the smell of alcohol. Someone or maybe all of the men in the room had a drink that morning. In a courtroom, the jury can detect any odor of alcohol, so drinking was prohibited during trial days.

He also focused on the jury and noted that Nucky had a strong following in the black community and wanted every effort to select as many people of color on the jury as possible, since they "will be your strongest allies over any other group or religion." Gray said he also understood the numbers bankers were going to testify that they paid Nucky money. Most blacks have played the numbers, and they know the bankers make a great deal of money for themselves and pay out small amounts to the few winners. They also know the bankers are gambling that they won't get caught. If they do get caught, they won't generate any sympathy. "You win some; you lose some," he said. However, blacks have a strong dislike for anyone who cooperates with the police to bring others down; this is against the law of the street.

Nucky also needed to start lining up his friends in state and federal officeholders, and from Broadway and the sports world, who would be willing to testify about his reputation for truth and veracity. But Gray wanted Nucky's friends to attend as much of the trial as possible and for all of them to sit together in the courtroom so the jury could view them as his concerned loyal supporters. The jurors needed to know Nucky's friends were genuinely concerned about his welfare.

It wasn't necessary for Nucky to tell him whether he received money from the numbers bankers or from Corio, but for the purpose of their discussion, they assumed Nucky did. "That is what the witnesses will say," said Gray. "Judge Corio will be an unlikable pathetic witness for the government and not worthy of belief," he said. He betrayed his friend and in-law, Tony Miller; he lied to the IRS agents in his own sacred court chambers, and he filed a fraudulent income tax return when he was given the money to pay the tax. In fact, he never paid the tax on his ill-gotten gains. He will be viewed as a desperate man, willing to destroy Nucky to save himself from prison.

The numbers bankers obviously gave money to someone for protection from the police, but the jury will expect to hear who received the money in the police department or vice squad. They are not going to tell who in law enforcement they paid since they will never be able to operate again in Atlantic City if they do. And to protect themselves and stay in business, their only convenient escape is by fingering Nucky.

A full-scale assault on the credibility of all three government witnesses would be in order after Nucky testified in the opening statement that he never received any money. That should create a reasonable doubt in the jury's mind and result in an acquittal or, at the very minimum, a hung jury. That is as good as an acquittal since Gray said that the government would never want to try Nucky again because witnesses have a short shelf life and will have less credibility the second time at bat. After Gray finished dispensing advice, he said, "I want to remind you that should you be so inclined to engage my professional services that my fee will be slightly higher than today's."

Two weeks after the meeting, D'Agostino called Nucky and said he was coming over to see him that evening, and some people were going to stop by. He said it was critical that he be there. After D'Agostino arrived, Kessel went to answer the knock at the front door. He saw two "button men," as some hit men are called, in dark clothing wearing black felt hats with wide brims; their hands tucked into their deep coat pockets. The larger, expressionless one with a flat nose and cauliflower ears stared straight ahead. The smaller one said, "We have an appointment to see Mr. Johnson."

Kessel was suspicious but escorted them into the living room where Nucky and D'Agostino were drinking bourbons. Nucky stood up and welcomed them; no names were exchanged. Kessel moved to the chair on the opposite side of the two guests with his back to the wall. He slowly reached under his jacket and released the shoulder holster safety strap over his pistol as Nucky started talking.

Nucky offered them a drink, but they declined. Nucky reassured them that they could talk freely in front of Kessel and D'Agostino, so they explained that they were there out of respect and to repay him for past favors. They knew that numbers bankers Weloff and Towhey flipped and want to put Nucky out of business. They had been in Atlantic City for the past week with our guys, watching them every day. They were now in the Club Harlem with two other guys who offered them a piece of gambling action in New York to hold their attention until the meeting with Nucky was done. The two men wanted to return to New York that evening and take Weloff and Towhey with them. It was simple: They will go away, and Nucky's problems would "go away." They just wanted Nucky's permission to make their move.

Nucky realized that if the witnesses against him disappeared, he would be the No. 1 suspect, and the *New York Evening Journal* would crucify him. Bad publicity isn't what he needed just before his jury trial started. Nucky told the men that their trip to see him was deeply appreciated, but his legal team assured him he had nothing to worry about. The men said if he ever changed his mind, they would gladly return to the shore. They left leaving Nucky feeling better about what was ahead for him.

Nucky needed inside information, so he decided to throw a party at the Ritz-Carlton and invite some political friends, lawyers, and public officials to ask about the charges against him. At the party, Nucky cornered his friend Jimmy Walker, also known as the "night mayor of New York" who enjoyed the club nightlife: He earned the moniker by sleeping during the day and working at night.

Walker said that politicians accumulate many friends as well as a few enemies. Some of these friends eventually drift away, but the enemies remain and spend all their energy trying to destroy them, including getting the IRS and newspapers involved since they can't defeat them at the ballot box. He remembered when he had trouble with the Seabury investigation. FDR, who was then governor of New York, threw him to the wolves so FDR could look as though he was the people's guardian of virtue. That was the reason he resigned as mayor of New York City in 1932, he said. When he left office and went to Europe, it took all the steam out of the investigation. The press was no longer trying to cut his legs from under him and drive him out of office. With FDR as president, he wouldn't hesitate to destroy a powerful Republican like Nucky.

Years ago, before New Jersey Governor Wilson became president of the U.S., he had indicted Nucky on a trumped-up election charge because he supposedly turned voters in South Jersey against him for the New Jersey governorship in 1910. But Nucky beat the charge; Wilson took that political setback as a personal affront and looked for an opportunity to take another shot at Nucky to prove he was right the first time.

And the underlying feud continued. FDR and Wilson were personal friends from the time Wilson appointed FDR as assistant secretary of the Navy during World War I, explained Walker. He said that was FDR's payback when he supported Wilson for the presidency the first time; they were cut from the same cloth. Neither of them ever had a real job; Wilson spent his life in colleges, and FDR lived off his family fortune controlled by his mother.

Walker said FDR continually fought his friends at Tammany Hall and lost in the Democratic primary in 1914 for the U.S. Senate from New York. Tammany leader Charles Murphy was not going to let a spoiled Harvard graduate dictate his personal agenda to the Democratic Party. FDR wanted Wilson to become president, but he was too liberal for Murphy and fought Wilson to the bitter end. FDR quickly learned who the boss was in New York. He always resented his setback from the Tammany machine and had an instant dislike for any political leader he could not control like Nucky, especially Republicans. Newshound William Randolph Hearst was close to FDR, and the photo of Nucky's stroll on the Boardwalk with Al Capone in 1929 was all he had to see before launching a full criminal investigation.

"Nucky, I said it before and I'll say it again," said Walker. "There are three things a politician must do alone ... be born, die, and testify. When a politician testifies, it usually destroys him." Walker suggested William E. Leahy as his attorney. He was highly regarded and frequently hired by the Department of Justice for difficult high-profile cases. Walker told Nucky he successfully guided him through the Seabury investigation. Nucky thanked Walker, but he was still leery of anyone who had worked for the government.

D'Agostino came to the party with Charlie Margiotti, an attorney he wanted Nucky to meet. Having served as attorney general in Pennsylvania, he also was defense counsel in more than 100 homicide cases, had a record of 26 cases ending in verdicts of not guilty, and was very selective about which clients he defended. But one of the main reasons that D'Agostino favored Margiotti, aka "The General," to defend Nucky was that Margiotti had recently won a case for U.S. Senator James J. Davis from Pennsylvania. The U.S. federal court case alleged that the senator operated a lottery through the Loyal Order of Moose. The jury acquitted Davis and gave Margiotti national attention; he was used to the spotlight and knew how to handle the press in high-profile cases.

Before the meeting was over, D'Agostino was sure Nucky would choose Margiotti. The general agreed to represent him provided he was notified in the next two weeks since his trial calendar was full after that time. But there was another guest at the party: prominent North Jersey attorney Walter Winne, who had been U.S. Attorney for New Jersey in 1922. With Nucky's help, he received the appointment from President Herbert Hoover, and Winne never forgot Nucky's strong backing. When they met at the party, Winne reminded Nucky that if he ever needed a favor, all he had to do was ask.

Nucky figured this was a good time to say that he was looking for a lawyer in this federal income tax evasion case, and he knew Winne had a pretty good idea what actually went on in Atlantic City. Winne knew about the charges and said he still had some close friends in the Department of Justice who gave him some background on the case. That was one of the reasons he decided to come to the party. The Department of Justice had orders from Washington not to cut any deals with Nucky and to use every means possible to put him in jail as long as they could. Nucky asked whether he could beat the charges if Winne represented him. While there were no guarantees, Winne acknowledged that he had won tougher cases in federal court. The jury is the key, he said. "You never know what they will do."

Nucky returned to the party in good spirits and with three good lawyers to choose from. However, the problem that two of them were from Pennsylvania and could spell trouble with a South Jersey jury. Nucky thought that they might not take kindly to strangers, just as the Pineys did not accept the islanders from Atlantic City. After much thought, Nucky selected Winne as his attorney, a decision he would later regret.

CHAPTER 15

READY FOR THE UNITED STATES OF AMERICA

Just as everyone was seated in the golden oak-paneled federal court-room at Fourth and Market streets in Camden, the side door to the judge's chambers opened, and the bailiff announced, "Hear ye! Hear ye! Please stand. The Honorable Judge Albert B. Maris of the U.S. Circuit Court temporarily assigned presiding!"

The spectators were ready for action. On July 11, 1941, the trial of Enoch L. Johnson, who was 56 years old, was about to begin after a four-and-a-half-year federal investigation by the FBI and the IRS. The corruption investigation of Atlantic City and Atlantic County officials had generated so much publicity that the federal court made special arrangements for the crowd: There were tables to accommodate 30 reporters, and visitors were required to have admission passes to enter the courtroom.

After Maris took his seat at the bench, he looked at Assistant U.S. Attorney Joseph W. Burns and asked, "Is the government ready?" Burns, the government prosecutor, stood and replied, "Ready for the *United States of America v. Enoch L. Johnson.*" The judge then directed his attention to Walter G. Winne, Nucky's attorney, and asked, "Is the defense ready?" The defense counsel stood and said, "Good morning ... Ready for Mr. Johnson."

Nucky listened to the words of the assistant U.S. attorney resonate in the courtroom: the case of the *United States of America v. Enoch L. Johnson.* He mused that the wording made it sound that it would be unpatriotic for the jury not to convict him.

Seated by his attorneys, Nucky appeared confident, buoyed by the ace in the hole in his briefcase: his lucky Irish brick. John Rauffenbart, local co-counsel, had earned a reputation for being an effective criminal attorney by his folksy manner when talking to a jury. He looked at the jury pool in hopes of recognizing a friendly face to concentrate on during the trial.

The judge directed the court clerk to start the jury selection process. The clerk walked to a small hexagonal wooden box that contained the names of the entire 54-juror panel seated in the courtroom. He spun the box on its axle, opened a small wooden door, reached in, and then pulled out a slip of paper with a juror's name on it. He called out the name, and the prospective juror was directed to take the first seat in the jury box. He continued this process until 12 jurors were selected and took their seats. The attorneys' *voir dire* began, the process by which the attorneys questioned jurors about their backgrounds to ensure impartiality during the trial.

The judge looked out over the packed courtroom of prospective jurors, reporters, cameramen, spectators, and Nucky's loyal supporters. "I would like the entire jury panel to pay strict attention," said the judge. "I am going to ask the twelve seated jurors some questions. Rather than repeat all the questions to the balance of the prospective jurors who may be selected, I want you to tell me at that time you are seated if any of the questions pertain to you. For example, do you know Enoch L. Johnson, also known as Nucky Johnson." The judge's questions were reported in the *New York Journal* on July 12, 1941.

In response, most of the members of the juror pool raised their hands. The judge then said to the jurors in the spectator area, "Please wait till you are selected and seated to raise your hand." The judge directed his attention to the 12 seated jurors and asked, "The fact that you know Nucky Johnson or his lawyer, would that fact alone prevent you from rendering a fair and impartial verdict based on the evidence that is presented in this courtroom?"

Juror No. 1 and Juror No. 8 raised their hands. The judge asked Juror No. 1 why he couldn't be impartial. "Judge, Mr. Johnson put my father to work in the late 1920s building the Atlantic City Convention Hall when there was no work in Atlantic City in the winter and I could never do anything to hurt him after what he did for my family."

The assistant U.S. attorney moved to disqualify Juror No. 1 immediately, and the judge granted his request. The clerk spun the box, drew another name, and another juror took a seat in the vacant chair.

The judge then directed his attention to Juror No. 8 who had raised her hand and explained her situation. "Judge, I am a devout 'church lady' and we believe gambling and drinking is the devil's work and anyone who helps the devil works against the Lord and becomes my enemy," she said. "From what I hear, Mr. Johnson encourages gambling and drinking to bring visitors to Atlantic City and this is the devil's work."

Winne immediately moved to disqualify her. The *voir dire* process continued for hours until 12 jurors—eight men and four women—were seated, plus two alternates. G. Rex Shawell Jr. of Riverton, a member of the Burlington County Republican Committee, was seated as foreman. The judge directed the clerk to swear in the 12 jurors, the two alternates, and the four bailiffs. The judge then ordered the U.S. Marshal to take the jurors into custody and away from the news media until a verdict was reached. The judge announced that the start of the trial and directed Burns to make his opening statement.

Burns was seated at the prosecutor's table piled high with files. Next to him were two IRS agents, specially assigned to assist him during the trial. Burns walked over to the jury railing and said, "I want to give you an outline, a road map, a picture of what the government intends to prove against this defendant to show his willful and intentional failed to report substantial income for 1935, 1936, and 1937. The government will prove he owes taxes of $1,232.18 for 1935; $19,957.30 for 1936 and $18,759.10 for 1937. There are three separate counts. Count I charges he failed to report income of $28,000 he received as a kickback for the railroad terminal construction contract in Atlantic City plus $46,400.00 for protection from the numbers syndicate, an illegal lottery, that operated openly in Atlantic City. Count II and III are the same, charging him with failure to report $62,400 each year from the numbers syndicate. The defendant wanted to turn Atlantic City into his own private 'Monte Carlo' as his cash cow to finance his lavish lifestyle and political organization."

He said Nucky had been the recognized political leader of South Jersey for more than 30 years, and in such a position, he was able to provide protection for the numbers syndicate to operate an illegal lottery without police interference. He was also able to keep outsiders from muscling into the Atlantic City numbers operation. For that influence, the government was intent on proving that he was paid handsomely. He noted Nucky's history as sheriff, as well as that of his father and brother. In fact, the Johnson family has controlled the office of sheriff and under-sheriff since 1887.

Burns described Nucky's service as Atlantic County Treasurer for the past 29 years. As sheriff, the chief law enforcement agency of the county, and as head of the treasurer's office, Nucky controlled the purse strings and law enforcement of Atlantic County. When the numbers syndicate wanted protection, from the inside and the outside, Nucky was the man to see, said Burns. The active vice squad in Atlantic City had a purpose. The vice squad didn't eliminate gambling; it controlled it. When there were police raids and numbers slips seized, a member of the syndicate would pick up a box of old slips and go to the police station and trade them for seized ones so their gambling action would not be interrupted.

He highlighted the activities of two members of the numbers syndi-cate who could explain how the syndicate operated. Ralph Weloff, who has known the defendant for 25 years, was assigned to carry the $1,200 protection money each week to Nucky at his cottage or at the Ritz-Carlton Hotel. On July 1, 1935, James Towhey was assigned to alternate with Weloff. The syndicate grossed $1,800,000 a year, paying Nucky $62,400 each year at $1,200 per week, starting in June 1935, with each syndicate partner receiving $200,000 to $250,000, for their year's work. This was a large and profitable operation out of their numbers bank—the Belmont Hotel at 37 North Kentucky Avenue in Atlantic City. The num-bers syndicate had 800 writers, 20 luggars whose job it was to bring gam-blers to town, and 70 pick-up men bringing in the bets and cash—no checks accepted.

As a political leader, Nucky had a complex machine that needed plenty of oil to keep it running smoothly. The numbers syndicate in Atlantic City supplied the oil. Burns started with the first indictment, outlining the government's proofs showing a conspiracy to evade taxes by the contractor, Anthony P. Miller, his attorney, Joseph A. Corio, and Nucky in the building of a new train terminal in Atlantic City at a cost of $2.4 million that began in 1933 and was completed in 1935.

The Miller Construction Company's books showed a profit of $240,000 and a legal fee of $60,000 to Corio. This fee appeared to the examining IRS agent to be an exorbitant legal fee and represented one-quarter of the profit from the construction of the new train terminal. The Miller Construction Company issued two checks for $30,000 each to Corio who cashed them at the bank and when his tax returns were examined, he did not report this $60,000 as income. When the judge was initially interviewed, he castigated the revenue agent for questioning his integrity and chased him out of his court chambers after telling them he only reported $20,000 since the $40,000 represented "operating expenses."

When he failed to explain who received the $40,000, he was indicted on charges of tax evasion and making false statements to the treasury agents on May 10, 1938. This emotional pressure caused him to have a nervous breakdown and was confined to a sanitarium for summer 1938. When his case was set for trial, he finally broke down.

Miller, Nucky, and Corio devised a plan to avoid taxes by the company paying Corio a legal fee of $60,000, said Burns. Corio was to cash the two $30,000 checks, pay Nucky $28,000, retain $13,220 to pay the taxes, and keep $9,400 as his share of the profit for acting as an intermediary in obtaining the contract with Nucky's approval for Miller. Miller also kept $9,400 for himself from the scheme. Miller went with Corio to the bank to cash the checks, and then they both went to Nucky's cottage and personally handed him the $28,000 in cash.

Burns said, "Corio will tell you from the witness stand that Johnson was getting concerned during the construction of the terminal, that he was not going to get his cut, and insisted on a written contract from Miller. Nucky sent his attorney, who was also his nephew, Judge W. Lindley Jeffries, to see Corio where a contract was drawn. He will tell you that Jeffries knew that evidence of this graft contract was very dangerous and instructed Corio's secretary to destroy her steno pad when they were finished. The secretary had just started a new steno book and being a very frugal person, she continued to use it and saved it. Fortunately, it was turned over to the government and will be presented here in court for you to see."

In 1933, Corio said the State Public Utility Commission ordered the two railroad companies coming into Atlantic City to consolidate under the name of the Pennsylvania Reading Seashore Lines, Inc. and to build a new terminal. Harry Bacharach, the mayor of Atlantic City, was on the Public Utility Commission and was elected mayor of Atlantic City by the Nucky's organization. State legislation was required and the president of the Senate was Emerson L. Richards from Atlantic County who was also elected to the State Senate by Nucky's organization. Approval of the Atlantic City Commission, Burns said, was required; the location of the terminal and right-of-way. With influence with the Public Utility Commission, state legislature, and city commission, Nucky was the only person who could control the awarding of the contract, and Miller was the highest bidder at three-fifths of the net profits for Nucky.

Burns urged the jury to find Nucky guilty beyond a reasonable doubt on all three counts of the indictment. He returned to his seat waiting for the defense to make their first move to challenge the government's case. The *New York Journal* assigned a full-time reporter to the trial, and the daily events were carried in detail in the New York newspaper.

Maris then directed his full attention to the defense table, instructing Winne to proceed with his opening remarks. All eyes of the jurors were focused on Winne, but he stood up, remained at the defense table, and asked to reserve his opening statement until after the government's case was finished. The packed courtroom was bewildered by Winne's legal strategy as the judge announced a 10-minute recess. The courtroom emptied into the hallway, and John D'Agostino, who was visibly upset, approached Nucky and said, "What the hell is this guy doing? He just blew the first round!"

Nucky tried to calm him, saying that Winne didn't want to show their strategy this early and that, once the government had Nucky's ungrateful friends testify, then Winne could calculate the best defense. But D'Agostino didn't like the strategy. Nucky told D'Agostino that he trusted Winne's judgment as U.S. Attorney for New Jersey, and the federal court was his territory.

Corio, appearing as a star witness for the government, gave his self-serving testimony. He had served two five-year terms on the Common Pleas bench and admitted during direct examination that he pocketed the money that Miller gave him to pay the income taxes on the $60,000 he received. This was the reason Miller, Nucky, and Corio were indicted in the first place.

He outlined the power Nucky had in obtaining public contracts and said he wanted Miller, his in-law by marriage, obtain a sizable construction contract. Miller was a small struggling contractor with few work options in the mid-1930s, so Miller, Nucky, and Corio met at the Ritz-Carlton Hotel where they agreed to a deal to pay Nucky $28,000. He further stated the construction project was welcome news to the Italian community since Miller promised to hire many Italians from the Ducktown section of Atlantic City.

Corio said he went to Nucky's cottage and handed him $28,000 in cash on September 26, 1935. He also remembered that Miller was present and saw Corio give the cash to Nucky, who apparently counted the money and separated the bills into $1,000 stacks before agreeing that the amount was correct. Through Corio, the government introduced an unsigned copy of an agreement to pay Nucky, but the original document was never produced.

When Winne cross-examined Corio, he left him a battered man. Winne's stock suddenly skyrocketed with Nucky's supporters. Corio admitted that he could have stopped the IRS investigation by paying the $13,200 from the beginning. In fact, he never paid the taxes as of the day he was sitting in the witness chair. He agreed to cooperate with the government to avoid going to jail, and Winne's skillful cross-examining implied that the government was not going to try to collect the taxes if his testimony implicated Nucky.

Corio came across as a man who betrayed a close family member and would implicate any friend without hesitation, if it served his purpose. Winne's argument showed that Corio could only strike a deal with the government if he squealed on Nucky. Corio also said Miller was present when the cash was delivered to Nucky, but Miller was not cooperating with the government and was not called as a government witness. This left Corio's testimony uncorroborated. With Corio's credibility destroyed and all the tax money still in his pocket, the defense's hopes soared.

When the government produced Weloff and Towhey, the two numbers bankers testified they paid Nucky $1,200 per week for protection for the three years named in the indictment. If there was a raid by the vice squad, they were allowed to deduct any fine from the protection money they paid Nucky. When Winne cross-examined the witnesses his manner

and voice changed dramatically; he began questioning them in a friendly tone about the necessity of maintaining the strong Republican Party
and Nucky as the leader. After all, it was good business and brought jobs
and fame to Atlantic City.

Weloff said, "I have known Nucky for over 20 years and have always
supported him even before I went into the numbers business. I have a
picture of him hanging in my numbers bank." The two numbers bankers
praised Nucky for his leadership and initiating projects in Atlantic City
that created jobs, especially the Atlantic City Convention Hall and the
train station.

The numbers bankers told the jury they had "pick-up men" who collected the policy slips they wrote for a bettor and took to the headquarters. Often the bettor looked for a number in a Dream Book (a list of
words with a matching set of numbers); the bettor selected a number
from a hunch or dream and bet on it. They explained that many of the
bankers were well-dressed to give the impression they had the ability to
pay off. They also admitted that they believed some or all of the money
they gave Nucky was used for political purposes and build his image as a
political leader.

Winne didn't attack the credibility of the witnesses. He also didn't try
to imply that if these numbers bankers wanted protection from being
arrested, they had to give money to certain top law enforcement officials
and not to Nucky as county treasurer. Burns realized that Winne was taking a high-risk strategy by letting Nucky take the witness stand and admit
that he received the weekly payment that he used for political purposes.
Burns knew he had a chance to cross-examine Nucky and considered this
an early Christmas gift.

Witness William Sheppard, Nucky's former part-time bodyguard and
chauffeur, offered the final damaging testimony for the government,
telling the jury he was given a list of people who were allowed into the
cottage, a list that included "nearly every cop in Atlantic City." He
claimed that Weloff and Towhey usually stayed long enough to drop off
an envelope, which Nucky placed in a tin box in his bedroom. Sheppard
recalled seeing the tin box packed with cash. Usually Nucky paid him his
wages from that very box. When the government rested its case, the court
directed Winne to make his opening statement to the jury.

Winne described how Atlantic City had grown as a gambling town before the turn of the century and how it contributed to having Atlantic City recognized as the World's Famous Playground. Then he surprised some of the courtroom by announcing that Nucky would take the stand and admit he received the money from the numbers bankers but will deny he received any money from Corio. He added that most of the numbers money was used for political purposes and the balance was reported on Nucky's income tax return as commission of $60,000 each year. Then court recessed for the day, and Nucky and his friends went back to their rooms at the Walt Whitman Hotel. Nucky's hotel suite had all the luxuries: a service bar, a bartender, a full buffet, and even an ice carving.

Winne explained the defense strategy to Nucky's friends, saying that if Nucky denied getting the numbers money, the jury may not believe him and could find him guilty. But if he said he received the money and used it for political purposes, there was a credibility issue for the jury to decide.

Jimmy Boyd, Marie Boyd's husband, and Mae Paxson from the county treasurer's office had delivered plenty of receipts for political expenditures to the courtroom to corroborate Nucky's statement. Nucky paid taxes each year on $60,000 in commissions as reported on his federal tax return. This made it easier for the jury to accept the defense.

When the trial resumed, Nucky took the witness stand in a packed courtroom of supporters and news reporters from all over the East Coast. Nucky appeared very dignified, tailored conservatively for the occasion. He remembered Billy Gray's advice: Look the jurors directly in the eyes when answering a question.

Winne put Nucky at ease by asking easy questions about his public service background to enhance his credibility before the jury. The jurors were paying close attention to his every word and seemed ready to hear him explain his actions, leaving the door wide open for Nucky's acquittal.

Nucky testified that he never received any money from Corio for helping Miller get the contract to build the Atlantic City railroad station, but he did admit that he helped Miller get the contract. Miller had agreed to hire local people, especially from the Italian community in Ducktown, which was close to where the terminal was to be built. He said any North

Jersey contractor would bring in workers from out of town, and it was just good politics to keep the jobs local.

Then Winne asked Nucky to talk about the money he received each week from the numbers bankers. Nucky admitted that in early 1935, Weloff came to him and said a numbers syndicate had been formed and that he was going to bring $1,200 per week to him for the Republican organization. Nucky insisted that the money was not intended for police protection but for political purposes and to advance his leadership. This sum was later increased to $1,500, which he said he used mostly for campaign purposes. His accountant reported the balance on his income tax returns for 1935, 1936, and 1937 under the heading of Commissions of $60,000. Nucky repeated, "I paid taxes on everything I had the benefit of personally."

When Winne asked him to explain how he distributed the numbers money, Nucky said, "Electing candidates that were friendly to my policies, building up the Republican organization, taking care of the poor—paying rents and hospital bills, buying them coal, food, and fuel." Helping people was good politics, he said. They remembered to vote on Election Day. He also said he sent cash weekly to Jimmy Boyd, the Fourth Ward Republican Leader and the Clerk of the Board of the Atlantic County Freeholders. Boyd's job was to distribute the cash to people who came to his county treasurer's office for help and those he sent directly to Boyd. At the end of each year, Nucky met with his accountant John Bewley and Mae Paxson, who kept his daily records. After deducting all political expenses, he reported the balance on his income tax return as commissions. During the year, he often sent a memorandum to Paxson about the money he spent as personal income.

At this point, Maris interrupted Nucky's direct testimony and asked why he didn't report the entire amount he received and then take the deductions. Nucky admitted that he had made a mistake. When Maris asked whether Nucky had ever requested contributions from the numbers bankers for the November political campaign, Nucky explained that they came voluntarily.

Burns was eager to attack. Nucky admitted that he kept the minutes of the meetings as secretary of the Atlantic County Republican Committee, and then Maris interrupted again and asked whether Nucky had any authority from the county committee to receive political contributions on behalf of the Republican Party in Atlantic County for the three years in question. Nucky said he did not. When the judge asked whether Nucky provided an accounting for the money he received, Nucky said that there's wasn't any account; he only had a few receipts and didn't file any expense account in any public office.

D'Agostino left the courtroom with Taylor and Kessel and walked to the end of the hallway where they could talk. D'Agostino saw the judge put the proverbial nails into Nucky's coffin. Nucky admitted he not only pocketed the money each week but that his tax returns were false and that he violated Jersey law by not filing an accounting with the state. The judge did in three questions what the prosecutor was unable to do all day, D'Agostino said.

Nucky explained to the prosecutor that during each of the three years in question, he kept a memorandum of the money he spent for political purposes, but he said he seldom received receipts. He sent money to Boyd to give to the people who were in need, and periodically, he gave memos for the balance of the numbers money he reported on his tax returns to Paxson. Burns was strategically testing Nucky's credibility by asking him about the payments he received in 1938, one year removed from the scope of the indictment. But Nucky's counsel objected since it could tend to prove another crime for 1938, and there had been a recent article in the *Philadelphia Record* on July 1, 1941, noting that Burns said Nucky was the target of an additional indictment on income tax evasion for 1938, 1939, and 1940. The court accepted the prosecutor's argument that the defendant claimed that he did not violate the law by his record-keeping and reporting practice for 1935, 1936, and 1937, and then he would not incriminate himself for the full impact if he followed the same practice for 1938.

The judge gave Nucky the option of testifying or invoking his privilege against self-incrimination under the Fifth Amendment. Nucky was legally caught between a rock and a hard place. Winne conferred in private with Nucky before he returned to the witness stand to explain the judge's ruling and his options.

Nucky had a flashback to Walker's comment about looking out for "the sucker punch," but he braced himself. He quickly understood that it

had been a bad idea for him to take the witness stand, but he intended to
play the hand he was dealt by taking the Fifth for his dealings in 1938 and
finish it. But once Nucky began taking the Fifth Amendment, the jury
appeared to lose all interest in his explanations. Nucky said he did not get
any money from the numbers bankers for some weeks, and the prosecutor asked him why. Nucky said it was due to police activity. "If they did-
n't operate, they didn't pay," he said.

He said that he knew writing lottery numbers violated state law "but
only if you got caught." Nucky's defense was now legally hemorrhaging.
The government concluded its questioning, satisfied that Nucky was the
government's strongest witness who had just sealed his own fate on the
stand. When Nucky stepped down, he couldn't even look at the jury.

The court took a much-needed recess before Mae Paxson took the witness stand, which gave Nucky a chance to regain his composure. He
walked over to court stenographer Charlie Degan and said, "I left my briefcase in the courtroom last night and it had my good luck charm in it—an
Irish brick." Degan said he would check around for it in the court clerk's
office. Nucky thanked him and mumbled, "I need all the luck I can get."

Paxson impressed the jury with her candor and loyalty to Nucky after
working for him for nearly 20 years. She explained that she received daily
notes from Nucky, who she referred to as "Mr. Johnson." The notes, written on small scraps of paper, paper napkins, or brown paper bags, asked
her to send a letter to a constituent. She composed a letter of condolence,
congratulations, speedy recovery, or whatever required. Ruppert Chase,
who was Boyd's aide, carried these special letters and incoming mail by
hand to Nucky's Iowa Avenue cottage. Nucky then signed and mailed the
letters.

Paxson maintained an "income file" for Nucky: When Nucky sent a
memo with monthly income, she placed it in this file. At year's end, she
gave him the file before he met with his accountant. Upon cross-examination, the prosecutor tried to imply that her loyalty for her employer
was obviously the motivation behind her testimony and designed to
make his defense more credible. But she was unshakeable and credible.

Jimmy Boyd's testimony added more details to the payment arrangements and did his best to cast a favorable light on Nucky. According to
Boyd, Chase would deliver an envelope from Nucky with cash almost on

a weekly basis to distribute to those who called upon him for help. The reason he received the cash was that part of Nucky's plan was not just to give the cash but to help solve the person's problem as well. When someone came to Boyd's office and said Nucky sent him and needed food for his family, Boyd testified he would not give him cash to go shopping. Instead, he called a grocery store where the person's neighborhood and asked the store to send one week's worth of food to the needy family.

The next step would be to get the person a job. Boyd testified that the Republican Party ran a monthly tab at restaurants, clothing, grocery, hardware, and furniture stores, as well as oil and coal companies. The cash he received from Nucky was used to pay these monthly tabs. Boyd said never asked the person whether he was a Republican when he came in for help, but once he helped him, he had one of his precinct captains walk him to the city clerk's office so he could register as a Republican. He testified that he received political contributions from other sources and turned them over to the treasurer of the Republican Party, but he said he always kept cash for Nucky's special people. When Boyd was investigated by the feds, his lifestyle left little room for the prosecutor to pry. After a few questions, the prosecutor realized that Boyd was helping Nucky's image in the eyes of the jury and quickly dismissed him.

The defense then presented a parade of recognizable character witnesses who testified to Nucky's reputation for truth and veracity. Former Governor Harold Hoffman spent many days in the courtroom and testified that he had known Nucky for more than three decades and that his reputation for truth and veracity was excellent.

Likewise, former U.S. Senator David Baird Jr. took the stand and concurred with Hoffman's assessment of Nucky's character. Jimmy Walker, the former mayor of New York, said that he was proud to vouch for a fine Republican like Nucky. A procession of public officials, sports figures, celebrities, and ministers sang Nucky's praises hour after hour.

As he walked over to the jury rail for his closing argument, Winne began to unravel the government's case in a friendly, conversational tone. He said that when Nucky received money from the numbers bankers, he admitted it. Nucky has firmly denied he received any money from Corio. The judge personally kept all the money Miller gave him out of pure greed, never paid any tax on this money in the past, and from his testimony, he will not pay any tax in the future. Why? Because the government wanted him to say he gave money to Nucky.

Winne said the only evidence have before the jury on Count I was the uncorroborated testimony of an admitted liar and admitted tax evader. The government had failed to prove this charge beyond a reasonable doubt and asked for an acquittal.

Winne tried to rationalize the money Nucky received from the numbers bankers, saying that every political party needs money to run its organization and to pay election-related expenses. This is true for every political party in the United States. Under Nucky's leadership, the Republican Party of Atlantic County is different than most, said Winne. Nucky strongly feels that there are many people who need financial help sometime in their lives, and he had an obligation as a political leader to step up to the plate. The money from the numbers bankers supported his political organization so he could help people who could also support the Republican candidates. Winne said that Nucky had reported the $60,000 in commissions on his tax returns. Maybe his recordkeeping and reporting system didn't follow the IRS guidelines, but he would never have taken the stand and testified he received the money if he didn't think he was filing a correct tax return.

Winne said the government failed to prove a willful and conscious intent to evade taxes and filing false tax returns and urged the jury to acquit Nucky on Counts II and III. He pointed to Nucky's unblemished record of public service for more than 30 years that was enough to raise a reasonable doubt as to the validity of the government's charges. Then Winne thanked the jurors for their attention for the past two weeks.

Since the prosecution has the burden of proof in a criminal case, Burns was the last to speak to the jury, saying that they had just witnessed a most unusual spectacle, the trial of a corrupt political official. He said Nucky admitted that he was on the take, but he did not ask for the weekly payments from the numbers syndicate. The numbers syndicate operated openly in Atlantic City, but the payments Nucky received were not for protection. But when there were arrests of the numbers writers, Nucky did not receive a payment. Burns asked the jury whether it would be reasonable to conclude that the payments were for protection; no protection, no payment.

Burns said Nucky didn't report his gross income from the numbers bankers, but he did include his net income in commissions on his returns. So he decided how much he reported to the IRS without substantiating the deductions, a luxury not offered to other taxpayers. Burns explained that Nucky had no authority from the Republican County Committee to receive donations and did not report the donations to any state agency as required by law. He also created his own rules and did so to purposely conceal the weekly payoff he received from the numbers bankers.

Nucky invoked the Fifth Amendment when he was asked who gave him protection money in the year 1938 after admitting he received money from the numbers bankers for that year. Burns asked the jurors if they could believe him about anything he said after he admitted that the truth about 1938 would incriminate him. The government fulfilled its burden of proof beyond a reasonable doubt on Counts II and III, said Burns, and urged the jurors to find him guilty on both counts.

On Count I of the indictment, the government charged that Nucky received $28,000 in cash from Corio for help in obtaining a construction contract to build a new railroad terminal in Atlantic City at a cost of $2.4 million, said Burns. The government produced a copy of a written agreement to pay Nucky his share from the award and admitted it was unsigned. The government did not have a signed agreement since the evidence of this deal was destroyed once the money was paid. The government didn't produce Miller since he was awaiting trial.

Burns admitted that Corio was not the most convincing or reliable witness, since he originally denied his involvement to save his reputation and career. But when the pressure was on, he corroborated the unsigned payoff agreement. Burns said that Corio had an unblemished reputation throughout his distinguished judicial career, and he urged the jury to take that into consideration. He also urged a verdict of guilty on this count.

Nucky admitted he violated the law of the state of New Jersey by accepting and not reporting political contributions to the state authorities and accepting money from the numbers syndicate for all three years, according to Burns. The fact that he intentionally disregarded the state laws points to the fact that he intentionally violated the income tax laws of this country. Burns accused Nucky of dragging the Republican Party into the mire and urged the jury to save the people of Atlantic County from the disgrace of having him as their leader.

When Burns returned to his counsel table, Winne requested permission to approach the bench, which the court granted. Winne challenged the inflammatory statement Burns made to the jury by asking them to make the connection that if Nucky violated state law, he must have violated the federal income tax law. Winne said that one offense has nothing to do with the other; it was a complete misstatement of the law and the facts in this case, and the court should direct a mistrial. Secondly, he said, counsel made the argument that this jury should take on the role of crusaders, reformers and do-gooders, and rid the Republican Party of Nucky as the evil leader. Again, Burns was creating a motive for finding the defendant guilty, which has nothing to do with the charges. Winne was urging the court to declare a mistrial.

Finally, Winne said Burns basically told the jury that because Nucky took protection under the Fifth Amendment, he wasn't worth believing. Such an attempt to destroy the defendant's credibility is a fundamental ground for a mistrial. But Maris said he was surprised by the objections on all three grounds. Though he expressed regret at Burns' remarks, he denied a mistrial. He felt he could correct the misstatements in his charge to the jury. The judge then charged the jury on the law they should apply to the facts in reaching their verdict. He included a highlight of the facts he considered significant for the jury to consider in his recitation of the law.

Winne had to restrain himself from interrupting the court since he felt the judge was slanting his charge in favor of a guilty verdict. Facial expressions, tone and infliction of his voice, and body gestures are not recorded by the court reporter who was listening to the judge and speed writing his every word in his ink pen at the foot of the dais. The court reporter was constantly refilling his pen with ink and shaking the excess on the green carpet. An experienced trial judge, Maris knew that the official record on appeal will not contain his manner of delivery of his charge but only his spoken words through the transcribed record. When the judge was finished, Winne asked to approach the bench.

"I assume you have an objection, Mr. Winne," Maris said. "Please place it on the record." Winne continued, noting that the judge's comments to the jury about the government counsel's remarks only accentuated the problem rather than neutralized the impact and importance in the jury's mind. "Allowing the government to question the defendant about income for 1938, a year for which he was not indicted, was a fatal and uncorrectable error no matter what is said by the Honorable Court to the jury," said Winne, before he renewed his motion for a mistrial. And with that, the lawyers returned to their respective counsel tables, and all the exhibits had been turned over for the jury to review after the eleven-day trial.

At 12:10 PM on Friday, July 25, 1941, the jury began deliberating. The attorneys and court personnel thought it might take several days, but that wasn't the case. The jury reached a decision at 5:10 PM after three ballots and five hours of deliberations. In the federal courthouse, there was a dash to the phone to reach Nucky and his attorneys who were at the Walt Whitman Hotel a few blocks away. Nucky anxiously returned to the courthouse with his friends to hear the verdict.

The courtroom was silent as Maris asked the clerk for the jury verdict. The foreman had a small piece of paper in his hand and slowly read, "We find the defendant, Enoch L. Johnson, not guilty on Count I." The clerk then said, "So say you each and every member of the jury?" In unison, the members of the jury replied, "Yes." With that, applause erupted from Nucky's supporters. Maris admonished the spectators and said he would have them cleared from the courtroom if there was another outburst. The foreman continued with guilty verdicts on Counts II and III.

Nucky was visibly shaken for a moment; he had been prepared for the worst, but he never thought it would actually happen. The judge ordered Nucky released on bail with sentencing set for August 1, 1941. The press was clamoring in the hallways to interview Nucky, and photographers were camped outside to snap his picture as he left the Market Street courthouse.

At Nucky's suite at the Walt Whitman Hotel, Winne tried to console Nucky. "Our chances on appeal are great," he said. "The judge should never have allowed any testimony for the years outside the indictment that forced you to take the Fifth. Let's hope Maris lets you stay out on the bail after sentencing—we can take this case to the U.S. Supreme Court if we have to. It's full of procedural and substantive errors."

Nucky had accepted his fate. "If the jury didn't let me go, I know the government is going to throw the key away," said Nucky. "They will let me out when I am 'old and cold.'" He reminded Winne that he could keep the appeals going, but going to prison meant he would be out of work without an income.

Nucky spoke to his friends and said that he noticed that the jury didn't look at him when they re-entered the courtroom with their verdict. He knew that was a bad sign. They reminded him of the death jury when Judge Trenchard directed them to witness Joe Labriola's hanging in 1907.

When he lost his lucky Irish brick, Nucky knew he had lost the case.

LIFE BEHIND BARS

CHAPTER 16

PRISON DAYS

On July 31, 1941, the day before the federal judge was going to sentence Nucky to prison, Nucky imposed a "life sentence" on himself: He married his longtime companion Florence "Floss" Osbeck.

Though Nucky had lost his beloved Mabel nearly three decades ago and deeply mourned her loss, Floss had been his partner for many years and they enjoyed many good times together. She was "a real looker," an attractive showgirl with the New York Ziegfeld Follies who was often featured in Broadway shows with the help of Nucky's friend Earl Carroll, the renowned Broadway producer.

Floss and Nucky understood each other. Both had stormy personalities, and on occasion, they ended up in a heated argument after too much drinking. In fact, these outbursts caused some patrons to leave restaurants and bars and others to duck for cover. Among their favorite haunts were Louise Mack's Entertainer's Club at 169 South Westminster Avenue (aka "Snake Alley" by locals since it twisted from New York Avenue to Kentucky Avenue) or Babette's Night Club, owned by Daniel Stebbins, at the corner of Mississippi and Pacific Avenues. But the shouting matches never lasted long.

William "Bill" Farley, nephew of Senator Frank S. "Hap" Farley, told me he had known Nucky ever since his childhood days. At age 17, Bill had a summer job at The Entertainer's Club as a bartender and recalled Nucky and Floss being in the club one evening. They slowly began a shouting match that escalated in an all-out verbal assault on each other. The language became so loud and foul that every patron left the club leaving him as the last person standing.

The independent-minded Nucky decided it was time to marry Floss for two reasons: First, she could visit him in prison and keep him up-to-date on the Atlantic City scene, and second, and more importantly, he really loved her.

Nucky and Floss's nuptials were the most talked about event in Atlantic City in years; it was as though the newlyweds were going on a pleasure cruise and not to jail. At 9:20 AM, select guests were allowed into the First Presbyterian Church at Pennsylvania and Pacific Avenues, as several thousand curiosity-seekers gathered outside. Traffic was stopped for blocks, and the police had to escort invited guests into the church. Nucky didn't make news; he was the news.

Floss wore a white crepe street-length dress with an orchid corsage pinned to her shoulder, with a white feather tiara and a white-flecked veil. Not to be upstaged, Nucky wore a cream-colored mohair suit, yellow tie, and white shoes. His best man was his attorney, Walter Winne, and his attendant was his brother, Al. Harry Osbeck, the bride's father, gave his daughter away at the ceremony as Nucky's longtime friend, The Reverend Henry Merle, officiated.

The 100 invited guests inside the church included many leading local political figures: the newly elected Atlantic County State Senator Hap Farley and his wife, Honey, Assemblyman and Mrs. Vincent S. Haneman, Assemblyman and Mrs. Leon Leonard, U.S. Commissioner Bruce Surran, and all the Atlantic City Commissioners along with their wives, as well as members of the Board of Freeholders and their wives. Other notables included Dr. John McQuade, Dr. J.P. Martucci, Mr. and Mrs. Max Malamut of the Shelburne Hotel, Atlantic County Chief Probation Officer Vince Lane, and, of course, his faithful Treasurer's office staff, Mae Paxson and Marie Boyd and her husband, Jimmy, the Fourth Ward political leader.

After the ceremony, the newlyweds left the church and were faced with a barrage of photographers from Philadelphia, New York, and other locales. Their wedding picture appeared in the nationally circulated *Time Magazine* on August 11, 1941. Amid the flurry of flashing light bulbs, the crowd screamed as the newlyweds rushed to their waiting car and headed to the reception at their cottage at 110 South Iowa Avenue. Marie Boyd took care of most of the reception details. She ordered the wedding cake from Inky Bruenig, the owner of the Vienna Restaurant, a popular dining establishment for all the city and county officials across from city hall, and occasionally Nucky. Marie wanted a cake that was not "too girly" and refused to tell Inky who the cake was for, since she wanted to keep the upcoming wedding a secret for as long as possible. The newlyweds posed for photographs against a background of palms and huge bouquets of white lilies. The police controlled the restless crowd outside the cottage.

Nucky was not looking forward to prison, but he knew what to expect since he was raised at the Mays Landing jail when his father was sheriff. The two years that he spent as sheriff and several years as under-sheriff also gave him a unique insight of the inmates' network that controlled most prisons. As a young boy, he went into the jail with his father to do some minor chores, and he went from cell to cell to pick up letters that had to be mailed from inmates. Some prisoners were classified as "trustees" and worked in maintenance around the prison and in the Johnson household. There was an informality that made a stay at "Johnson's Hotel" far from unpleasant.

Over the years, he frequently saw the same offenders return to serve another sentence, and they called each other by their first names. "Welcome back!" Nucky said, to which the offender usually replied, "It's good to see you and your Pa, Nucky. I know I'll get three squares and a good bed, which is better than what I was doing on the outside."

Nucky's Chicago connections also reassured him that he would have protection from the other prisoners' scams, since some of the Chicago mob frequently rotated through Lewisburg Federal Penitentiary and had been alerted to protect Nucky. Frank Hague also called Nucky before he was scheduled to leave for "graduate school." It seems that some of his Jersey City boys were aware he was coming, and they were planning on showing him the ropes and "watch his back."

Once he was sentenced on August 1, 1941, Nucky was quickly hand-cuffed, and U.S. Marshal Stanley Seamen escorted him from the federal courtroom in Camden. Judge Albert B. Maris gave Nucky five years on one count with a fine of $10,000, and he gave him the same sentence on the other count. He then said the sentences were to run consecutively, and the fine was cumulative. It was what Nucky expected: 10 years in prison and a $20,000 fine. Judge Maris rejected the plea from Nucky's lawyer to let him out on bail pending his appeal, which is the general practice in income-tax evasion cases. His first step en route to Lewisburg was a brief nine-day stay in Trenton State Prison. U.S. Marshal Stanley Seaman drove him there in his car along with Nucky's brother, Al, who was then-sheriff of Atlantic County.

The New Jersey Senate in Trenton was in session that day, and the newly elected Senator Hap Farley from Atlantic County, was in the downstairs Senate cloakroom when he received a call. It was from Nucky who had just arrived in the Mercer County Jail near the capital building, saying, "Hap, I want to see you today—it's important." Hap replied, "I'll be right over, I know where you are."

Hap's driver drove him to the jail where a prison guard was waiting for him at the main gate. Warden George Widmann instructed him to take Hap directly to the private conference room. When Hap opened the walnut door to the conference room, Nucky and the warden were regaling each other with stories, since they had known each other during the time Nucky was sheriff. The warden excused himself to let the two men have some private time to talk.

"Maris had direct orders to bury me," said Nucky. "Al Capone got 11 years in prison and he did a hell of a lot more than me. I should have gotten three years max, but when you are in politics, they always triple the time—it makes a good press release for the IRS."

"I know my conviction won't be reversed on appeal since the judges on the Third Circuit Court of Appeals in Philadelphia will not want to reverse one of their own brothers," said Nucky. "Maris is part of the Appellant bench in Philadelphia and was especially assigned to sit as a trial judge in New Jersey for my case, so you know they are not going to question his ruling during my trial."

Nucky told Hap that the government was going to make him do most of the 10 years unless he gave them information on Edge, Kean, Morrow, Smathers, Hoffman, and others he helped get elected with a lot of their cash, and some of Nucky's that was over the legal limits. "You know me well enough to know I will never bring them down," he said. "The FBI knew Smathers got cash from Corio, but the Bureau couldn't prove it. The FBI told me, 'Let Smathers do a couple of years in prison'—they would take it off my time—I refused."

Nucky told Hap about his future. "Hap, I am going to be out of circulation for awhile, and I want you to take full control of the leadership of our party. We have no College of Cardinals; therefore, I am appointing you. I have sent in my resignation to the Board of Freeholders as County Treasurer. It will become effective on August 4, 1941, and this is a job you should take over in the future. It is good for all the county employees to see your name on their paychecks."

And Nucky talked to Hap as if he was admitting that his leadership days were over. "Let me give you some sound advice that Frank Hague gave me, but I foolishly did not follow," said Nucky. "Elections are won with money and it is not always easy to get. You need money from legitimate sources and some not so kosher, but whenever someone wants to give money personally to you regardless of the reason, don't take it! They may profess their undying loyalty to you at that moment but, when the heat is on, they'll cave and claim 'you shook him down.' The next time you will see them is when they are sitting in the witness chair testifying against you as the star canary for the prosecution."

Jimmy Boyd was someone Hap could trust, according to Nucky. He knew the Republican organization needed a good treasurer, and Boyd was the man for the job. The Republican organization mandated the post in its bylaws. He was street smart and knew everyone in town, and, more importantly, he knows how to handle cash. "Jimmy tried to help me at my trial and is a real stand-up guy," said Nucky. Make sure that any donations, especially cash, go right to Jimmy, said Nucky. Once someone puts cash in your hand, they can brag that you can be bought—it's just a question of price.

Nucky knew the political landscape would change after he was out of circulation for four or more years. He had been at the head of the line for more than 30 years and didn't intend to go to the end of the line and start all over again after he was released from prison. With that, Nucky said it was Hap's turn now, and his next stop was Lewisburg, Pennsylvania.

Situated on nearly a thousand acres in Pennsylvania's Allegheny Mountains, Lewisburg Federal Penitentiary is an imposing facility near the Susquehanna River. Its adaptation of Italian Renaissance architecture, constructed of brick, stone, and cement, has the simplicity of an old-world monastery, offering an ideal setting for an orderly life for the disorderly.

Lewisburg, which was the place for inmates who could be reformed, was a central induction center for all federal criminals convicted in the Northeastern section of the country. Warden Henry C. Hill was considered to be one of the most progressive prison officials in the federal prison system. His mission, though not giving to "coddling," was to release a prisoner back into society as a better person than when he first came through the prison gate.

As the human grist was sorted out in the legal and court systems, the hardcore repeaters were sent to the Federal Penitentiary in Atlanta, Georgia the younger prisoners to the Federal Penitentiary, Chillicothe, Ohio, and the "older improvables" remained in Lewisburg. Nucky, who was called many things over the years, including the Jersey Devil, picked up a new moniker when he entered the gates on August 11, 1941. The U.S. government officially designated him as prisoner No. NE 11207 USP, and described him as "improvable," along with 1,500 other inmates.

Nucky knew what life was like behind the prison walls: Rise at 6 AM, breakfast at 6:45 AM, dinner at 11:30 AM, the final meal at 4 PM, and then the bugler's taps at 9:35 PM. Most inmates were expected to work in the clothing factory where uniforms were made for the guards and prisoners. A few were assigned to the garden and lighter duty in the infirmary. For the unruly, the isolation cells were the maximum-security quarters for those who would not "shape up." Extreme discipline problems were shackled in leg irons and shipped to Alcatraz in California to do hard time.

For Lewisburg's "dressing-in" procedure, Nucky was led into the shower area, where he stripped and showered. For the next four years, his distinct custom-made suits were replaced by a gray prison uniform. When Nucky was dressed in his new attire, he asked the guard, "Where can a guy buy a fresh red carnation around here?"

With his ration of blankets in hand, Nucky's next stop was the warden's office. Warden Hill said he had read Nucky's entire file from the IRS and FBI, and it looked as though he told the truth even when it was not in his best interest, especially at his trial. He asked Nucky for help in encouraging prisoners to attend classes and get some training, since most prisoners respected Nucky and were likely to listen to him. The warden told Nucky that he was sending him to the doctor for a complete check-up and then to the Catholic priest for a spiritual check-up. Nucky was a

Protestant, but was told by the warden there was a minister on back order. He agreed to all the terms.

Nucky decided to make the best of a bad situation in prison. He passed the complete physical and dental evaluation with "flying colors." Then Nucky arrived at the Catholic chaplain's office for the standard interview. The chaplain congratulated Nucky on his recent marriage. "Our diocese has a summer cottage at the shore—Stone Harbor—and we get the *Atlantic City Press*, Cape May Edition," the chaplain said. "The *Press* covered your trial and marriage. I was looking forward to meeting you since we do get a lot of guests from South Jersey."

Nucky liked the priest from the start and asked him how he ended up in prison. The priest explained that he was an orphan and learned early what it's like to have no one who wants you or to care for you. He felt a calling to volunteer to be the prison chaplain and gave Nucky a Bible with the instructions that the good book was there to help him, especially the words in red, while in prison and the rest of his life.

Armed with his new reading material, he settled in to his first dorm assignment, which was functional, but his goal was to get an honor room without bars or locks on the doors.

The prison rules were more restricted than he anticipated for visitors and correspondence, far from the open policy the prisoners enjoyed in the Mays Landing county jail. Only blood relatives were permitted to correspond during the initial 30-day quarantine, which excluded his new wife, Floss. No visits were permitted during the first 30 days.

After one month, he was able to add seven visitors to his designated list. Nucky selected Floss, Lou Kessel, John D'Agostino, Carmen D'Agostino, Jimmy Walker, Herman "Muggsy" Taylor, and Emerson Richards. When he was putting the list together, Nucky joked with the clerk in the warden's office: "This is like selecting your own pallbearers!"

The visiting hours were limited to one hour from 8:30 AM to 11:30 AM and from 1 PM to 3:30 PM weekdays, except Saturdays and holidays. A guard was present at all time to listen to the prisoner's conversation, except for those with the prisoner's attorney. Legal counsel could come and go as they pleased as long as they gave 48 hours' advance notice.

Mail was also restricted. Nucky could only receive seven incoming letters per week, and he could send out only two letters per week. Every inmate was required to file a designated list of seven persons he wanted to hear from, and all other letters were stamped "return to sender" by the prison. Every prisoner could also receive books, but they had to be mailed directly from the publisher for security purposes. And each inmate was also required to work somewhere in prison, whether it was on the farm, bindery, kitchen, clothing factory, laundry, library, hospital, or the schools.

Nucky was only in prison a few months when the U.S. entered World War II on December 7, 1941. The Atlantic City he knew and loved changed dramatically when the U.S. Air Force took over 27 of the major hotels for barracks. The first hotel to be "drafted" was the Ambassador, aka The Monarch of the Boardwalk. Atlantic City became Camp Boardwalk, the largest U.S. Air Force domestic training center.

U.S. Senator William H. Smathers and Atlantic City Mayor Thomas D. Taggart Jr. invited the friendly invasion to Atlantic City since it would help the city recover from the Depression that devastated the entire country. Smathers boasted that Atlantic City had the largest convention in the country: the U.S. Air Force.

The convention auditorium was converted into a training center where troops conducted drills in the massive hall. The Boardwalk became a parade ground, and the tourists were treated to the sights of the Air Force troops marching in formation down the wooden walkway proudly singing the Air Force hymn: "Off we go into the wild blue yonder, flying high into the sky!" Early in the morning, the new recruits were busy doing their calisthenics on the beach at the cadence of the demanding drill instructor.

The local merchants welcomed the soldiers and often sold their merchandise at half-price to anyone in uniform. Since many local residents volunteered in the military hospitals, it was common to see the volunteers pushing limbless soldiers in wheelchairs for a stroll along the Boardwalk.

The Coast Guard protected and patrolled the beach and coastline on horseback, since there was a constant threat of German U-boats launching spies ashore. When I was an Atlantic City Life Guard, I had to get a note from the Chief of the Beach Patrol for me and my partner to take a lifeguard boat out for a row each morning. When we were launching the boat one time, a Coast Guard on horseback approached us and asked for the permission note. After we showed him our note, he told us to "Have a good row!"

The military ordered all the Atlantic City hotels to dim their lights to prevent any of the beachfront hotels from being silhouetted on the horizon, an easy target for patrolling German U-boats. In self-defense, many of the beachfront hotels installed black window shades so guests could have light in their rooms and comply with the blackout.

The Chalfonte-Haddon Hall, at North Carolina Avenue and the Boardwalk, which was converted into a hospital, took in the wounded as they returned from overseas. For three years during the war, the hotel complex treated more than 150,000 wounded soldiers. It became known as the England General Hospital named for Lieutenant Colonel Thomas M. England, who spent time on research for a cure for yellow fever. The dedicated Army nurses took over the Colton Manor Hotel, on South Pennsylvania Avenue, a short distance from Haddon Hall.

Floss kept Nucky up-to-date on local politics and the changes in Atlantic City during her frequent visits to Lewisburg. He was delighted when she told him the Air Force took over the Ritz-Carlton. "Nothing is too good for our guys," said Nucky. "I hope they enjoy it as much as I did." Floss told Nucky that the military converted the Graham Hotel at States and Pacific Avenues into a USO Canteen where soldiers could dance and where movie stars frequently entertained the troops. She also told Nucky that William Graham Ferry was the Director of Civilian Defense for Atlantic County and was enlisting Air Raid Wardens for homeland defense. Marie Boyd, from the county treasurer's office, volunteered as a nurse's aide at the England General Hospital, where the most seriously wounded were taken.

And there were plenty of patriotic celebrities parading around in uniform: Clark Gable from *Gone With the Wind* fame occasionally visited with relatives Marie Cicero and her son Larry at 31-C North Maryland Avenue. Floss also saw Ronald Reagan, the actor who later became the 40th U.S. President. Captain Glen Miller's band entertained the troops frequently at the Steel Pier and the convention auditorium. He joined the Army Air Force at the height of his career to organize bands for the Air Force. Unfortunately, his plane crashed in the English Channel killing all aboard on December 15, 1944.

Harold "Doc" Winter, who was drafted in the summer of 1942, was assigned to New Jersey's Fort Dix and then sent to Atlantic City. He was in charge of all bandleaders for all marching bands on the Boardwalk. The entire country was treated to the first national radio broadcast from Atlantic City featuring Kate Smith singing a medley of patriotic songs including her signature tribute, the second national anthem, "God Bless America." The Philadelphia Flyers hockey team would later have Kate Smith on the ice to sing her stirring rendition of "God Bless America" for winning the Stanley Cup in 1974 and 1975.

Nucky wanted to find out what happened to one of his favorite drinking spots, the Tuna Club, and whether the Coast Guard was letting the sportfishing boats out in the ocean. Floss said that some boats went out, but the Coast Guard searched them when they returned to the Tuna Club. The Tuna Club also made national headlines for its flock of carrier pigeons that used to carry messages from the boats to the club. The club donated the pigeons to the Army Signal Corps so they could be used to ferry airborne communications as needed. Floss also told Nucky that the Air Force did something special for his Pineys by setting up a "Hillbilly School" at the Chelsea Hotel so the Pineys could learn to read and write in order to join the Air Force. Nucky often said that the Pineys might not know how to read or write, but they sure as hell knew how to fight.

The war effort also changed spring training for the major baseball teams in the area. Floss said she had run into Pop Lloyd, a star of the Negro League, who told her the Boston Red Sox had been training over in Pleasantville near Atlantic City for the past two years. At the end of the training camp, they graciously donated all their uniforms to the kids who played in the field across from the All Wars Memorial Building at 1510 Adriatic Avenue in Atlantic City.

Inside prison, many of the convicts knew about Nucky from the publicity he had received and wanted to talk to him. One day, an inmate by the name of Karl Schultz from Egg Harbor City struck up a conversation in the prison library. Schultz, who had met Nucky at the Aurora Hall at a political rally in Egg Harbor City some years ago, was a master boatbuilder by trade and a distant relative to Commodore Louis Kuehnle. Nucky asked him why he was in prison, but Schultz wouldn't talk about the past since he couldn't change it. He simply said he was looking forward to getting out of here in a few years.

Schultz was the prison casket maker. The prison assigned him to the woodworking shop and said if he could build a boat, he could build a wooden casket that was watertight. Schultz said that there was at least one funeral a week from suicides or occasional stabbings, but most inmates die of natural causes since they didn't have much to live for. But Schultz had his work to keep him busy. He built oblong pine caskets—usually 7' long—since one size fits all. He said he even built one for himself, just in case. In his, he stapled a white-linen lining in the top half to rest his weary head. He jokingly said he put it high on a shelf in his shop under "Lay Away." Some of the prisoners lost all contact with family members, and when they died, they were buried on the prison grounds. Nobody wanted them, dead or alive.

On July 12, 1942, after Nucky had served a year in prison, a team of his local lawyers came to discuss his appeal to the U.S. Supreme Court, the final effort to have his conviction overturned. The group included experienced criminal trial attorney John Rauffenbart, his civil attorney Martin Bloom, and the aggressive criminal lawyer Jim McMenamin Jr., aka "Young Jim." His father, also Jim, was the Atlantic City chief of police.

Young Jim tried to join the Army soon after World War II broke out, but he couldn't because of a heart condition. This rejection disturbed him since every able-bodied man at that time was considered a "slacker" if he was not wearing a military uniform. Young Jim thought he was bulletproof and brushed off the Army's diagnosis and never sought treatment.

Jim drove the legal entourage with their wives to a Harrisburg hotel where they checked in for the night. On Saturday morning, all three lawyers went to Lewisburg prison, and after they went through security, Young Jim suddenly collapsed. He was rushed to the nearby Evangelical Hospital, but it was too late. He was pronounced dead on arrival.

When Nucky heard about Young Jim, he was shocked and refused to talk to anyone for more than a week. He told Floss, "Young Jim went out too soon—he had a great future and would have made an outstanding Judge had Tom Taggert not taken the spot for himself. If I wasn't in here, I would have put Jim on the bench."

Nucky's appeal to the U.S. Supreme Court was eventually filed but was denied by the court; the legal battle was over. Although Nucky was routinely scheduled for a parole hearing after serving three years, he did not think it would be granted after he refused several requests to be interviewed by FBI agents. The Department of Justice thought that Nucky, who was 59 years old, would crack under the pressure of prison life, but they underestimated his ability to cope in prison.

Prison life was uncomfortable for him, but he made friends quickly as he did in public life. He took pride in encouraging some prisoners to attend classes and to obtain a high school diploma as the warden urged him to do. The other inmates looked up to him, especially the prisoners who knew about his assistance to the black community in Atlantic City.

Each day, Nucky had a fixed routine, which improved his physical health and mental stamina. If he had talked to the FBI agents, word would have spread quickly throughout the prison population, and the rest of his time would be miserable. The warden urged Nucky to listen to what the FBI agents had to say since it could help him with his parole. Nucky repeatedly refused such requests.

Nucky knew before he went to prison that "snitches get stitches and end up in ditches." Some informants were moved out of the general population and placed in "rat row" for their personal protection. Some inmates paid a "rat hunter" to track a snitch down for their brand of swift justice. Nucky was determined to remain silent; when he eventually left prison life, he could proudly hold up his head and say, "My word is my bond and the government will never take that away from me." Nucky kept that promise not only for his four years in prison, but the rest of his life.

CHAPTER 17

PEN PALS

By the time Nucky entered Lewisburg Federal Penitentiary in 1941, Prohibition had been over for more than eight years. But Nucky was still a legend to many inmates who were once involved in the flourishing liquor trade. Everyone knew he had been a part of The Big Seven, the cartel that had been busy making vast sums of money distributing liquor illegally on the East Coast.

The inmates at Lewisburg not only wanted to meet Nucky, but they wanted to say they were friends of his when they were back on the street. Nucky enjoyed telling stories about his lavish parties at the Ritz in Atlantic City, the celebrities who attended, his meeting with The Big Seven, the Carpentier-Dempsey fight in 1921, and meeting Al Capone and Johnny Torrio for the first time. As an encore, he regaled his entranced audience with the story of how he later met Capone and Torrio again in 1927 at the Dempsey-Tunney fight, and the first Crime Convention in Atlantic City in 1929, of course.

One day, Moe Annenberg, an old acquaintance of Nucky's who was near the end of his three-year stint for income tax evasion, stopped by to see him. Annenberg wasn't sure whether Nucky would remember him, but Nucky had an excellent memory for faces and events. In spring 1929, Nucky readily recalled that Capone, Torrio, and the Chicago and New York mobs gave Annenberg the nod of approval for his horse-racing wire. When Nucky asked how he ended up in prison, Annenberg was quick to share his side of the story about the largest income tax evasion in the history of IRS at that time, which was more than $1 million. He said he paid $8 million for income taxes and civil penalties but was still sentenced to prison and ended up in Lewisburg.

Obtaining permission to operate the horse-racing wire in Atlantic City created funds to finance all his businesses for the next decade. He used telephones and teletypes to transmit the odds and winners of horse races direct from the racetracks to every bookmaker parlor that subscribed to his wire service across the country and overseas. Payment for the wire service was due each week or the wire went dead and the parlor was out of business, he said. The bookies all knew Capone and Torrio were getting a cut, so they were not about to cross them.

Annenberg also published the *Wall Sheet* showing the daily thoroughbred racetrack action; every horse room received a copy that explained what horses were running, the weather conditions, the jockey, the pole position, and the track. He admitted that it wasn't easy getting total control of the operation, but his Chicago friends struck a deal where he bought out all the competition. Of course, he had to pay dearly for their help.

He kept investing cash in other publications and eventually gained control of the *Daily Racing Form*, *TV Guide*, the *Philadelphia Daily News*, *Morning Telegraph,* and *The Philadelphia Inquirer*. He outbid all the competition to get 108-year-old *Inquirer*, which he considered the prize trophy in the world of journalism and his passport to respectability. He said he wanted to gain some stature and give his kids a chance to go to the right schools and travel in the best social circles.

Annenberg, with a wife and eight children, had a good life, but he says he was never satisfied and was addicted to work and gambling. He had a ranch in Wyoming, a home at Miami Beach, and a penthouse suite at The Warwick Hotel in Philadelphia. But some of his choices weren't all that wise: The IRS discovered some of his more creative accounting procedures, including the time he charged his daughter's wedding in 1934 to the *Daily Racing Form* business and chartered two Pullman railroad cars to bring his friends from Chicago to New York for the ceremony. He picked up the tab for their luxury hotel rooms at The Pierre in New York City where the wedding was held. His accountant listed the entire bill as a "convention expense."

His children apparently reported dividends from his holding company on their returns, which the IRS reported was a way to avoid a high surtax. Some of his gambling debts were also charged as legal expenses on his company books. At any given time, he said he was handling 80 or 85 corporations, and his publishing empire "just got out of control."

Annenberg's only son, Walter, was also indicted. One of the reasons Moe said he pleaded guilty was to strike a deal with the government to drop the charges against Walter. Moe needed him on the outside to run the business. The feds knew he was close to Capone, which originally triggered the IRS interest in him, figuring that Annenberg gave Capone cash to operate, but it was something that the feds couldn't prove.

In the early years, William Randolph Hearst hired Annenberg to boost the circulation of his *Chicago Evening American* newspaper, which he did with great success. Later, Hearst gave him control of the entire circulation of all his newspapers and magazines, which was the No. 1 circulation job in the world of journalism. Before long, Annenberg became publisher and president of the *New York Daily Mirror*.

Many people thought Annenberg's horse-room wire service was against the law, but it wasn't. He paid some people to keep the peace, and for the others, he called one of his Chicago friends to keep them quiet. He said he even sent some IRS agents on vacation, but each time he found a way to get rid of one of them, another agent appeared and looked even deeper into his finances. The agents managed to find enough wrongdoing to build a solid criminal case against him that he ended up spending his days and nights in Lewisburg. Nucky and Annenberg had much in common and spent part of the day whenever they could to talk about their past escapades and their mutual friends involved.

On another afternoon, inmate Poppy Ippolito, who had worked as a rumrunner in New York, came to see Nucky and told him about his experiences with the U.S. Coast Guard in New York harbor. In those days, some U.S. Coast Guard captains were paid to take their ships in opposite directions so the rumrunners could come ashore; other enforcement officials were paid $2 per case. Some wanted the good whiskey for themselves or to sell ashore. Once Ippolito had shared his adventures, he wanted to hear more about Nucky's role in The Big Seven.

Nucky was ready to tell some tales now that the statute of limitations had expired about his group in New York run by Meyer Lansky, the brains of the mob. The other six consisted of the Brooklyn gang of Joe Adonis; Abner "Longy" Zwillman and Willie Moretti in North Jersey;

Harry "Nig" Rosen and Waxey Gordon in Philadelphia; Charles "King" Solomon in New England; Johnny Torrio and Charles "Lucky" Luciano for part of New York; and Nucky in Atlantic City and Cape May in South Jersey. The seven territories had been carved out in the past but were only enforced after The Big Seven had its meeting at Atlantic City's President Hotel in May 1929.

The Big Seven finally realized it was bad business to compete with each other; the entire country was thirsty, and there was enough business for everyone. From Nucky's vantage point in Atlantic City, there were only a few Coast Guard stations along the entire South Jersey coast that looked the other way for the most part. Sometimes, he had to pay for the Coast Guard not to be around when a shipment was coming in; otherwise, it was clear sailing. Rumrunners who were busted were taken to friendly judges and usually given probation. Some of the local Atlantic City ABC agents, George Tracy and Joe Sussman, were tough on bootleggers, but they could not keep up with all the booze traffic that was coming in from the back bays and the mother ships anchored beyond the 12-mile legal limit in the Atlantic Ocean off Atlantic City. The country was thirsty for liquor, and the members of The Big Seven were happy to do what they could to quench that thirst.

In 1933, everything changed when Prohibition ended. President Franklin D. Roosevelt campaigned for the repeal of the "great experiment" to boost revenue from the legal liquor industry and to create jobs to help the country out of the Depression. On December 5, 1933, after the required 36 states ratified the 21st Amendment, Prohibition ended in the U.S., everywhere except New Jersey, that is. New Jersey bootleggers were not about to give up their lucrative business to Uncle Sam. Illegal alcohol continued to flourish, a product of the South Jersey stills that served nightclubs in Philadelphia, New York, and Atlantic City with their high-proof alcohol for the carriage trade.

Prison time gave Nucky time to think about what he wanted after he was released. Life outside prison had definitely changed as Nucky had known it, but he was determined to pick up where he left off with his businesses and political connections. That's why he knew he had to find people who might help him in prison and after he was released. When he was considering hiring attorney William E. Leahy to represent him, he remembered a conversation he had about Leahy trying to get a federal judge out of Lewisburg. Judge Martin T. Manton, the senior judge for the U.S. Court of Appeals in New York, was serving two years in Lewisburg. He was still there, so Nucky decided to look him up.

Manton, who had been in Lewisburg since 1940, was considered an "assault risk" the day he went behind the gates since he was a senior federal judge. He was secluded from the rest of the prison population, since all enforcement officials, especially judges, were fair game for revenge by prisoners who felt victimized in the past by the police and the justice system. Manton accepted this protection willingly; he didn't care to socialize with anyone in the prison since he felt they all deserved to be there except him. He was assigned to work in the greenhouse, and his free time was spent in the library and learning to speak Spanish.

In prison, cigarettes were the only currency, and Nucky always had a stash. He gave two cartons to a trustee who confiscated a copy of the complete prison file jacket on Manton. Nucky read his prison record and the account of his conviction for obstructing justice: The jury concluded he accepted bribes to fix cases. Nucky mused to himself, "Where was this judge when I needed him?"

Nucky chose Manton's home ground at the library as a good place to strike up a conversation. They had several things in common: Both were staunch Republicans, both were of Irish descent, both of their trials were sensationalized in the press, and in their minds, both had been wrongfully convicted.

Nucky's old nemesis President Woodrow Wilson had selected Manton for the federal bench in 1916, as the youngest federal judge in the country at age 36. After listening to Nucky tell the story of his case, Manton thought Nucky should never have been convicted and considered whoever told him to take the witness stand was guilty of criminal malpractice.

When Nucky heard the judge's opinion, he said, "Many people have told me the same thing after the trial, but only a few warned me before the trial." Manton couldn't wait to talk about Nucky's defense. Walter Winne may have been a good U.S. attorney, according to Manton, but he certainly was not a seasoned trial lawyer. Winne was an office administrator and hadn't spent time in the trenches as did the assistant U.S. attorneys who try cases every day.

When Nucky told Manton that he still had an appeal pending, Manton set the record straight and told Nucky how the system really worked. He said Maris was specifically sent to Camden from the federal circuit court across the Delaware River. The appellate court was going to give Maris the benefit of all his rulings, and unless he committed a gross error, his decision wouldn't be reversed. The court of appeals wouldn't upset the Department of Justice and IRS to save Nucky's hide. The judges were too worried about protecting themselves and possibly advancing to a higher court, senior judgeship, or getting a salary increase.

Manton shared the details of his trial with Nucky. He said he testified at his own trial, but he was required to do so. As a U.S. Circuit Court judge, Manton had to refute the charges and take the stand; otherwise, the jury would have reacted negatively. He admitted to receiving some loans from litigants, but it did not influence his decision. That was hard for jurors to accept, but that was why he never admitted that he was guilty of any of the government charges. This gave Nucky a new inside view of the legal process and what the years ahead held for him.

Nucky's first parole hearing was scheduled for December 7, 1944, and Floss took action since Nucky was helpless behind bars. She took the bold step of personally going to see Judge Maris in Philadelphia, two months before the hearing on October 6, 1944, to ask for her husband to be released early. Lou Kessel drove her to the courthouse where they met in the judge's private chambers, but no promises were made. Tragically, as Kessel was driving home with Floss, they were involved in a head-on collision in dense fog on Albany Avenue Boulevard near the bridge into Atlantic City. The other car had crossed over the road; the driver was killed almost instantly.

Both Kessel and Floss were injured in the crash and taken to the Atlantic City Hospital; Kessel had a punctured lung. It looked as though his injuries weren't bad at first, but he died at 11 AM on October 7, 1944. Floss suffered extensive facial cuts but survived. When Nucky heard that Kessel was dead, he withdrew. He blamed himself for the tragedy and was inconsolable for months. His request to attend Kessel's funeral was denied, which left Nucky embittered against federal authorities for the rest of his life.

Nucky's parole hearing went as he expected: He was denied parole in spite of a perfect record while in custody. Nucky represented himself at this hearing and later lamented, "I had a fool for a client."

Nucky believed that it was a political vendetta that put him in prison and that it kept him there. His only hope was to call in some of his political IOUs that he had earned by his four years of silence. U.S. Senator William H. Smathers was the first to come to Nucky's mind. Smathers came to Atlantic City in 1912 from North Carolina and began to practice law and entered politics as a Democrat. He defeated Nucky's candidate for the New Jersey Senate in 1935, but Nucky helped him become U.S. Senator in 1937, primarily to get him out of South Jersey. He remained in the U.S. Senate for one six-year term.

During his criminal trial, Nucky remained silent when the FBI was investigating Smathers. By all accounts, Smathers had received money from Corio in order to use his political influence to derail the government's case against Corio. Had Nucky cooperated with the government, Smathers would have been disgraced, disbarred, and forced to resign from the U.S. Senate. Smathers was indebted big time to Nucky for his career, and when he received the call from Nucky to represent him at his second parole hearing, he readily agreed. Smathers had just been defeated for re-election to the U.S. Senate by Republican Albert Hawkes on November 3, 1942. However, Smathers still had a great deal of influence with the Roosevelt administration for supporting the president's New Deal policies. Smathers had a home in Ventnor City, at One North Oxford Avenue, but he frequently commuted to the capital on business to keep up his political contacts and serve as a lobbyist for several large corporations.

On December 10, 1945, the atmosphere at the second parole hearing was vastly different than the first with Smathers as his counsel. This time, the board was looking for reasons to let Nucky out. The board decided that in view of Nucky's perfect record and the death of his friends, Kessel and Young Jim McMenamin Jr., that he should be released. Although the review board cited those reasons for his release, Nucky knew better.

When Nucky left the hearing room with Smathers, he said that political clout put him in the can and political clout got him the hell out. He thanked Smathers for his help, and Smathers thanked Nucky for his silence. Although Nucky was released in 1945, he still owed the original $20,000 fine and the cost of the trial. Looking fit and weighing 20 pounds lighter, Nucky told the reporters waiting for him when he was released that he received many job offers, but he was looking forward to settling in at a local company in Atlantic County.

When Floss and Nucky drove home, they knew they were starting a new chapter in their lives. They knew their future wouldn't be as exciting as their past, but then again, that's just the way they wanted it.

THE FINAL DAYS

CHAPTER 18

TIME TO SMELL THE ROSES

Time in prison gave Nucky a chance to contemplate what his life would be like after his release from Lewisburg, and he was sure he would never regain his past political stronghold role in the Republican Party.

When Nucky went to prison in 1941, a battle for Republican Party leadership in Atlantic County erupted between rising stars Thomas D. Taggart, Jr. and Frank S. "Hap" Farley. Nucky took in all the excitement from the sidelines of his prison cell, betting on the sure winner in his book—Hap.

In one corner, the Taggart name was well-established in Atlantic County. Taggart had been elected to the State Assembly from 1935 to 1937, and to the State Senate for Atlantic County from 1938 to 1940 with Nucky's endorsement. Thomas D. Sr., a physician, had been chief surgeon of the Atlantic City Hospital for 25 years.

Taggart's friends knew about his aspirations to become mayor of Atlantic City, but many tried to talk him out of this venture and vacating his state senator post because they believed political power rested in the state senatorship. When Taggart opted not to run for a second term as senator, Hap, then an assemblyman, took the vacant Senate seat in 1941. The *Atlantic City Press* celebrated the changing of the political guard with a front-page photograph of Hap and Taggart strolling down the street, locked arm in arm. The article in the newspaper simply reported that Nucky was in Trenton, but not at the election ceremony.

When Taggart ran for mayor of Atlantic City, he was elected in 1940 on Nucky's coalition ticket of three Republicans: Taggart, Joseph Altman, and William S. Cuthbert, along with Democrats William F. Casey and

Daniel S. Bader. Taggart was thrilled with the number of votes he received and thought this would guarantee him the leadership position for the Republican Party.

Taggart had staked his claim on the chairman's post based on his seniority and longtime loyalty to the Republican Party in the State Assembly and as mayor of Atlantic City. But Hap's popularity not only far exceeded Taggart's, but he already had Nucky's endorsement, and a vote of confidence from Nucky trumped everything else.

Taggart's term as mayor was rife with turmoil and bitter infighting with his fellow commissioners. First, he decided to fire Police Chief William S. McMenamin Sr. and his secretary, Lieutenant William Mulloy, and then replaced them with Captain Earl Butcher and Detective Jerry Sullivan, respectively.

Taggart named Detective James Maley, the police department's best marksman, as his personal bodyguard and began leading raids on gambling parlors. He loved the publicity and always notified the press about his continuing efforts to drive every underworld character out of town. He personally led the charge, toting two pearl-handled pistols in his belt Western-style with gun butts forward. The *Atlantic City Press* responded by giving him the moniker of "Two Gun Tommy."

Atlantic City's gambling fraternity wasn't happy with Taggart's crackdown, and neither were the other city commissioners. They felt Taggart was constantly interfering with their departments; worst of all, city business was being neglected. Taggart's turmoil generated such animosity that residents wanted to start a recall petition to remove him from office. But the city commissioners found an easier way to disarm Two Gun Tommy.

While Taggart was out of town in 1942, the commissioners passed a resolution that stripped the mayor of all authority except for the city solicitor's office that handled routine civic disputes and contract preparation. Taggart's political career started to freefall, which escalated in continual litigation against his past political friends. Hap emerged the winner.

With Hap in the political limelight, Nucky had lost his grip on gambling, illegal liquor trafficking, brothels, and "ice money" (a percentage of the salary that each municipal employee was required to make to ensure his job) from city and county workers, especially when he went to prison. He also figured that those cash streams weren't likely to reappear for him or any other political leader in the future either.

But Nucky's entrepreneurial spirit prevailed. Fellow inmate John H. Stoneburg Jr. coaxed Nucky into writing his memoirs in Lewisburg prison. Nucky knew Stoneburg was trying to make a quick buck for himself from his colorful past, but he decided to go ahead anyway with the project.

Initially, Nucky enjoyed recounting the details of his life. As he shared his stories, he remembered more and more events and colorful characters from his past. But as Stoneburg committed Nucky's amazing life to paper, he had trouble discerning fact from fiction and embellished many of the events beyond all recognition. When Nucky discussed this with Stoneburg, he always assured Nucky that any inaccuracies could easily be changed when the book was finished.

Despite their literary differences, Nucky and Stoneburg agreed on the title of the book: *The Boardwalk Empire*. After all, Nucky ran his political empire from the ninth floor of the Ritz-Carlton Hotel overlooking the Boardwalk, and the title said it all.

Stoneburg left Lewisburg on June 14, 1945, two months before Nucky. They agreed to meet in Atlantic City after they were released to finish Nucky's memoirs, and they did. Once the book was finished, Nucky gave Floss a copy of the manuscript to read. Floss hated it. She thought Nucky was portrayed as a petty criminal and the events and people in his life were sensationalized. Family friend Marie Boyd said that Nucky and Floss threatened to sue Stoneburg if he ever tried to publish the book. Nucky's contempt for Stoneburg was clear and unbridled.

But the manuscript was the least of Nucky's worries. When he stepped out of Lewisburg on August 14, 1945, Nucky was far from being a free man: His parole was set until 1952, and he still owed the government the $20,000 fine that Judge Maris imposed more than four years before.

Floss and Nucky settled back into the Atlantic City community as best they could. They moved into a beach block home in Atlantic City owned by Floss's mother, Anna Osbeck, at 103 South Elberon Avenue. Al, Nucky's brother, also moved in. Some of Nucky's friends believed that Nucky actually owned the property but didn't want any assets in his name that the government could seize. Meanwhile, Al carried on the Johnson family tradition, serving as sheriff of Atlantic County from 1932 to 1941 and then as undersheriff with Sheriff James Carmack from 1941 to 1944.

Finally in 1947, Nucky was offered and accepted a job as a public relations consultant for Renault Winery, owned by the D'Agostino family. Nucky had been close to the family for many years, especially John, who was his longtime business partner. It was a good fit for Nucky too; he personally knew all the nightclub operators and the bar managers for most of the South Jersey bars. He had also been one of their best customers for years.

But getting a job after a felony conviction and prison term wasn't easy, even with good connections. Carmen D'Agostino, John's brother, notified Nucky that the New Jersey Alcoholic Beverage Control Commission would have to approve any job candidate as part of the standard procedures who was connected to the sale or dispensing of alcohol. Employees have to be fingerprinted, answer a barrage of questions, and undergo a police background check.

One of the first questions on the application asked the obvious: Have you ever been convicted of a crime? Of course, Nucky was honest and checked the box marked yes. In turn, the state authority quickly rejected his application. But Carmen found a way around the problem and used his political affiliations to full advantage: Governor Alfred E. Driscoll could waive Nucky's conviction charge.

Carmen and Nucky agreed that if Hap asked the governor for a favor, the waiver would be granted. Driscoll, a Republican from Camden County and friendly with Hap, worked with Hap when they became state senators in 1941. Carmen was also one of Hap's childhood friends at the Wenonah Military Academy in 1921. Hap was receptive to Nucky's request and asked him to gather a few letters of recommendation from his friends to help the case and give the governor a sound footing for granting the waiver.

Driscoll, who was elected in November 1946 and took office the following January, was aware that granting Nucky a waiver would be a popular move in Atlantic County but not in the other 20 counties that he depended on for votes in the next election. Driscoll was wary of causing any waves that might tarnish his image. He already expected a contentious campaign against South Jersey Congressman Elmer H. Wene, a popular Democrat. Wene was elected to Congress in 1941 and 1943 and to the New Jersey Senate from Cumberland County in 1946.

Hap met with Driscoll several times at the state capital in hopes of persuading him to approve the waiver for Nucky but without any success. Hap wasn't happy. His Republican organization had overwhelmingly supported Driscoll for governor; they had even worked together on a number of the governor's legislative initiatives and had served together in the Senate.

Nucky was quick to recognize the political stalemate and devised a plan of his own. He met with the D'Agostino family and suggested that Floss be added to the Renault payroll instead of Nucky. He could work with her on the sidelines in contacting and developing clients. The proposal worked, and Floss became the new public relations consultant. Each day she called on places based on Nucky's suggestions. She kept a daily log of her activities in case any law enforcement agency ever challenged the authenticity of her work. She didn't want anyone to think she was a shill for her husband.

Hap knew that Floss's salary from her Renault job wouldn't support the lavish lifestyle that they had come to know and love. Nucky billed his official employment status as a promotional salesman for A. P. Miller, Inc., a general contractor firm in Atlantic City owned by Anthony P. Miller. Miller was indebted to Nucky for his silence during the federal investigation of Corio and Miller. But for more than 30 years, Nucky had helped launch the political careers of many in the Republican Party, including Hap. In early 1948, Hap met with Jimmy Boyd and they agreed to help Nucky and Floss financially. Hap asked Jimmy, who still held the pursestrings for the reserve funds for elections and the needy, to use his discretion in making sure that Nucky received some financial support each week, which he did for the rest of Nucky's life.

As a staunch supporter of the Republican ticket, Nucky went out of his way to support Hap as his successor. Even in prison, Nucky sent Hap letters via Floss telling him how pleased he was with Hap's Republican Party leadership. They remained close friends and met at civic and political functions every so often.

Hap and Nucky agreed not to be seen together in public on a regular basis since the *Atlantic City Press* and the *Newark Star Ledger* found ways to use their relationship against Hap. Hap did not want to give the impression that Nucky was somehow still in control of the Republican organization behind the scenes. Plus, the Newark paper wanted a reason to attack Hap. The newspaper strongly opposed Hap's success in bringing thoroughbred horse racing to New Jersey in 1946. Hap was also concerned about his political opponents charging him with being associated with a convicted criminal in their campaign literature and casting Nucky in an unfavorable light. Neither of them wanted that kind of publicity.

Since he was still on parole until 1952, Nucky was always mindful that any adverse publicity might cause a violation of his parole. So Nucky and Hap deliberately limited personal or political contact but remained friends.

Nucky still made headlines, even in his quieter years. The *Atlantic City Press* made it an annual ritual to send a reporter to interview Nucky at his home on January 20 (his birthday) after he was released from prison. Headlines each year confirmed Nucky's status: "Nucky Still Looks Dapper," "Still Robust …. Debonair," or "Chipper as Ever." One of Nucky's favorite reporters at the *Atlantic City Press* was Sonny Schwartz who often published glowing reports about Nucky.

Ever the night owl, Schwartz became friendly with Skinny D'Amato of the 500 Club, along with many of the celebrities who played in the Atlantic City clubs. Most of the older performers knew Nucky personally from the days when Nucky arranged his elaborate galas.

Local restaurants including Conrad's Colonial Steak House & Cocktail Lounge, the Knife & Fork Inn, and Pal's Cocktail Lounge, all within walking distance of his Elberon Avenue beachfront home, were just a few of Nucky and Floss's favorite places. The door to their own cottage was always open to friends who often appeared to regale each other with stories of their glory days in Atlantic City. Every so often, Floss and Nucky still enjoyed the spotlight and attended political functions near election time each year. Wherever they went, they were always greeted warmly, especially among the black organizations.

But Nucky couldn't help but notice that his name had been removed from the letterhead of many Republican clubs that he helped in founding; instead, Hap's name had been substituted. However, the organization leaders still greeted him with the respect due a political boss.

Life seemed to be on the upswing for Nucky but not for long. On July 21, 1948, John D'Agostino was killed in a car accident; he was 53. Nucky was devastated by the news. They had been friends and business partners for years through good times and bad, and their loyalty to each other never wavered. D'Agostino took care of Nucky, especially financially in his later years, at least while D'Agostino was still alive. Nucky was concerned that after D'Agostino's death, Johnny's brother and sister would take Floss off the payroll, but that didn't happen. Floss had settled in to her job and continued to generate more new business for the Renault Winery. On January 12, 1951, Nucky attended the installation of new officers for the Hap Farley Second Ward Republican Club and the auxiliary at the West Side Memorial Building. Many members were among his lifelong friends. The next day, the *Tribune*, published by the *Ventnor Town Crier,* printed a picture of Nucky with all the officers. Nucky was the only white face in the picture.

Periodically, Nucky's old prisonmate John H. Stoneburg contacted him, ostensibly to discuss publishing *The Boardwalk Empire*. However, Stoneburg's real reason of contacting Nucky was actually an appeal for financial help after he had been arrested again for passing worthless checks in fall 1952 in Washington, D.C. Under the circumstances, Nucky did not want to get involved with Stoneburg and told him so.

In spring 1952, Nucky was finally discharged from parole, which ended over 13 years of federal prosecution. He still faced the sizable IRS liability, and in order to avoid any collection action, he took his attorney Edward Feinberg's advice and took a pauper's oath declaring he had no assets. The oath did not affect any of Floss's assets that she held in her own name. Floss paid the usual household bills from her checking account, and Nucky continued his lifelong practice of paying cash for anything he wanted, usually with $100 bills, which he felt showed the public that he may be out of power, but he certainly wasn't out of cash.

One summer day in 1958, Nucky was enjoying a casual breakfast in his sun-filled parlor at his beach block home at 103 South Elberon Avenue in Atlantic City, when Jimmy Boyd stopped by to see him.

Boyd had just read the July 26 issue of *The Saturday Evening Post* that hit the newspaper stands. Actor David Niven was interviewed by a reporter named Dean Jennings who wrote an article called "I Learned to

Be a Playboy." The article detailed Niven's escapades after he served in the British Army Rifle Brigade during World War II and his early years as a Hollywood actor.

Apparently, Niven was involved with a group that called themselves "The American Pony Express Racing Association." Niven claimed that after Prohibition ended in 1933, he teamed up with the promoters Maurice "Lefty" Flynn and Douglas Hertz. Flynn was called Lefty from his days at Yale when he played football and kicked with his left foot. His other partner, Hertz, was the owner of the Pegasus Club, an indoor polo club in New York, and Damon Runyon, the sportswriter and New York columnist for the Hearst papers. Their scheme was to race polo ponies in small auditoriums around the country running counter-clockwise since the ponies could handle the short turns. Niven and his cronies hired Indians off the reservation and cowboys as the jockeys dressed in colorful costumes.

Niven claimed that opening night at the Atlantic City Auditorium was a sellout. Niven booked himself as "Captain Niven of the Royal Mounted Police" and carried an American flag as he galloped in on horseback during the opening Grand March of all the performers into the center ring.

The day after opening performance, Niven claimed Nucky and four other rough guys burst into his office in the Atlantic City Auditorium. Niven said Nucky told him he was taking over the beer and popcorn stands. The story also said that Nucky asked Niven for the names of the winners of four pony races in advance so he could feed this information to his bookies.

According to the article, Niven said he refused to go along with Nucky's demands, and within an hour, all the local licenses for the show were revoked, and trucks carted away all the beer, hot dogs, and other food. This broke the company and they went out of business after only one performance.

When Nucky finished reading the article, he was shell-shocked, calling the story "libelous" and said it was a "cheap shot that [Niven] waited 25 years to hit me with." Nucky knew *The Saturday Evening Post*, founded by Benjamin Franklin in 1728, had its signature all-American scenes painted by artist Norman Rockwell, which portrayed the publication as wholesome and trustworthy. Nucky knew he had to have the best legal help he could get, especially after his criminal trial in 1941. He intended to fight this "last campaign" with everything he had. He wanted to get the best lawyer who specialized in libel cases against high-profile national publications since he knew they would mount a vigorous defense and make it expensive to litigate his claim. Since libel litigation is a specialty, Nucky decided to consult Edward A. Costigan, one of the leading lawyers in New Jersey.

Nucky and Carmen D'Agostino met Costigan at his office at the Broad Street Bank Building in Trenton to discuss the merits of his claims and to agree on a fee arrangement for legal services. Costigan told Nucky that he had read the article and considered it libelous under New Jersey and Pennsylvania law. The complaint highlighted the facts in the article that portrayed Nucky as an extortionist, gunman, underworld boss, and bookie, and then the complaint quoted the exact language from *The Saturday Evening Post*.

Nucky liked the idea his complaint was filed in Atlantic County. He felt this gave him the home field advantage, and he would have a friendly judge and jury. However, truth is a complete defense to libel. If it is true, Nucky would be thrown out of court and would owe Costigan a substantial legal fee. But if Niven produced witnesses to say that he tried to shake them down, it would be front-page fodder in every newspaper on the East Coast.

Nucky's spirits fell when Curtis Circulation Co. had the case moved to the federal court in Camden, based on diversity of citizenship and the amount of the claim met the federal jurisdiction exceeding $10,000. But Nucky's friends and colleagues stepped in to help.

Boyd called Nucky the next day to tell him that a former state trooper and a retired Atlantic City detective were digging into the facts of the Niven story and were going to get the records of the show and background of everyone involved with the American Pony Express Racing Association. The work was all pro bono to pay Nucky back for all his past favors.

Costigan said Dean Jennings, the reporter who interviewed David Niven and wrote this article for *The Saturday Evening Post,* never contacted Nucky to verify the facts, which is a basic violation of impartial reporting. Juries penalize reporters who are unfair and don't want to hear both sides. Since this was a civil case, Costigan was entitled to take the depositions of Jennings and Niven, who would have to testify under oath to establish the truthfulness of their charges.

A judgment against Niven would be hard to collect the way he bounced around Europe, according to Costigan. In his experience, an apology was worthless since people believe what they want to believe. But Costigan was out for a sizable settlement, and the litigation began with a complaint in the Superior Court of New Jersey in Atlantic County for $1 million in damages against Curtis Circulation Co., a Delaware corporation that circulates *The Saturday Evening Post* nationally and internationally.

CHAPTER 19

THE LAST CAMPAIGN

A t 75, Nucky was sure that David Niven must have thought he was dead or too decrepit to take him on in the courts. Nucky remembered *The Saturday Evening Post* blasted him back on August 26, 1939, when he was first indicted by the government. The magazine tied him into Frank Hague's problems in North Jersey and printed the picture of Nucky with Al Capone walking down the Boardwalk.

As for Niven, he appeared in a number of significant Hollywood films in the 1930s including *The Charge of the Light Brigade* with Errol Flynn in 1936, *The Prisoner of Zenda* in 1937, and his first major role in 1938 in *The Dawn Patrol, Wuthering Heights* in 1939, and *Separate Tables* with Deborah Kerr in 1958, a role that earned him an Academy Award for best actor.

After 1949, Niven formed a television company with Dick Powell, Charles Boyer, and Ida Lupino, appropriately called Four Star Productions. Niven chose dramatic roles, becoming one of television's first and most prolific stars. In the 1950s, he starred in the controversial, *The Moon Is Blue* followed by the mammoth *Around the World in 80 Days*. His appeal was legendary as an impeccably dressed gentleman with a slight British accent; he also became one of the most highly paid actors in Hollywood.

At first, Nucky was concerned since the case would be tried in the same federal court in Camden where he was convicted in 1941. However, times had changed. The trial judge was Thomas M. Madden, a former assistant U.S. attorney and a staunch Democrat appointed to the federal bench by President Harry S. Truman, a lifelong Pendergast-machine

Democrat. These two credentials would have normally upset Nucky but not this time.

Madden's close friend was Angelo D. Malandra, a Democratic leader in Camden County, a noted criminal lawyer and godfather of one of Madden's children. His law office at 509 Market Street in Camden was just a few blocks from the federal courthouse at Fourth and Market streets. Malandra was also a close friend of Skinny D'Amato, the operator of the 500 Club in Atlantic City and godfather to Skinny's son, Angelo, who was named after Malandra. D'Amato, who grew up in Atlantic City, was involved in gambling in one form or another all his life with Nucky's blessing. Nucky felt that if he needed a favor from Skinny, he would be glad to make the necessary contacts.

At a conference with Costigan, Nucky started to describe a possible connection to the judge, if needed. Costigan quickly interrupted and asked that he be kept out of Nucky's political world so he could focus on the law, which he was firmly convinced was on Nucky's side. The less Nucky said about his connections, the better for Costigan. Since rumors spread quickly in Atlantic City, he didn't want to have Nucky's legitimate claim damaged by a federal probe of the relationship between the judge and Nucky. Of course, Nucky agreed.

Nucky was not used to answering to anyone throughout his life, even in prison, but Costigan was different. He had read the transcript of Nucky's testimony in his criminal case and realized that Nucky was always anticipating the next question instead of focusing on the question at hand, which weakened his credibility. He pointed out that Nucky was also trying to analyze the person who asked the question as he did with people throughout his life. He had to be convinced that the attorney for *The Saturday Evening Post* was a professional, that there was nothing personal, and that his case was just another file in his office. After a week of grueling preparation for the depositions, Nucky finally understood what he was in for, but he didn't like the ground rules.

On September 2, 1959, Nucky started his deposition began in the law offices of Starr, Summerill and Davis in Camden. Attorney Wilbur H. Haines asked Nucky questions on behalf of David Niven, the defendant, and Costigan sent James J. Armstrong, his office associate, to protect Nucky's interests.

Q: *Would you state your full name?*
A: *Enoch L. Johnson.*
Q: *Are you the plaintiff against Curtis Circulation Company and Curtis Publishing Company who circulate and distribute The Saturday Evening Post?*
A: *Yes.*
Q: *Where do you live?*
A: *103 South Elberon Avenue, Atlantic City, for the past 14 years.*
Q: *What is your occupation?*
A: *I am promotional salesman for A. P. Miller, Inc., who are general contractors, for the past 14 years.*

Haines then began focusing on the article that appeared in *The Saturday Evening Post*, attempting to show it was true. And even if it were not true, he tried to show how Nucky did not suffer any financial damages. Nucky testified he had never personally seen or met Niven. In fact, he had never heard of him until four years ago but may have seen him on television once. Nucky also said he had never heard of American Pony Express Racing Association until he read about it in *The Saturday Evening Post*.

Haines wanted to know what Nucky claimed was libelous in the article. *"Well, I object to Niven asserting that I came to see him in the morning at the Convention Hall office with four other men and tried to stick him up for an interest in some popcorn...and that I wanted to put some bookmakers in the auditorium...and that my pockets were bulging and that I carried a gun."* Nucky added that the entire article was ridiculous.

Haines continued the following questioning:

Q: *Well, I refer you to the third paragraph where Niven says: "I looked up to see a group of five men who walked into my office without knocking. Four of them had hats pulled down over their eyes and wore long tight overcoats which had bulged in the wrong places. The fifth introduced himself as Mr. Nucky Johnson, whom I knew to be the underworld boss of Atlantic City."*
Q: *Now the article doesn't say that your pockets bulged, does it?*

A: *It certainly intimates that I was associated with someone that does.*

Q: *What else are you complaining about in the article?*

A: *The local Atlantic City Press featured me in the advertisements to sell The Saturday Evening Post several weeks before it was published.*

Q: *In your complaint, Mr. Johnson, you stated the article caused you to be held up to ridicule, scorn and wrath as a result of the publication and that your name, character and reputation has been damaged.*

A: *Damn right!*

Q: *Tell us how the article affected you.*

A: *I was humiliated on several occasions, along with my wife. I had numerous telephone calls and anonymous letters that were very nasty. There was a decrease in my regular invitations. The colored Elks Club stopped calling me to come to their installations and events. I have been an honorary member for a half century.*

Q: *Did any member of the colored Elks say anything to you about The Saturday Evening Post article?*

A: *Yes. Margaret Creswell—she is a longtime police officer in Atlantic City and a good friend. She is an Associate Directress or similar title with the Elks.*

Q: *What did Margaret Creswell say to you about the article?*

A: *It was terrible! You should sue them—they know nothing about the way you treat everyone.*

Q: *Who else spoke to you about the article?*

A: *General Daniel DeBrier—he is a prominent lawyer in Atlantic City—he also said I should sue the magazine—the article was disgraceful and that I was the one responsible for having the Convention Hall built and I would have been the last one to damage the reputation of the Hall.*

Haines then asked about Nucky's position with the county, where he served as county treasurer from 1911 to 1941, and his political position as secretary of the Atlantic County Republican Committee. Nucky also mentioned that he was Atlantic County sheriff in 1911 and clerk of the

Supreme Court for five years. He was then examined about his conviction in 1941 and his eventual release from prison in 1945.

Haines began asking Nucky about the sources of the monies he received in his criminal conviction for income tax evasion in 1941, as well as his relationship with Judge Corio, rumrunning, and bootlegging. Haines concluded his examination, and then Armstrong asked Nucky some questions for explanatory and procedural reasons. He wanted Nucky to be more specific as to how the article offended and libeled him. He also wanted to have a complete record of his client's testimony for the case in the event he should die before the trial. That way, the transcript could be introduced to keep his claim alive for his wife. He was also well aware that *The Saturday Evening Post* wanted to drag out the case to discourage Nucky financially.

Armstrong started by asking Nucky if he was offended by the reference in the article about him looking like Dracula.

"Surely," said Nucky, "that's a terrible comment to make about anyone."

Q: *Did you and Mr. Costigan conduct an investigation?*

A: *Yes.*

Q: *In the article of The Saturday Evening Post it states the opening night was a sellout [the first performance of Captain Niven of the Royal Mounted Police]—what did your investigation disclose?*

A: *An absolute lie—the total income was $600.00 and they had over 10,000 seats set up.*

Q: *Did the event last more than one night?*

A: *It lasted four nights and the total receipts for all four nights was less than a thousand dollars.*

Q: *The article mentions you were in the Convention Hall office in the morning, is that correct?*

A: *No! I don't get up until late in the afternoon and around that time I may have been in Newark working a gubernatorial campaign.*

Q: *Did you check to see if they had a license?*

A: *Yes—they never had a license.*

Q: *What does you investigation disclose why they closed?*

A: *The Society for Prevention of Cruelty to Animals, S.P.C.A.,* went after them after they received many complaints. The American Pony Express left town owing a lot of bills.

Q: What is the difference in your social life as a result of this article in The Saturday Evening Post?

A: There was a lack of social invitations, speaking requests, some people stopped coming by my home to see me—this was very hurtful.

Q: Prior to the article, how many people would stop by your house?

A: Probably an average of 25 to 30 each week.

Q: After the article came out, how many came to see you?

A: Very few—except some personal lifelong friends who would always come by.

Q: How did it affect your relationship with your wife?

A: She would become upset very easily—affected her job—she was a salesperson for Renault Winery. Some places refused to see her or talk to her—her orders dropped off.

Q: How else did this article affect your social activities?

A: I was always invited personally by Mary Roebling to a very lovely event she had each year in Atlantic City—this stopped.

Q: For the record, who is Mary Roebling?

A: She was the first woman to be Chairman of an American bank—the Trenton Trust Company in 1937—that later merged and became the National State Bank in Elizabeth, New Jersey. She was a staunch Republican—always supported the Republican ticket. She gave great parties. She used to come to my parties at the Ritz. A few years ago in 1955, the journalist Edward R. Murrow interviewed her at her home for his popular national television show, 'Person to Person' in which he interviewed celebrities.

Q: Have you applied to the United States Pardon Attorney for a pardon of your criminal conviction in 1941?

A: Yes, I applied several years ago and it was denied. I applied again, shortly before the article came out, and it looked like it was going to be approved until The Post article hit the newsstands.

Nucky had learned the FBI had conducted a background investigation of him and had contacted all his past neighbors at 43 South Annapolis Avenue, where he lived for the first year after his release from prison. This is a standard procedure for every pardon application. The FBI also spoke to all his neighbors surrounding his home at 103 South Elberon Avenue and many past and present political figures. Members of the Atlantic County judiciary interviewed included Judges George Naame, Leon Leonard, and Vincent Haneman. Judge Albert McGee, an active Democrat, a past state president of the N.J. Bar Association, and a former U.S. commissioner, told the FBI the same thing all the other persons said, "Nucky was a model citizen and urged his pardon be granted."

The only unfavorable information uncovered was the fact that Nucky had filed a lawsuit for libel against the Curtis Circulation Company for the distribution of the July 26, 1958 publication of *The Saturday Evening Post*. The alleged events contained in the article occurred in 1933—25 years ago and before Nucky went to prison in 1941, but they nevertheless were fresh in the public's mind. Of course, this dampened Nucky's chances for the U.S. Pardon Attorney to recommend to U.S. President Dwight D. Eisenhower that Nucky be pardoned. His pardon was never granted.

Nucky's attorney continued to ask him questions to show there was malice in the reckless manner the article was researched by not attempting to corroborate the facts from other sources, particularly about Nucky. His lawyer was pushing the case through the judicial system and because of his procedural skills, he was able to have Niven answer interrogatories under oath before Sidney E. Paulson, vice consul of the U.S. in Rome, Italy, where Niven was then living. The deposition took place on June 21, 1961 at the American Embassy.

Costigan flew to Italy and attended the deposition to cross-examine the actor since this would be his only opportunity to show the recklessness of Niven's statements. The questioning began as Costigan gathered the basic background information about Niven and his contact with reporter Dean Jennings, who wrote the story for *The Saturday Evening Post*.

Niven admitted that he had a series of interviews with the reporter, and he was given a final draft for him to review before it was sent for publication. The witness stated he was secretary and treasurer of the American Pony Express Racing Association for the purpose of having indoor races in large auditoriums with the first preference at the Atlantic City Auditorium on the Boardwalk. He claimed the opening night was a big hit with a large audience in the auditorium.

Niven testified, *"The next morning in the little office, three or four men walked in and the leader plunked himself down in front of the desk. The others took up positions around the room. Naturally, after 25 years, I do not remember the exact words, but they said to the effect, 'The show is great and this is what we will do. We will take over things like peanuts, bottled drinks, popcorn. We will want to know the results of four out of the six horse races the night before they go off.' I asked him who he was and he said, 'Nucky Johnson.'"*

Niven said that he had heard about Nucky from many New Yorkers who said he was the boss of Atlantic City and controlled every racket that one could think of. He referred to Nucky as an extortionist who controlled all brothels in the city, claiming that the information came from Damon Runyan, the sports reporter and Maurice 'Lefty' Flynn, the president of the association. He had been associated with Jack Kindler and Charles Burns and their 21 Brands Liquor Company, but before that, they had run the famous speakeasy Jack and Charlie's. Many of their old contacts went into legitimate businesses and they all knew about Nucky Johnson in Atlantic City.

Q: *What happened to your Atlantic City venture after your visit from Nucky Johnson?*

A: *It folded after one week, on two or three occasions the lights went out, large number of our bridles or saddles were stolen— word went around that people at the box office were recommending customers to stay away.*

Q: *Did you believe that the man who identified himself as Nucky Johnson was in fact Nucky Johnson?*

A: *No.*

Q: *Did you subsequently change your mind?*

A: *Yes.*

Q: *What made you change your mind?*

A: *My description of the man prompted anyone to whom I told the story to tell me that I made a hideous mistake and that in their opinion, he was indeed Nucky Johnson.*

Q: *Where did Dean Jennings conduct these interviews with you?*

A: *My house in Pacific Palisades in California.*

Q: *When you were given the manuscript of your story to review did you make any changes?*

A: *I made a charming reference to myself and the Duke of Edinburgh and a reference to my first wife, Primula Rollo Niven, who had died accidentally. It was very tragic. We were at my friend, Tyrone Power's house, playing a game of hide and seek. My wife opened a door to the basement to hide, thinking it was a closet. She fell down the stairs and was fatally injured. She died the following day from her injuries.*

Q: *Mr. Niven, when did you take up residence in Switzerland?*

A: *February 29, 1960.*

Q: *Where did you live during the period from March 1, 1958 to approximately July 1, 1958?*

A: *I think it was the time my wife and me took a trip around the world. I believe I even did a film in Europe. One picture I made in 1958 was Ask Any Girl with Shirley MacLaine—No, I did two pictures in 1958—the other was Separate Tables. I received an Academy Award for that picture.*

Q: *Did you give final approval to publish the article involving Nucky Johnson?*

A: *Yes.*

Q: *Did The Saturday Evening Post or Curtis make any independent investigation of the facts you reported about Nucky Johnson?*

A: *I do not know.*

Q: *Mr. Niven, is it not true that the Atlantic City show, in theatrical terminology, was truly a flop?*

A: *If you are referring to the end result, you could not be more right.*

Q: *One last question. Did you know at the time you and Dean Jennings wrote this article in 1958 whether my client, Enoch L. Johnson, was alive?*

A: *I never gave it a thought.*

Niven was then required to sign the transcript of his testimony since it would be introduced at the time of trial in the United States if he were not available. Costigan was quite optimistic after listening to Niven's testimony and the casual manner he accepted rumors as fact. Niven also had no living witness to establish his defense of truth, and he could never positively identify Nucky as the person, if there was one, in his office at the auditorium. Costigan was now ready to talk about a settlement.

Extensive negotiations continued between the attorneys to settle the case. Initially, *The Saturday Evening Post* felt Nucky's conviction and the sordid background that led to the guilty verdict would minimize any recovery before the jury, but Nucky's attorney obtained a preliminary ruling from the court that the conviction for income tax evasion would be allowed to be told to the jury, but none of the underlying facts would be allowed to be brought to their attention.

With that news, the negotiations quickly changed from denial of liability to the amount of damages that *The Saturday Evening Post* would have to pay to minimize its $1 million possible judgment before a sympathetic jury at trial. Nucky then stepped into the impasse in a meeting with Costigan. Nucky didn't want an apology if he could get enough money. But getting a sizable settlement might awaken the IRS to any outstanding liabilities or the government for that $20,000 fine Maris imposed in 1941.

He decided the best deal would be to split the difference on our claim, even take less if necessary, with Nucky's cut going to Floss so the government couldn't touch it. He wanted to dismiss the case without any paperwork and make arrangements to give the lump sum to Floss. In turn, she would pay one-third of the fee for the legal costs. Costigan said that *The Saturday Evening Post* also didn't want to disclose the amount paid since it could trigger other lawsuits.

On December 19, 1961, Federal Judge Arthur S. Lane in the U.S. Federal Court in Camden signed an order of dismissal, with no mention of the amount of the settlement. But in 1965, Nucky received letters from the U.S. Attorney's Office in Camden, asking him to pay the $20,000 fine stemming from his 1941 conviction for tax evasion. Nucky was convinced that some past political enemy was seeking a finder's fee and reported to the IRS that he settled his libel case with *The Saturday*

Evening Post and Niven for a substantial sum, and this alerted the U.S. Attorney's Office to initiate a collection action to collect the $20,000 fine after his case was dormant for 20 years.

He also did not rule out the possibility that Lyndon B. Johnson, a Democrat who was elected president in 1964, could have triggered collection efforts in all federal agencies to raise money for his social programs. Throughout his life, Nucky always believed when Democrats were in charge, it usually meant trouble for him. Nucky decided to call Frank S. "Hap" Farley, who was the influential Republican leader in New Jersey and senator from Atlantic County.

By then, Nucky and Floss had moved to 20 South Marion Avenue in Ventnor, about a mile from Elberon Avenue. Hap told Nucky that he would be sending me as his law associate. I had just served almost four years with the U.S. Attorney's Office in Camden and was familiar with the government collection practice. The next day, I met Nucky and Floss at their apartment for a meeting that lasted several hours. Nucky had an excellent memory and surprised me about how much he knew about my family, especially my father, Graham Ferry, who was a Republican supporter all of his life.

Nucky told me that he had taken a pauper's oath in early 1952 at the urging of his local attorney, Edward Feinberg, since he said he was being harassed by the IRS and this calmed their collection efforts for 10 years. When Nucky asked what could be done to stop the government dragging him back to federal court, I replied, "The 'Pauper's Oath' should have been sufficient to close the file, but your application for a Presidential Pardon awakened the government there may have been some assets available to satisfy the $20,000 fine, plus the court costs from the criminal case that could easily be over $100,000."

Since Nucky had no assets in his name and his health wasn't good, I wanted to get a letter from Nucky's doctor highlighting his medical problems and a current financial statement. I told Nucky the fine would expire upon his death and the government could not try to collect from his estate.

Hap asked me if I had ever met Nucky before our first business meeting at his Marion Avenue home in 1964. I replied that I hadn't officially met him, but I did see him for the first time early in the 1950s. It was in the Cotton Club on North Illinois Avenue, when I was with two of my lifeguard buddies, John Daley and Art Brown. We were listening to the live music when suddenly the house lights went on and the entire place became dead silent. A large man strolled in wearing a long, black full-length coat with a red carnation in the lapel. He had a beautiful sepia showgirl on each arm. The audience immediately recognized him and people began standing, smiling and chanting, "Nucky, Nucky!"

When the band started a drum roll, Nucky was escorted to a table at the front where he enjoyed the show the rest of the evening. It was as though a rock star had just entered the club. A steady stream of people were going over to his table and shaking his hand.

"That's Nucky," said Hap. "He lights up a room. The black people love him; do what you can to help him."

When Hap asked how the meeting went with Nucky and Floss, I said I could readily see why Nucky was so popular for more than 33 years: He has a magnetic personality and is so appreciative of anything you do for him. He makes you feel important, when in reality, he is the important one.

But in those days, Nucky was battling myriad health issues. His physician submitted a medical report to me outlining Nucky's medical conditions: He had been under constant care for chronic arteriosclerotic cardiovascular disease and lymphatic leukemia. I sent the medical records to U.S. Attorney David Satz, who I knew from my government service and who came to my departure ceremony when I left the Department of Justice on October 6, 1961. Satz told me that Nucky was a high-profile case, which is the reason he was personally handling the file. After a number of telephone conversations, I gave Nucky the good news that the government finally agreed to close its collection file. Nucky didn't have to pay a penny. Nucky and Floss were overjoyed.

Floss continued to work at Renault and was always on the job. As part of her public relations duties, Floss encouraged the Renault to enter a float each year in the Miss America Boardwalk Parade. It was good exposure for the winery since the parade was viewed by thousands who lined the Atlantic City Boardwalk during the day to see the present and future Miss America. In the pre-television days, the Miss America Boardwalk Parade and beauty pageant was often highlighted in the Fox Movietone News, which aired just before the evening's main feature. Clips of

Marilyn Monroe as the Grand Marshal in 1952 can still be viewed as part of vintage documentaries of the time.

In 1961, Floss's initiative paid off. Renault's float was awarded the Grand Sweepstakes Award for the best float in the Boardwalk parade. On the opening night of the Miss America Pageant and in front of a large audience, Floss stepped on center stage of the mammoth convention hall in Atlantic City to accept the award on behalf of Renault Winery from local resort hotelman Mike Fiore.

Nucky sat in the audience and watched Floss walk across the largest stage in the world, a hall he helped build more than 30 years ago. He was justly proud of Floss and the legacy he left Atlantic City. Fiore was a personal friend of Nucky's and operator of the Penn Atlantic Hotel, home to the Riptide Room where Nucky and Floss often dined.

Nucky continued to support the community whenever and wherever he could. He attracted attention to the local chapter of the national lampoon society called the Circus Saints & Sinners Club. The club, which started in 1929 as a way to help elderly circus performers, raised funds for many worthwhile charities in later years. The Fall Guy Show, which was the club's annual fundraiser, showcased Nucky in early 1965, as the fall guy under the George A. Hamid Tent of the South Jersey Chapter of the Circus Saints & Sinners Club. The organizers began gathering anecdotes about Nucky from longtime Atlantic City residents highlighting his ledgendary generosity.

On December 5, 1965, nearly 500 members and guests from all over the East Coast crowded the showroom at the 500 Club to roast Nucky. Reporter Sonny Schwartz was on hand to cover the event for the *Atlantic City Press*.

Nucky sat at a table with his wife and 500 Club owner Skinny D'Amato. All evening, people stopped at Nucky's table to thank him for a favor he did for them years ago or just to wish him good health.

Many local officials in public office attended, including Hap, Senator John E. Hunt of Glouster County, and Atlantic County Sheriff Gerard Gormley, who touted Nucky's benevolence to those in need during his 30 years at the helm of the Republican Party.

The three-scene Fall Guy Production, directed by Pat Mussarra, featured parodies of Nucky in the Roaring Twenties with bathtub gin flowing, rumrunners landing on the Atlantic City beaches and in the back bay docking at Rum Point Harbor, gamblers, flappers, raccoon coats, silk stockings, and Nucky's coal fund for the needy.

One scene featured Nucky's father who had the distinction of being the last sheriff in Atlantic County to hang a prisoner in September 1907. Although the re-enactment was supposed to be humorous, the scene depicting the hanging of Joe Labriola brought back too many unpleasant memories for Nucky, including when he read the condemned man's final letters professing his innocence.

After the performance, Judge Raymond S. Stark presented Nucky with a life membership card in the Circus Saints & Sinners, a diamond pin and an engraved clown statute, which every awardee customarily receives.

At 82, Nucky stood in front of the audience and spoke in his signature gravelly voice, expressing his deep gratitude for the award. He received a standing ovation. Smiling and misty-eyed, Nucky gratefully acknowledged the applause and appreciation that had been absent from his life for the past 25 years.

Nucky's health continued to decline, and Floss knew she could not physically take care of him at home for much longer. In early July 1968, Nucky fell getting out of bed and fractured his hip. He was admitted to the Atlantic City Hospital where he was told surgery was necessary. When Nucky was discharged from the hospital, Floss called Marie Boyd and said Nucky wanted to go to the county nursing home.

Hap made the arrangements, and the county sent an ambulance the next day and transferred Nucky to the Atlantic County Nursing Home at Dolphin Avenue in Northfield, New Jersey, several miles outside of Atlantic City.

The staff at the nursing home welcomed Nucky. Many of the employees did not know Nucky personally, but most of them felt that they knew him because his reputation for fair treatment of county employees was legendary during his 30 years as Atlantic County Treasurer and Republican leader. Some of the personnel were second-generation employees, and their parents were always singing Nucky's praises.

Once Nucky settled into his new private living quarters, he wanted to bring his walnut roll-top desk to his room. He said he had work to do and his desk put him in the mood to write. Jimmy Boyd had the desk delivered the next day, and Nucky started sending out brief letters on Renault Winery stationery to his many friends to let them know where he was if they wanted to stop by to say hello.

Floss stayed with Nucky every day from morning until visiting hours ended in the evening. Marie Boyd not only visited every five days, but she brought with her specially cooked meals from one of Nucky's favorite restaurants. One day when she arrived at Nucky's room, Floss and Nucky had a gift for her in appreciation for all her help. It was the gold locket that Nucky had given to his first wife Mabel and then to Floss. Marie was touched by Nucky's generosity, especially since it was a gift to Mabel, the love of his life.

Nucky's friends visited him at the nursing home to cheer him up. With Nucky's dire medical problems, friends knew that each visit might be their last. Nucky was often in a very reflective mood. He had made arrangements to care for Floss financially, and all his daily needs were provided by Atlantic County at the nursing home. He had time to reflect on his life as each visitor brought back cherished memories of the times he spent with each of them.

When Marie Boyd visited one day, she asked Nucky if he ever heard from Walter G. Winne. Nucky said Winne contacted him at least once a year. Since the trial, Winne had become president of the Bergen County Bar Association in 1947 and prosecutor for Bergen County for six years.

"Walter felt very disappointed in himself," said Nucky. "He admitted to me after I got ten years in prison that he hadn't actually tried a case for over four years and quickly realized in the middle of the trial that he made some serious procedural errors—the most devastating one was having me testify."

It turned out that Winne was later indicted for not enforcing the gambling laws during the time he served as Bergen County prosecutor. But the decision was reversed on appeal and after a long trial, Winne was found not guilty on sixteen counts.

Then Marie asked about Governor Harold Hoffman. His election was the first time in 27 years that the Democrats had lost the governorship. Jersey City Mayor Frank Hague helped Hoffman push through the first state sales tax to help people who were still suffering from the effects of the Depression.

When Hoffman left the governorship, he went into the Army and came out a full colonel and worked with the N.J. Division of Employment Security to become the first director. Unfortunately, Governor Robert B. Meyner suspended Hoffman, after it turned out he had embezzled $300,000 from the South Amboy Trust Company where he was an officer. He died of a heart attack in 1954 in New York City before any criminal charges were filed.

But looking back over all the people Nucky helped, he said the most upsetting was Walter E. Edge. Nucky said he read the self-serving book Edge wrote in 1948 called *A Jerseyman's Journal*, which is Edge's life story and how he navigated the landmines of the political world by his own ingenuity. Nucky's name was never mentioned in the text. He even checked the index in the back to make sure. Shortly after the book was published, Nucky bumped into Edge on the Ventnor Boardwalk. He told Edge that he could have changed his entire life if he told the government that Edge gave him bundles of cash to get elected that were well over the limit. Edge's book should have been renamed The *Jerseyman's Journey to the Pen*. With that, Edge turned his back on Nucky and walked down the Boardwalk to his home on Oxford Avenue. They never spoke again.

In the fall of 1968, Nucky, now 85 years old, slept constantly and his physical condition continued to deteriorate. Floss had accepted the reality that her beloved Nucky would not be with her for much longer, maybe only days. She wanted to talk to him about the past.

"We had a great life together and I want you to know that every day has been better than yesterday," said Floss, "and I look forward to each tomorrow."

Nucky said he had so many pleasant memories that very few people have ever experienced, which was pretty good for a Piney. He knew he wouldn't be around much longer and asked her to make funeral arrangements with Sheriff Gormley, who operated a funeral home in Atlantic City with his brother, Ray.

On December 10, 1968, Dr. Arthur Lee, the Atlantic County assistant medical director, announced to the press that Enoch L. "Nucky" Johnson died at 7:40 PM on Monday, December 9, 1968. He had been a patient at the home since July 31, 1968.

Nucky's last words to Floss on Monday night were: "I love you, baby."

The announcement of Nucky's death was reported in all the major newspapers on the East Coast. The Associated Press had already prepared a biographical release that they sent to all their affiliated editors for immediate release upon confirmation of Nucky's death, along with stories about his life and his legendary generosity throughout the community. When the *Atlantic City Press* asked Atlantic City Mayor Richard "Dick" S. Jackson to comment on Nucky's death, he said:

"He represented an exciting period for Atlantic City for 30 years and upon his death that excitement is gone forever. I considered him a friend—he gave me my first job—he was responsible for my appointment to the Atlantic City Fire Department."

Former Mayor Joseph Altman told the *Atlantic City Press* that Nucky gave him his start in politics. "He started me as a Journal Clerk in the New Jersey Assembly," he said. "He helped me all my life. I became an Assemblyman, Atlantic County Prosecutor and finally, Mayor of Atlantic City for 23 years. Nucky had his Broadway friend, Earl Carroll, bring musical stage shows to Atlantic City. This added luster to the Resort. He was an imposing figure of a man—you would look around twice to see him. I always marvel how he was able to have the Auditorium built, the largest in the world, for a little city on a tiny island, during the Great Depression of 1929—that takes enormous financial courage and political muscle."

When Hap was asked about Nucky, he said, "He was very good to many members of my family. He had a great political mind. Very generous to many people—there were no state or federal welfare programs during Nucky's time—but Nucky always extended a helping hand."

When Floss called Gormley to make the funeral arrangements, the sheriff told her that Nucky finalized all the details this past summer. He assured her that everything was organized and already paid since Nucky didn't want Floss to worry.

Many public officials, past and present, began to call Gormley and Floss to be honorary pallbearers. Floss finally selected the ones she thought Nucky would like: Hap, Congressman Charles W. Sandman, Atlantic City Mayor Richard S. Jackson, and Atlantic City Commissioners Meredith P. Kerstetter, Karlos LaSane, Arthur W. Ponzio, and William Somers. Also included were former Atlantic City Mayor

Joseph Altman, Mayor Leon Leopardi of Longport Borough, Margate Mayor Martin Bloom, Somers Point Mayor George Roberts, Assemblymen Albert Smith and Samuel Curcio, Atlantic County Clerk Richard Blair, Sheriff Gerard L. Gormley, James "Mickey" McCullough, Dr. James Mason, Anthony Miller, Sr., Joseph P. McBeth, Carmen D'Agostino, Hugh McGinty, Captain Clarence W. Starn, John R. Siracusa, Paul "Skinny" D'Amato, Walter Ullrich and Roger Plager, his publicist.

Gormley told Floss that he had gone to the cemetery with Nucky many times and noted that Nucky was very respectful in remembering his parents and his first wife, Mabel. He called it a peaceful place for him. He knew many people who were buried there and used to say, "I sure lost a lot of good loyal Republican voters!"

The funeral was set for 2:00 PM Friday, December 13, 1968 at the Gormley funeral home in Atlantic City, with the Reverend H.S. Detweiler of the Calvary Methodist Church presiding at the personal request of Nucky. Final internment was in the family mausoleum at the Zion Cemetery in Bargaintown where Nucky had a place reserved for Floss, too.

The name Johnson-Shimp appears over the bronze doors, the resting place for Nucky's father, Smith and Nucky's mother, Virginia; Nucky's first wife, Mabel; and Ida Shimp Golden, Mabel's stepmother.

Though the viewing began at 7:00 PM Thursday at the funeral home, Hap was the first to arrive at 6:30 PM to pay his respects to Floss. It was the senator's practice to come early to every funeral service so he had uninterrupted time to talk to family members.

I went to the viewing with my mother Louise A. (Kirby) Ferry, and by 7:00 PM the line had already begun to form. Hundreds came by to say farewell as they passed the flower-banked bier of the one-time Atlantic County political boss for 30 years. Renault Winery sent a large floral spray arrangement in the shape of a champagne bottle, which was placed above the casket. Corney Bell of the Atlantic City Police Department took a picture of Nucky wearing a suit and signature red carnation in his casket.

For several hours, I watched the people from all walks of life, not only from Atlantic County but other parts of New Jersey, waited their turn to pay their final respects to Floss for the good times and memories they had with Nucky.

At 2:00 PM on Friday, December 13, 1968, the final service was held at the Gormley Funeral Home. The cortege then proceeded slowly across the meadows to Bargaintown to the Zion Cemetery for entombment. The Atlantic City Police Department Motorcycle elite squad escorted the procession, blocking all intersections so the procession could proceed interrupted.

Red carnations, Nucky's favorite flower and trademark boutonnière, were placed on his bronze casket before it was placed in the vault in the family mausoleum.

Marie Boyd remained by Floss's side at the viewing and all day. When they were returning to Floss's home in the chauffeur-driven limousine, Floss confided in Marie. "I wanted to tell you what happened at the viewing the other night, but you have to promise not to tell anyone."

Floss explained that while she was in the receiving line, a man introduced himself as William Kramer, the clerk in the federal court in Camden. He used to talk to Nucky when there was a recess in Nucky's trial in 1941. Kramer's office was directly across the hall from the courtroom. He said everyone in the clerk's office was hoping the jury would find him not guilty.

"Mr. Kramer then told me that several weeks ago, he was taking an inventory of the exhibits in the evidence vault in the clerk's office and came across a black briefcase that had Nucky's name on it," said Floss. He said he opened it and the only thing inside was some newspapers from 1941 that highlighted his trial and an old red brick. He remembered that Nucky had been looking for his briefcase at the end of his trial, and nobody could find it. It was accidentally placed in the evidence vault in the clerk's office."

Floss said that Kramer saw Nucky's obituary in the newspaper and decided to pay his respects. And he brought along Nucky's briefcase to give to Floss. Marie waited for Floss to continue.

"When I said my final goodbye before the casket was closed," said Floss, "I put the Irish brick next to his right hand so he could feel it. I now know he is resting in peace and in a good place for all eternity."

CHAPTER 20

EPILOGUE:
LIFE AFTER NUCKY

For those who casually stroll along the world-famous Boardwalk today, Atlantic City is a vibrant shore community. The city today reflects a legacy of the political power brokers who created it, built it, and kept it flourishing through the tough times in American history, the Great Depression, Prohibition, two World Wars, the Korean, Viet Nam, Desert Storm, Iraq and Afghan Wars.

Over the year, the city and its residents endured many changes. In 1910, Atlantic City's population was growing rapidly and reached 46,150 residents. The permanent population peaked at 64,094 in 1940 when Nucky was at the height of his power. Then, World War II dramatically changed Atlantic City from a thriving resort to a military base: Camp Boardwalk, and by 1978, casino gambling brought new life to the resort but not year-round residents. The population dropped to 35,000 in 2009, while at the same time the city welcomed more than 30 million tourists anxious to gamble.

By far, the one individual who gave Atlantic City pizzazz, fame, and it legacy of excitement was Nucky Johnson. His Atlantic City attracted the best and worst, but through his dynamic leadership and vision, the city prospered and the residents rejoiced.

The dynamic growth of Atlantic City came from the Republican Party through the stewardship of four visionary Republican political leaders: William Moore, John J. Gardner, Commodore Louis Kuehnle, and Enoch L. "Nucky" Johnson.

Moore, a product of Mays Landing, New Jersey, was one of the founders of the national Republican Party in Philadelphia in 1856, when Abraham Lincoln lost the Republican nomination for President of the United States. Moore had a long successful political and business career in Atlantic County. In fact, he served 41 years in public office as a judge, director of the Atlantic County Board of Freeholders, U.S. Congressman, and State Senator. He built a mansion on Sugar Hill, overlooking the Great Egg Harbor River, in Mays Landing, where he directed his ship-building, coastal trade enterprises, and disbursed political patronage to party members.

Moore, who died in 1878, passed the political baton to Gardner who served in public office in South Jersey for 46 years. When he returned from the Civil War in 1865, Gardner was elected in 1868 as mayor of Atlantic City, at age 23, (the youngest ever), then Atlantic County coroner in 1878, and five terms as State Senator. While serving in the Senate, he was chosen as chairman of a committee to investigate election fraud in Hudson County. As a result, a number of ballot-box stuffers were sent to prison. North Jersey returned the favor, and Atlantic County became the target of vote fraud near the end of Gardner's political career in 1910. As a U.S. Congressman for 12 years until 1912, he was described as a "political czar" of the Second New Jersey Congressional District in his obituary; Gardner died in 1921.

Gardner's successor was Commodore Louis Kuehnle, who dispensed patronage out of his family-owned Kuehnle Hotel saloon called "The Corner" in Atlantic City. He pioneered the development of Atlantic City with his numerous investments in a brewing company, a telephone company, a heating plant, building the Boardwalk, drilled the first artesian well and building homes. He was convicted of personally benefiting from a public contract while serving as a municipal official and went to Trenton State Prison in 1913 and was released almost six months later on June 1, 1914. He was elected to public office in 1920 when he ran for city commissioner in Atlantic City, a post he held for 12 years; Kuehnle died in 1934.

Frank Hague, who shared political favors with Nucky throughout his political career, was the powerful Democratic mayor of Jersey City for three decades. He was also a Democratic National committeeman from

New Jersey and vice chairman of the Democratic National Committee from 1924 to 1949.

Some critics challenged the source of Hague's wealth since he enjoyed palatial homes, European vacations, and a private suite at the fashionable Plaza Hotel in New York. At the time of his death in 1956, Hague's wealth was estimated at $10 million, which just illustrated what a great saver he was on his annual city salary of $18,500.

Hamilton F. Kean, who Nucky orchestrated his U.S. Senate election in 1928, had two sons, John and Robert Winthrop. Robert was elected to the U.S. Congress from Essex County for 10 terms and then ran for the U.S. Senate against Democrat Harrison Williams in 1958. But without Nucky, Robert was defeated. However, Williams didn't last long; he was later involved in the Abscam scandal and went to federal prison in 1982.

The Kean name continued in the political world as Robert's son, Thomas H. Kean, became the 48th governor of New Jersey and headed the investigation of the terrorist destruction of the Twin Towers in New York City on September 11, 2001. His son, Thomas H. Kean, Jr., Republican State Senator from Union County, made an unsuccessful bid for the U.S. Senate seat in 2006, but no doubt will try again to carry on the family tradition.

In 1929, Al Capone, Nucky's longtime business associate, was convicted in Philadelphia for gun possession after attending the first national convention of crime figures in Atlantic City in 1929. He served one year at Eastern State Penitentiary, a gothic-style structure in Philadelphia built in 1829. Although the prison officially closed in 1971, it is now a tourist attraction that features cell block No. 1, where Capone served his time. His cell has been restored to its original 1929 splendor with Capone's personal Oriental rug gracing the cell floor.

In May 1932, Capone was sent to Atlanta Federal Prison where he took over control and obtained an assortment of special privileges. He paid his personal bodyguards with money he smuggled into prison. His next destination was Alcatraz in 1934 where he lived in isolation. After his release in 1939, his health started to deteriorate due to syphilis, and his power in the mob diminished just as quickly. He died in 1947 in Florida; he was 48.

Although Alvin Karpis, aka Public Enemy No. 1, may have escaped the Atlantic City police in the gun battle in 1934, he was personally captured a year later by J. Edgar Hoover, director of the FBI. Karpis served 33 years in federal prisons, 26 in Alcatraz, a term longer than any other of the 1,576 inmates. Capone was a prison mate of Karpis during his entire stay. After Alcatraz, Karpis was extradited to Canada, his birthplace, and eventually settled in France where he wrote two books about his life titled, *Public Enemy Number One* and *The Alvin Karpis Story.*

Earl Carroll, an American showman, songwriter, and director, was best-known for his *Vanities* productions, beginning in 1922, with showgirls in flashy and skimpy costumes. Unfortunately, in 1926, he did not fully dress some of his performers in a Washington's Birthday bathtub party on stage, a performance that resulted in Carroll being sentenced to the Atlanta Federal Penitentiary for one year and fined $2,000. He served four months of the sentence and then returned to the welcoming bright lights of Broadway. In 1935, Nucky recommended Carroll become one of the judges in the Miss America Pageant, a post he gladly accepted.

In 1932, Colonel H. Norman Schwartzkopf Sr., a graduate of West Point who became the first superintendent of the New Jersey State Police, was involved in the investigation of the Lindbergh infant kidnapping. In 1991, the Colonel's son, H. Norman Schwartzkopf Jr., who was born in Trenton and attended West Point, became the general in charge of all coalition armed forces for Operation Desert Storm.

Martin T. Manton, the judge of the U.S. Circuit Court of Appeals for the Second District of New York and was Nucky's prison mate in Lewisburg in 1940, had the ability and political connections for uncommon greatness. He was convinced that his loan practices were completely legitimate until his dying day and not bribes as the jury concluded.

Manton was personal friends with several renowned political figures: John W. Davis, Democratic presidential candidate who ran against Calvin Coolidge in 1924; Alfred E. Smith, who testified as a character witness at Manton's criminal trial in 1939, was governor of New York and Democratic candidate for the presidency in 1928 against Herbert Hoover; and Woodrow Wilson, Democratic governor of New Jersey in 1910 and 28th U.S. President from 1913 to 1921. Wilson appointed

Manton, at age 36, to the federal bench and appellate court, secondly only in prestige to the U.S. Supreme Court.

William Randolph Hearst, a successful publisher who established a nationwide chain of newspapers, wasn't as successful in politics. He had two passions: One was public office, and the second was to put Nucky in jail in 1941. His first failed, but his second succeeded. He lost all of his bids for public office, including as mayor of New York City in 1905 and 1909, as governor of New York in 1906, and as the Democratic presidential nominee in 1904.

Moe Annenberg made a fortune through transmitting horse racing results, after receiving approval in 1929 to operate a national wire service to horse rooms throughout the U. S. and in Atlantic City. He was convicted for income tax evasion and became Nucky's prison mate in Lewisburg Federal Penitentiary. Annenberg died in 1942, shortly after he was released from prison. His son Walter H. Annenberg used his father's wealth wisely with donations to the arts and charities. He was a silent power broker in the Republican Party (Richard M. Nixon appointed him ambassador to Britain), and *Forbes* Magazine listed Walter H. Annenberg as one of America's wealthiest men; he held the No. 39 spot with an estimated wealth of $4 billion in 2002.

Frank S. "Hap" Farley took over Nucky's position as Atlantic County treasurer and the chairman of the Republican Party. Farley took a different route to political power in 1942; he had a solid educational background having attended the University of Pennsylvania and Georgetown Law School, where he graduated in 1925. He served as president of the Atlantic County Bar Association in 1941 and was elected an Atlantic County Assemblyman for three years, Atlantic County State Senator for 30 years, majority leader of the Senate, president of the Senate on two occasions, and acting governor on six occasions. Farley passed more legislation than any other legislator in the history of New Jersey. In his entire 34-year career, he only missed two legislative sessions, both due to illness.

Each county in New Jersey, with its own Republican chairman, formed a statewide Chairman Association and selected Farley as chairman of the statewide parent organization in 1952. His influence was much broader than all his political predecessors. He became a frequent delegate to the Republican National Convention and, because of his leadership role with the 21 county chairmen, he had a voice in selecting statewide and national candidates for the presidency. Farley attended the Inauguration of President Dwight D. Eisenhower in 1957, as a guest of his Georgetown friend Judge John J. Sirica, who gained national fame as presiding over the Watergate scandal in 1973.

Farley was instrumental in having Richard M. Nixon nominated on the first ballot in Florida in 1968 and attended Nixon's inauguration and Presidential Ball in 1969. He was instrumental in having Republican presidential candidates visit Atlantic City to energize the local Republican base in South Jersey. Farley's career ended differently than Nucky's: In 1971, the Dean of the New Jersey Senate was defeated for re-election and gracefully retired from public life except to assist in bringing casino gambling to Atlantic City in 1976.

The Republican Party in South Jersey survived many investigations that periodically surfaced: Governor Woodrow Wilson's task force in 1910 sent several office holders to prison, including Republican leader Commodore Louis Kuehnle; the federal probe, triggered by William Randolph Hearst, in the late 1930s sent the Republican leader Nucky Johnson to jail in 1941; and the Kefauver Investigation of 1951 tarnished the image of Atlantic City but left the Republican leader Farley unscathed and the Republican organization firmly in tact.

One of Nucky's personal friends and a strong Republican supporter was Skinny D'Amato who operated the 500 Club at 6 South Missouri Avenue in Atlantic City. This was a frequent stop for Nucky on the way home after partying in the evening.

In early 1960, at the request of the John F. Kennedy political organization, Paul "Skinny" D'Amato, owner of the 500 Club in Atlantic City, and friend, Angelo Malandra, criminal attorney and Democratic political leader from Camden, agreed to go to West Virginia to campaign for JFK in his Democratic Primary effort to defeat the U.S. Senator from Minnesota, Hubert H. Humphrey. West Virginia, which was 95 percent Protestant with a large Italian population, was the key to winning the Democratic nomination. D'Amato and Malandra, armed with a bundle of cash, used their natural charm to convince many doubtful voters to cast their ballots for JFK. Their efforts contributed to the Kennedy victory and launched him on the road to the White House.

Floss, Nucky's wife, lived for almost three years after her husband. She died in 1971, and she was entombed in the family mausoleum next to Nucky and his family at the Zion Cemetery in Bargaintown, Egg Harbor Township, New Jersey.

Herman "Muggsy" Taylor continued to promote world championship boxing events including Rocky Marciano versus "Jersey Joe" Walcott, Bob Montgomery versus Ike Williams, Joe Louis versus "Two-Ton" Tony Galente, and countless others in his 70-year boxing career. In 1977, David Niven wrote his autobiography titled *The Moon is Blue*, which was a best-seller. On page 167, he retells the cleansed story of the American Pony Express Racing Association escapade in Atlantic City's Municipal Auditorium. However, he did not mention Nucky by name and refers to the person who tried to extort his group as "Pinkie." Nucky disappeared and "Pinkie" became the new bad guy.

The Albert brothers' love for bluegrass music began at the Home Place in the early 1930s and never vanished from the heart of the Pinelands; in fact, bluegrass is more popular now than ever in local and national music circles. Today, there is a popular theater appropriately named The Albert Musical Hall that opened in 1997 in Waretown, Ocean County, in South Jersey that features a series of country playing musicians every Saturday night from all over the East Coast. In keeping with their spirit of independence and self-reliance, the Pineys built and paid for their theater themselves.

In 1929, Charles Darrow invented the game of *Monopoly,* named for the streets and setting property values in Atlantic City. It became the best-selling board game in the world, still produced by Parker Brothers, a division of Hasbro. In fact, a prime location was taken over by Bally's Park Place Casino when it acquired the former 900-foot-long Young's Million Dollar Pier in 2002. The corporation converted the pier into an upscale shopping mall that opened in spring 2006 with a *Monopoly* theme throughout, including Tiffany's, Louis Vuitton, White House Black Market, Burberry, Ltd., BCBG, Kenneth Cole, and other high-end stores.

When Nucky was convicted of income tax evasion in 1941, he served time for essentially opening the door to gambling in Atlantic City. For years, the state was vigorously against all gambling for a host of moral reasons: It was destructive to family life, it brought criminals and undesirables into the community, and it was considered to be morally reprehensible. The state tried to stamp it out at every opportunity. Religious leaders vociferously protested when legalized gambling was mentioned and if it became law, doomsday would follow. But that never happened. In 1976, the New Jersey State Constitution was changed by the voters to allow casinos in Atlantic City, and the city has never been the same.

Nucky's cottage at 110 South Iowa Avenue near Atlantic City's Boardwalk, where he played and ruled during twenty of the thirty years of his public life, is gone today; the Tropicana Casino & Resort now occupies the site. Also gone is the home at 103 South Elberon Avenue where Nucky resided after he returned to Atlantic City from Lewisburg. The Hebrew Old Age Center of Atlantic City, now known as Seashore Gardens, acquired the property and built an annex to the building at 3850 Atlantic Avenue (formerly known as the Cosmopolitan Club Hotel), which was managed by my father, William Graham Ferry, from 1942 to 1945. All of Nucky's favorite nightspots are gone: The Entertainer's Club, the Silver Slipper Supper Club, Babette's Night Club, The 500 Club, Hialeah Club, The Cotton Club, Club Nomad, Club Harlem, Grace's Little Belmont, Bath and Turf, Trench's Neptune Inn, the Dennis Hotel Fjord Room, the Ambassador Hotel's Merry-Go-Round Lounge, Conrad's Restaurant, Clicquot Club, the President Hotel's Round the World Room, the Claridge Hotel Mayfair Lounge, the Traymore Hotel's Submarine Grill and the Penn Atlantic Hotel's Riptide Room, with its famous cheesecake. The four-story Flemish structure, Knife & Fork Restaurant built in 1912, was restored to its original grandeur in 2005 by the Dougherty family, and is the lone survivor of Nucky's reign.

The popular oceanfront family amusement sites are gone. The casinos have taken their places, replacing wholesome family attractions for high-end merchandise stores for lucky gamblers. The aristocratic Quaker oceanfront hotels no longer exist where alcoholic beverages were once forbidden. In fact, all the beachfront hotels are gone or have been turned into casinos where alcoholic beverages flow 24/7 and now spill over the Boardwalk into beach bars in the sand.

Nucky was a strong supporter of the Miss America Pageant and Boardwalk parade and helped revive it when it ceased for several years.

In 1940, the Miss America Pageant moved into Nucky's Atlantic City Auditorium (Convention Hall) where it remained until 2005 (except during the war years 1942–1945). Unfortunately, after 84 years, the management of the pageant decided to leave Atlantic City for Las Vegas in 2005. The crowning of Miss America, a huge television ratings success for many years, is not even carried on network television today.

Convention Hall has been remodeled several times since 1929 and was renamed Boardwalk Hall in 2001. Unfortunately, during the renovations, the largest pipe organ in the world, designed by Senator Emerson Richards, was severely damaged. It is in the process of being restored. Convention Hall housed many national conventions including the Democratic National Convention in 1964 where Lyndon B. Johnson was selected as the Democratic candidate for President of the United States.

The Hall has been host to a great variety of special events such as world championship boxing, the Little Army-Navy Football Game (Pennsylvania Military Academy v. Kings Point Merchant Marines), the Liberty Bowl football game, horse, dog and livestock shows, rodeos, basketball tournaments, midget auto racing, professional wrestling, ice hockey, the Ice Capades, and concerts featuring artists from opera singers to rock stars.

These days, the gaming resort, with its bounty of casinos and bright neon lights, has even adopted new slogans: "Atlantic City—Always Turned On" and the more recent "Do AC". Atlantic City remains a destination location for the fun-loving crowds Nucky always envisioned.

Nucky's hometown lives on, as does its legacy as "Playground of the World."

BIBLIOGRAPHY

Original Sources

Atlantic County Board of Elections
5903 Main Street
Mays Landing, NJ 08330

Atlantic City Election
Returns 1920 through 1940.

Atlantic City Free Public Library
Atlantic City, NJ

Microfilm of Newspaper articles of the
Atlantic City Press.

Atlantic County Library
Mays Landing, NJ

Background Articles.

Atlantic County Historical Society
Somers Point, NJ

Background Articles.

City of Atlantic City
Bureau of Vital Statistics

Death Certificate of Louis Kessel,
October 7, 1944.

Correspondence with Darrell Byerly
Historian

Lewisburg Prison background.

Correspondence with Benjamin R. Fitzgerald, RMC

Former Atlantic City Municipal Clerk,
Re: Resolutions to build Atlantic City
Auditorium.

Correspondence with Thomas Somers

Clerk of the Atlantic County Board of
Freeholders, son of Mayor William Somers
of Atlantic City, Re: Appointment of Enoch L.
Johnson as County Treasurer.

Correspondence with Stephen Townsend

Clerk of the New Jersey Supreme Court
Re: Enoch L. Johnson .

Ellis Island Passenger List

Louis Kessel arrived in 1912 from Russia.

Federal Bureau of Investigation
Washington, D.C.

Records of Enoch L. Johnson's background
Investigation for his Parole Application
Records of Paul "Skinny" D'Amato
Records of Moses L. Annenberg
Records of Federal Judge Martin T. Manton
Records of the Investigation of U.S. Senator
William Smathers.

Friendly Sons of St. Patrick of
South Jersey Minutes 1935 to 1968

Attendance at Annual Banquets of Enoch
L. "Nucky" Johnson and public officials.

Genealogical & Memorial History
of the State of New Jersey

Biography of Johnson Family.

Legislative Manuals of the
State of New Jersey

Re: Walter Sooy Jeffries background Enoch L.
"Nucky" Johnson as member of New Jersey
Assembly Legislative Committee, County
Committeeman & Clerk of the Supreme
Court of New Jersey.

National Archives, Philadelphia, PA

National Archives Trust Fund
Washington, D.C.

New Jersey Bureau of Vital Statistics
Trenton, NJ

Marriage record of Mabel S. Jeffries &
Enoch L. Johnson, September 12, 1906.

New Jersey Real Estate Commission
Trenton, NJ

List of real estate license
holders included Enoch L. "Nucky" Johnson.

New Jersey State Archives
Trenton, NJ

Transcript of the testimony of the 300
witnesses in investigation
of 1911 Atlantic City vote fraud.

New Jersey State Library
Trenton, NJ

Oath of Enoch L. Johnson upon his
appointment as Clerk of the New Jersey
Supreme Court.

Pennsylvania Crime Commission Report of 1980

Personal correspondence & files of Frank S. Farley

New Jersey State Senator 1940-1971.
Acting Governor on five occasions.
Partner Farley, Fredericks & Ferry.
Died on 09/24/77 .

Personal correspondence & files of Frank J. Ferry

Law Partner of Senator Frank S. "Hap"
Farley. Correspondence from Enoch L.
"Nucky" Johnson re: termination
of criminal fine of $20,000.

Personal recollection of Carl Aschenbach, Jr.

Native of Atlantic City re: early background
of Atlantic City and political system for
employment.

Personal recollection of Thomas Baker
Atlantic City Bookmaker

Re: background on horse
racing rooms and bookmakers.

Personal recollection of James H. Boyd
the 4th Ward of Atlantic City Leader; Clerk of
Atlantic County Board of Freeholders

Re: background of Enoch L. "Nucky"
Johnson. Attended criminal trial of Enoch L.
"Nucky" Johnson in 1941. Died on
04/11/74.

Personal recollection of Marie Boyd
Employee of Atlantic County Treasurer's
Office and wife of James Boyd, Fourth Ward
Leader in Atlantic City

Re: attendance at 1941
criminal trial of Enoch L. "Nucky" Johnson.
Died on 08/23/06.

Personal recollection of Helen (Kirby) Carmack
Lifelong resident of Atlantic City; shook the
hand of Jack Dempsey in his training camp
in Atlantic City in 1921

Acquaintance of Nucky Johnson.
Aunt of Frank J. Ferry.
Died on 08/06/98.

Personal recollection of Bob Chambers

Numbers runner in Atlantic City. Re: back
ground on numbers operation.

Personal recollection of Frank DeCarlo
Violations Clerk of Atlantic City Municipal Court

Johnson having Italian dinners at his home.
Re: Enoch L. "Nucky" Died on 05/24/05.

Personal recollection of Charles Draper
Atlantic City Beach Patrol Historian

Personal recollection of Agnes G. Dwyer
Teacher at St. Nicholas R. C. School
in Atlantic City for 35 years

Re: early life in Atlantic City in the 1900s.
Died on 11/09/03 at age 99.

Personal recollection of Dr. Andrew D. Dwyer
Son of Democratic Magistrate
& U.S. Internal Revenue Service Auditor

Re: Democratic Organization and
Lafferty/Farley connection.
Died on 12/21/06.

Personal recollection of Barbara (Dunn) English
Daughter of Atlantic City Convention Hall Engineer

Employed by Enoch L. "Nucky" Johnson.

Personal Recollection of Frank S. Farley
New Jersey State Senator from Atlantic
County for 30 years

Numerous accounts of Nucky
Johnson and political activities.
Died on 09/24/77.

Personal recollection of Paul J. Farley

Law partner—Farley, Fredericks & Ferry.
Brother of Senator Frank S. "Hap" Farley
Personal acquaintance of Enoch L. "Nucky"
Johnson. Died on 11/18/74.

William Farley
Nephew of Senator Frank S. "Hap" Farley

Account of Enoch L. "Nucky" Johnson and
wife at Entertainer's Club in Atlantic City,
N.J. Died on 09/13/02.

Personal recollection of Louise A. (Kirby) Ferry
Lifelong resident of Atlantic City;
Mother of Frank J. Ferry. Personal acquaintance
of Enoch L. "Nucky" Johnson

Attended Dempsey-Carpentier fight.
Died on 11/08/79.

Personal recollection of William Graham Ferry
New Jersey Senate Journal Clerk

Father of Frank J. Ferry. Personal acquain
tance of Enoch L. "Nucky" Johnson.
Died on 08/09/50.

Personal recollection of William Graham Ferry, Jr. President, Atlantic City Board of Assessors for 20 years. Brother of Frank J. Ferry

Re: accounts of Enoch L. "Nucky" Johnson's nightlife.

Personal recollection of Audrey L. Foster Atlantic City Friends School Teacher; Atlantic County Employee

Re: Albert Music Hall & Country Expressions.

Personal recollection of Murray Fredericks Law partner of Senator Frank S. "Hap" Farley

Numerous accounts of gambling & bootlegging in Atlantic City.

Personal recollection of Herbert Freedman Associate of Paul "Skinny" D'Amato

Re: background of "Skinny" D'Amato. Personal friend of Sally (Ferry) III.

Personal recollection of Martin Friel Atlantic City Police Department Officer; Liaison with the Criminal Courts

Re: Anthony Miller's association with Nucky Johnson.

Personal recollection of Jake Glazer Lifelong resident of Pleasantville; former boxer & Egg Harbor Township Councilman

Re: Laoma Byrd Boxing Gym in Pleasantville.

Personal recollection of Gerard "Jerry" Gormley Sheriff of Atlantic Co.

Re: Still operation background of Enoch L. "Nucky" Johnson. Died in September 1984 .

Personal recollection of Leo J. Howlett Mayor of Absecon; personal friend of Sen. Frank S. "Hap" Farley; Acquaintance of Enoch L. "Nucky" Johnson

Re: Ku Klux Klan in Atlantic County.

Personal recollection of Sally (Ferry) III Employee of Atlantic County Board of Freeholders, Clerk's Office & Atlantic County Purchasing Department; Sister of Frank J. Ferry

Re: accounts about Enoch L. "Nucky" Johnson. Died on 10/19/02.

Personal recollection of Mary (Cramer) III Personal friend of Senator Frank S. "Hap" Farley and his wife, Marie; Mother-in-Law of Sally (Ferry) III

Re: background of early Atlantic City and Enoch L. "Nucky". Johnson.

Personal recollection of Charles P. Jeffries Member of Atlantic Co. Board of Freeholders; Organizer of the Friendly Sons of St. Patrick

Re: early history of the Friendly Sons of St. Patrick and Enoch L. "Nucky" Johnson. Died on 11/02/79.

Personal recollection of Enoch L. Johnson and Florence (Osbeck) Johnson

Career highlights reviewed during interview with Frank J. Ferry.

Personal recollection of Peter Kreischer Former President of Ventnor City Council

Re: process of candidate selection.

Personal recollection of Reggie Lee
Personal friend of Senator Frank S. "Hap"
Farley; Morris Guard member.

Re: acquaintance of Enoch L. "Nucky"
Johnson.

Personal recollection of John Mathis,
Brother of Atlantic City Bookmaker Bill Mathis

Re: gambling activities in Atlantic City.

Personal recollection of John Mooney
Atlantic City Police Department Vice Squad
Commander; Atlantic City Councilman.

Re: background of Enoch L. "Nucky"
Johnson—gambling, bootlegging,
Dempsey vs. Carptentier Boxing Event.
Died on 10/13/05.

Personal recollection of Ed Nichterlein
Atlantic City Press Sports Editor

Re: Atlantic City boxing history.
Died on 03/09/95

Personal recollection of Arnold R. Orsatti, Sr.
Restaurant operator; Personal friend of
Sen. Frank S. "Hap" Farley

Re: Atlantic City politics & bootlegging.
Died on 10/14/03.

Personal recollection of Frank Pederson
Long time resident of Scullville, N.J.

Re: account of Irish bricks.
Died on 11/23/07.

Personal recollection of Donald D. Phillips
Atlantic City Attorney

Supplied copy of "Boardwalk Empire" by
John H. Stoneburg. Account of Detective
Richard Black, Enoch L. "Nucky" Johnson,
Skinny D'Amato, and movie star, George
Raft. Died on 09/10/02.

Personal recollection of William H. Ross, III
Employee of Atlantic County Board of
Freeholders; Mayor of Margate. Chairman
of the Republican Party of Atlantic County

Re: account of Enoch L. "Nucky" Johnson's
work routine at Atlantic County
Treasurer's Office.

Personal recollection of June G. Sheridan
Atlantic County Historian

Enoch L. "Nucky" Johnson's days
as sheriff and Johnson Civil War records

Personal recollection of John Siracusa
Atlantic City Real Estate Broker

Re: witnessed Nucky & Floss Johnson
drinking at Conrad's Restaurant. Supplied
photograph of Enoch L."Nucky" Johnson.

Personal recollection of Maxine Stonehill
Daughter of Atlantic City
Merchant (Hoffman Hardware).

Re: account of Enoch L. "Nucky"
Johnson's daily use of $100 bills
to purchase newspapers after his retirement.

Personal recollection of Jack Strotbeck
Owner of Strotbeck's Restaurant in Margate

Re: Floss Johnson working for Renault
Winery.

Personal recollection of Ishman Wallace
Atlantic City Iron Worker

Re: he volunteered to become a "Johnson
Democrat."

Personal recollection of Martin "Marty" Wilson, Sr. Atlantic City Precinct Captain—Fourth Ward; Clerk of the Atlantic Co. Board of Elections	Re: account of Enoch L. "Nucky" Johnson frequently going to Knife & Fork Restaurant. Died on 09/30/02
Polk Directory (various years)	Lists names & addresses of all residents of Atlantic City, Ventnor City, Margate City, and Longport Borough.
Punxsutawney Historical & Genealogical Society Punxsutawney, PA	Background of Charles J. Margiotti, Attorney
Republican National Convention published by Charles W. Johnson Minneapolis, Minnesota (1893)	Proceedings of the first three Republican National Contentions 1856, 1860, and 1864.
Rutgers State University Archives Archibald S. Alexander Library New Brunswick, NJ	
Social Security Administration	Application for Social Security number by Florence (Osbeck) Johnson and Enoch L. "Nucky" Johnson on August 1, 1941.
Superior Court of New Jersey	Declaration of Naturalization Record Intention to become a U.S. citizen filed by Louis P. Kessel, February 3, 1913.
Surrogate of Atlantic County	Probate pleadings for Florence (Osbeck) Mays Landing, NJ Johnson and her will dated July 9, 1955. Confirmation that Enoch L. Johnson did not have any will. Administration Pleadings of Louis P. Kessel of January 22, 1945. Smith E. Johnson will of October 19, 1917.
Testimonial Dinner Program for Hamilton F. Kean	October 25, 1930 – lists all public officials including Enoch Lewis "Nucky" Johnson.
U.S. Selective Service	Registration for Draft by Enoch L. Johnson on September 12, 1918 and Louis P. Kessel of June 5, 1917.
University Libraries of the University of Notre Dame Notre Dame, Indiana	Boxing background of Dempsey Carpentier boxing event.
Zion Cemetery Records c/o Maund Enterprises, Inc. Woodbine, NJ	Mausoleum record of Enoch L. Johnson.

NEWSPAPERS

Atlantic City Daily Press
November 29, 1911, December 8, 1911; June 9 & 10, 1914; June 21, 22, 23, 24, 27, 28, 29, & 30 of 1921; July 2, 4, 30 of 1921 December 8, 1944; July 20, 1958 February 1, 1959; January 20 & 21, 1961

Atlantic County Record
1910, 1911 & 1912 Articles of election fraud investigation. June 6 & 13, 1914 criminal trial.

New York Herald Tribune
January 1, 2, 3, 5, 6, 7, 10, 12 & 15 of 1930

New York Times
January 2, 1958 re: Frank Hague obituary; October 29, 1975.

Philadelphia Bulletin (Sunday)
February 28, 1965 re: William A. Gray obituary

South Jersey Republican
1886 & 1889

The National Police Gazette, New York
June 18, 1921; July 2 & 23, 1921

Wall Street Journal
Background Articles.

MAGAZINES

Boxing
London, England
June 29, July 6, & July 13, 1921

Philadelphia Daily News
June 15, 1949

Philadelphia Magazine
August 1971

Reader's Digest
September 1954

Seaview Country Club Promotional Literature
Clarence Geist, founder, background

The Nation's Pictorial Review & Digest
Article by William A. Haffert, U.S. Coast Guard War Correspondent
August 1945
Dempsey's background & military career in the U.S. Coast Guard.

The Saturday Evening Post
August 26, 1939 & July 26, 1958

Tlime Magazine
August 11, 1941

Woodbine Festival Museum of Woodbine Heritage
Background of Maurice de Hirsch.

ORIGINAL SOURCES

Brief of Appellant Enoch L. Johnson
to the United States Court of Appeals
for the Third Circuit Court of Appeals
of October 14, 1941 with supporting
Appendix containing the trial testimony
of Enoch L. Johnson.

Brief of the Respondent the United States
to the United States Court of Appeals for
the Third Circuit Court Appeals with
supporting Appendix containing the
indictment and the trial testimony of
Ralph Weloff and James Towhey and
Enoch L. Johnson filed on November 12, 1941.

Opinion of Circuit Court of Appeals Judge Biggs
denying the Appeal and sustaining the conviction
of Enoch L. Johnson filed on June 30, 1942.
Circuit Judge Jones filed a dissenting opinion.

U.S. Federal Court in Camden, NJ
Docket Register from
August 2, 1941 through June 3, 1950
for *U.S. v. Johnson*

United States Senate Reed Committee
transcript of the testimony of Enoch
L. Johnson and Hamilton Fish Kean
re: 1928 Republican Primary contest
for United States Senator

*Johnson v. Curtis Publishing Co. and
David Niven.* Deposition transcript of
Enoch L. Johnson in Camden, New Jersey
on September 2, 1959

Deposition transcript of David Niven
taken before Vice Consul of the United
States in Rome on June 21, 1961

Interview of Judge Alexander Holtzoff
on October 20, 1964 by Sidney Fine
and Robert Warner

PRINTED SOURCES

Atlantic County
Freeholders Minutes
   Supplied by Clerk of the Atlantic County
   Board of Freeholders, Thomas Somers
   re: Appointment of Enoch L. "Nucky"
   Johnson as County Treasurer.

Barrett, May Ellin
   Irving Berlin, A Daughter's Memoir
   Simon & Schuster (1994)

Beamish, Richard J.
The Novelty Cutlery Co.
   The Story of the Lone Eagle

Berg, A. Scott
   Lindbergh, G.P. Putnam & Sons (1998)

Carol, Joyce & Halpern
   "Reading the Fights" article by Elliot J.
   Gorn *The Manassa Mauler and the*
   Fighting Marine New York (1988).
   Henry Holt & Co. Publishing Corp. (2001)

Collins, Jef
   "International Boxing"–1968 Annual
   Jalart House, Inc., P. O. Box 175
   Port Chester, NY

Connell, Kate
   Underground Railroad
   Steck Vaughn Company (1993)

Cryst, George
   The Life Story of Harold G. Hoffman
   Terminal Printing and Publishing Co.,
   Hoboken, NJ (1934)

Dempsey, Jack
   The Ring Magazine, December 1967.
   Published monthly by The Ring, Inc.

Edge, Walter Evans
   A Jerseyman's Journal
   Princeton University Press (1948)

Edwards, Billy
   Legendary Boxers of the Golden Age
   Chartwell Books, Inc. (1990). Background
   On Jack Dempsey, "The Nonpariel"
   Middleweight Champion.

Engs, Robert F.
   The Birth of the Grand Old Party

Ewen, David
   The Story of Irving Berlin, published by
   Holt, Rinchay and Winston, Inc. (1950)

Fleischer, Nat
   50 Years at Ringside
   Greenwood Press, New York (1940)

Fleischer, Nat
   Jack Dempsey, The Idol of Fistiane

Fleischer, Nat & Andre, Sam	*An Illustrated History of Boxing* Citadel Press. Kensington Publishing Corp. (2001)
Frank, William E. (Special Agent, Intelligence Unit, U.S. Treasury Department) & Burns, Joseph W. (Special Assistant to the United States Attorney, Department of Justice)	"The Atlantic City Investigation and Trial of Enoch L. Johnson" (1941)
Gienapp, William E.	"The Origins of the Republican Party 1852–1856"
Goldman, Herbert	*Ring–1986 Record Book & Boxing Encyclopedia*
Gosch, Martin A. & Hammer, Richard	*The Last Testament of Lucky Luciano* Little Brown Co. (1974)–Account of Enoch L. "Nucky" Johnson as part of "The Big Seven" cartel during Prohibition
Hall, John F.	*The Daily Union History of Atlantic City and County*, Daily Union Printing Co. (1900)
Heston, Alfred M.	*Absegami, Annals of Eyren Haven and Atlantic City*, Sinnickson Chew & Sons, (1904)
Heston, Alfred M.	*Heston's Hand Book, Atlantic City Illustrated*, Franklin Publications (1895)
Heston, Alfred M.	*South Jersey–A History 1664–1924* Lewis Historical Publication Co. (1924)
Irey, Elmer	*The Tax Dodgers* Greenberg Publishers, New York Account of the investigation of Enoch L. "Nucky" Johnson for income tax evasion
Joseph, Samuel	*History of the Baron De Hirsch Fund* Augustus M. Kelley, Publisher (1978)
Kahn, Roger	"A Flame of Pure Fire–Jack Dempsey and the Roaring 20s"
Kearns, Jack "Doc"	*The Million Dollar Gate*, published by MacMillan Co., New York (1966)
Keylin, Arleen & Cotten, Jonathan	*The New York Times Sports Hall of Fame* Arne Press, New York (1981)

Konje, Professor Urlt

The H.P. Dream Book 1926 &1927
Reference book used to select a number
to place a wager

Langford, Gerald

The Murder of Stanford White
Bobbs Merrill Co. (1962)

Livesey, Robert E.

*On the Rock—Twenty Five
Years in Alcatraz, the Prison
Story of Alvin Karpis*
Beaufort Books, Inc. (1989)

Manual of *The Legislature of New Jersey*

Years 1923, 1935 & 1938

Marhall, Logan

"Sinking of the Titanic—1912"

McCarter, Robert, LLD

*Memories of Half Century at the New Jersey
Bar—New Jersey State Bar Association*
(1937). Background of Attorney General
Robert McCarter

McMahon, William

So Young, So Gay,
Press Publishing Company and William
McMahon (1970). Account of activities on
Atlantic City Boardwalk.

Mooney, Michael McDonall

*Evelyn Nesbit & Stanford White—
Love & Death in the Gilded Age*
William Morrow Co. (1976)

Morell, Parker

Diamond Jim—the Life & Times,
published by Simon & Schuster (1934)

Morley, Sheridan

*The Other Side of the Moon,
A Bibliography of David Niven* (1985)

Nelson, William

*Nelson's Biographical Cyclopedia of New
Jersey* re: background of John J. Gardner

Nesbit, Evelyn

*The Prodigal Days—the Untold
Story of Evelyn Nesbit*,
published by Julian Messner (1934)

Niven, David

The Moon's A Balloon, An Autobiography,
G.P. Putnam & Sons (1972). Life of David
Niven.

Peterson, Robert A.

Patriots, Pirates & Pineys (1998)

Ray, Chaplin and Max Call

Al Capone's Devil Driver,
Acclaimed Books (1979)

Rinhart, Floyd & Marion

Summertime, Photographs of Americans at Play 1850–1900, published by Clarkson N. Potter, Inc. (1978)

Roberts, James B. & Skott, Alexander

The Boxing Register, 2nd Edition, (1999)

Sacket, William C.

New Jersey's First Citizens, (1917–1918), J. J. Scannell Co. (1917)

Schaap, Jeremy

Cinderella, Houghton Mifflin (2005)

Shulman, Irving

Valentino

Souvenir Program of

Semi Centennial Celebration of Atlantic City–June 15, 16, 17 & 18, 1904

Souder, H.J.

Who's Who in New Jersey–Biography of Enoch L. "Nucky" Johnson

Sugar, Bert R.

The 100 Greatest Boxers of All Times (1999)

Symons, Julian

Crime, Crown Publishing Co. (1966)

Thompson, Jeff

Ocean County Sheriff's Department History, published by the Ocean County Sheriff's Department (2000)

Trent, Bill

Public Enemy Number One, The Alvin Karpis Story, Simon and Shuster (1971)

United Baptist Temple

Souvenir Program of January 1, 1937

Walker, Alexander

Rudolph Valentino (1976)

Waltzer, Jim

Tales of South Jersey, Rutgers University Press (1950)

Willis, Laura Lavinia

Early History of Atlantic County, First Years Work of the Atlantic County Historical Society (1915)